Accompanying
CD/CDs in the pocket
at the front/back of
the book

Contemporary Database Marketing:

CONCEPTS AND APPLICATIONS

Martin Baier
Kurtis M. Ruf
Goutam Chakraborty

Preface by
Thomas Stoneback, Ph. D.
President
Direct Marketing Educational Foundation

Racom Communications
Evanston, Illinois

© 2002 by Martin Baier, Kurtis M. Ruf and Goutam Chakraborty

Published by Racom Communications Inc.
815 Ridge Ave.
Evanston, IL 60202
www.racombooks.com
(847) 424-9300

Cataloging-in-Publication Data available from the Library of Congress.

Printed in the United States of America

ISBN: 0-9704515-1-2

To my wife, Dorothy, who has shared with me the emergence of database marketing recorded herein; and, to my daughter, Donna, who in her own professional work has nurtured direct marketing with creativity and enthusiasm.

Martin Baier

To the memory of my father, Jacob F. Ruf, who was the guiding and inspiring mentor in my life. To my mother, Sondra Ruf, whose patience and love has been the glue of our family bond; and to my brothers—Brian, Eric, and Jake—who are lifelong partners seeing our father's vision come to fruition.

Kurtis Ruf

With sincere appreciation to my family (Alison, Deven, and Ian) for their constant support and encouragement.

Goutam Chakraborty

Contents

Preface

"The Plastic of the New Millenium"

Hollywood recommended "plastics" as the chosen career when Dustin Hoffman starred as The Graduate in the 1960s. But if a sequel were filmed today, the advice would be marketing – direct and interactive marketing!

Indeed, this specialized discipline will grow at twice the rate of the general economy during the next five years. And it will start from the current base of approximately 10 percent of all business conducted in the U.S. Today, more than half of all advertising has a direct response component; no surprise since 52 U.S. industries use some form of direct marketing. Clearly the need for talented and trained direct marketers has never been greater, nor the opportunities more exciting...

Not that long ago, company leaders in the catalog industry began to open retail stores to complement their catalog, direct mail and telephone sales. (Similarly, neighborhood and national retailers began to market direct.) More recently, web sites were added as e-commerce was spawned. Businesses expanded, becoming multi-channeled, integrated and much more sophisticated in the process. Brands were born.

But who will grow them?

The publishing of *Contemporary Database Marketing: Concepts and Applications* is an important event in The Direct Marketing Educational Foundation's efforts to encourage and promote the advancement of direct marketing and database marketing education. Textbooks, educational and instructional programs, and other learning devices are only beginning to catch up with this large and fast moving industry.

This new book by Martin Baier, Kurt Ruf, and Goutam Chakraborty—industry leaders, marketing award winners, and professional educators—is timely, and it brings together the practical and theoretical, the strategic and tactical aspects of direct marketing. Each of the four sections reflects how direct marketing theory is related to the hard information of day-to-day business practices. Plus, an exciting addition is the Interactive Workshops and Exercises which reinforce learning through the manipulation of "live data" on the accompanying CD, among the first of its kind.

While no one knows exactly how digital interactive technologies are going to affect classic direct marketing – or vice versa – the transition of old economies to include the new will require talent, effort, and dedication.

Read this book.
Study smart.
Learn.

Because, as every direct marketer knows: the future is a very exciting place to be!.

Thomas Stoneback, Ph.D.
President, Direct Marketing Educational Foundation
dmef@the-dma.org

The DMEF is a non-profit educational foundation established in 1966. Its mission is to increase and improve the teaching of direct and interactive marketing attract new talent to the field of direct and interactive marketing provide career guidance and information

Introduction

Contemporary Database Marketing: Concepts and Applications has been conceived for structuring and teaching a college course in database marketing. It also has been developed to have practical relevance for professionals interested in, about to enter, or already involved in database marketing. It can be used for continuing study or for reference.

The impetus for this book has come from both the academic and professional communities including:

- Professors seeking teaching resources for planned or in-place database marketing courses.
- The Direct Marketing Educational Foundation, which has been a driving force in the development of a "model" curriculum for the multidisciplinary teaching of direct marketing.
- Corporate trainers and other direct marketing professionals in the trenches.
- Richard Hagle, our editor and publisher, who has been a source of encouragement throughout the process of bringing this work to market.

I serve as lead author, selected to combine theory and practice for use in the classroom as well as in the professional marketer's "war room." My objective has been to identify and organize the relevant concepts along with the proven applications of the database aspect of direct marketing. What appears here has been evolving for many years—in my own learning, in my own teaching, and in my own experience—coupled with that of dozens of others.

Kurtis M. Ruf, co-author, herein perpetuates the pioneering work of his father (and my good friend and colleague of many years), the late Jacob F. Ruf. Jake was the visionary who developed the very first relational database language commercially available (IMPRS) as well as the first systems for clustering both households and businesses. In the 1970s, Jake and I together developed the first ZIP Code area market segmentation models.

Goutam Chakraborty, co-author, provides considerable academic and practical, especially statistical and analytical, expertise and experience. He has been among the very first to offer courses in database marketing at Oklahoma State University, and the lessons of his extensive hands-on teaching are reflected in this book.

As direct marketing has emerged as a college discipline, it has become apparent that at its core is the technology of a database coupled with scientific utilization of information to create and cultivate long-term customer relationships. This has been especially notable as the powerful information dissemination capabilities of the Internet (and its commercial partner, the World Wide Web) have evolved as a mighty economic force.

Today, virtually every organized entity—whether for-profit or not-for-profit— is initiating or expanding direct marketing in their operations and, in the process, are developing and utilizing database information. This can be observed in a broad range that includes big corporations, small businesses, trade and professional associations, educational and healthcare institutions, theater and arts groups, services, financial firms—in fact, all types of enterprises. Effective use of a database has become one sure means of improving objectives to increase profits, fund-raising contributions, attendance, memberships, or political actions. The reason for this explosion is painfully simple: decision-making can be based more solidly (even if imperfectly) on the facts—on data.

This explosive growth of this data-based direct marketing has made it difficult to find enough people with the skills demanded by the discipline. By gaining the knowledge needed to guide firms and organizations to direct marketing success via a database, trained professionals also boost chances for their own career advancement.

How to Use This Book

The four major sections of this book, containing more than a hundred exhibits and illustrations, deal with:

1. **Fundamentals of Database Marketing**, with these chapters headed: The Basics of Direct Marketing (Chapter 1) Basic Principles for Developing, Maintaining, and Using a Database (Chapter 2); and Data Enhancements (Chapter 3).

2. **Essential Tools of Information Gathering and Analysis**, with chapters devoted to Information Gathering: Sources and Uses of Data (Chapter 4); Using Basic Statistical Concepts (Chapter 5); and Data Analysis Tools and Techniques (Chapter 6).

3. **Direct Marketing Strategies and Program Applications**, with individual chapters on "The Lifetime Value of a Customer" (Chapter 7), "Consumer Market Segmentation" (Chapter 8),"Business-to-Business Market Segmentation" (Chapter 9),

"Structuring and Evaluating an Experiment" (Chapter 10), "The Decision-Making Process" (Chapter 11), and Using Database Information to Create More Effective Promotions" Chapter 12).

4. **Cases**, two chapters of Comprehensive Case Demonstrations, culminates with the real-world database-driven Mountain & Valley Resort, presented in a manner that enables hands-on manipulation of information.

All chapters contain case examples and all conclude with Workshops and Exercises that emphasize each chapter's contents. Most of these are Interactive Workshops that direct the reader to the CD-ROM accompanying the text. The CD makes it possible to work with the actual data and exhibits in the text. Many of these enable using statistical techniques, such as experimentation, hypothesis testing, and calculation of sample size. Others instruct on the use of and demonstrate analytical tools such as correlation, regression and cluster analysis. And, still others enable determination of market segments and the lifetime value of a customer. Included on the CD-ROM are comprehensive summary records (transaction, demographic and psychographic data) for Mountain & Valley Resort, through which all of the techniques, concepts, and applications can be demonstrated.

Material herein has been classroom-tested; most is field-tested. Much has been put into practice. Instructors using this text may see fit to rearrange the teaching order of the fourteen chapters. Contemporary Database Marketing does not progress from the "easy" to the "difficult." Neither does the real world!

Acknowledgments

Although the three of us are co-authors, each responsible for this comprehensive textbook in database marketing, we hasten to acknowledge lots of input and lots of help from lots of others.

Much has been derived from our direct marketing experiences: from the firms and schools that provided us with the opportunities and field laboratories, from academic and professional colleagues as well as from literally hundreds of other direct marketers who have shared their own successes and failures with us. In various ways, those who taught us planted many seeds, as did the challenging and perceptive interactions with hundreds of students.

As the development of this work progressed over a long period of time, substantial contributions were provided by reviews and important input from academics and professionals alike. These included:

James Cortada
Consultant
IBM Consulting

Nina Diamond
Associate Professor
DePaul University

Tracy Emerick Ph. D.
Managing Consultant
Taurus Marketing

Robert MacArthur
Adjunct Professor of Marketing
Boston University

Randee Monitz
Vice President, Professional
Development and Education
Draft Worldwide

Joshua Moritz
CEO, J. Moritz & Company
Adjunct Professor
New York University School of
   Continuing Education
   Direct Marketing Program

Phillip Pfeifer
Professor of Marketing
Darden Graduate School of
   Business
University of Virginia

Lisa Spiller, Ph. D
Associate Professor of Marketing
Christopher Newport University

Ruth Stevens
President, eMarketing Strategy
Adjunct Professor
New York University School of
   Continuing Education
   Direct Marketing Program

Kurt Ruf acknowledges substantial contributions for original studies and support of exhibits provided by these colleagues of his at Ruf Corporation:

- Debra Churchill
- Sharon Crozier
- Bruce Hughes
- Henry Maddix
- Eric Ruf.
- And Mary Lou Hines, University of Missouri, the architect who developed, with him, the CD-ROM that accompanies this book.

Goutam Chakraborty acknowledges Laurie Spar of the Direct Marketing Educational Foundation for ongoing guidance, and Vishal Lala for his comments on data analysis.

Martin Baier   August/2001

I
Fundamentals of
Database Marketing

Chapter 1

The Basics of Direct Marketing

Key Concepts
- Direct Marketing
- Database Marketing
- Customer Retention and Loyalty
- Offer and Audience
- Lifetime Value of a Customer
- Direct Marketing Cycle and Full-Circle Marketing
- Continuity Selling
- Cross-selling
- Permission Marketing

Applications
- Marketing Strategy
- Market Segmentation
- Product and Promotion Management

Like all ideas, marketing and business ideas appear, grow, evolve and develop, and eventually are recycled. New terms and forms of expression replace old ones. Driven by advances in technology in particular, marketing since the 1990s has seen the proliferation of terms like *relationship marketing, one-to-one marketing, interactive marketing,* and *affinity marketing,* among many others to describe new forces, new operations, and new relationships. While most of these terms add a helpful perspective on the changing dynamics of the world of marketing, one idea remains constant: all business and marketing was originally done on a one-to-one, face-to-face basis; and most marketing, regardless of product, medium, market size, or message, reflects the character of that relationship.

Smart marketers have always strived to create that sense of personal relationship, and the new technologies of the past fifty years have made it increasingly possible to assert what direct marketers have contended for generations: It's all direct. All marketing is direct marketing. It is as true today as it was a hundred years ago: The quality of any organization's relationships with its customers (or benefactors or constituents) has always been the basis for its survival and success. That means the basic principles of direct marketing still apply and, if anything, in our contemporary impersonal world, it is more critical than ever: It's *still* all direct.

This chapter will introduce a term that puts all of the newer marketing concepts, terms, and approaches in perspective: **Full-Circle Marketing.** It captures the spirit of the best of face-to-face marketing as reflected in traditional direct marketing combined with the advanced tools and techniques of modern-day database marketing. Indeed, today's methodology, as old as the scientific method, makes it possible for organizations to have real relationships with their customers—whatever the medium for communicating—thus making other terms, such as *customer relationship management* and *electronic customer relationship management,* reality.

What Is Direct Marketing?

Direct marketing should be called *directed marketing* because that feature most distinguishes it from traditional mass marketing. It replicates the centuries old face-to-face selling process to communicating and selling in a way that includes three essential components:

1. A proposition that encompasses:
   - **The Offer** (an attractive product at an attractive price).
   - **The Audience** (customers/prospects who in some ways have indicated that they would be open to the offer).
   - **The Promotion** (benefit-oriented messages sent via print, broadcast, and/or electronic media that appeal to the audience and sent in a way—kind of media—that appeals to that audience).

2. Measurement of the response to the message and medium.

3. Valuation of the buyers and repeat buyers (customers):
   - What do they buy?
   - Why do they buy?
   - How often do they buy it?
   - When do they buy it?
   - How much do they spend?
   - Who are they?

Direct marketing has often been viewed as a business of numbers. All sorts of formulas have been developed over the years to expand on the list of operating principles above, but one of the old standards (40/40/20) has stood the test of time:

Offer (40%) + Audience (40%) + Promotion (20%) = Sale

In other words, 40 percent of success is determined by the offer, 40 percent by the audience chosen, and 20 percent by the promotion. Like all such formulas, this one is subject to the "magic words" of direct marketing: test and measure. That is a differentiating factor that distinguishes direct marketing from other kinds of marketing. Point 3—valuation of customers—follows easily from the previous actions.

You can say more about direct marketing, but you can't say less and cover the basic principles. Most important, direct marketing means asking for a response to a message sent via some form of media to a prospective buyer whose past or current behavior indicates the likelihood of interest in the marketer's offer; i.e., the prospect has demonstrated both the *ability* to spend as well as the *propensity* (the willingness) to buy.

Different behaviors indicate different levels of potential interest, but the customer contact is predicated on the belief that the buyer's past behavior can be linked to the present proposition. The traditional use of the term *junk mail* has become a misnomer. Sending an irrelevant sales message to someone who is clearly not a reasonable target or candidate for the offer is as much a "waste" to the seller as it is a "nuisance" (often called an "invasion of privacy") to the disinterested prospect.

Database Marketing: The Next Step

Direct marketers of an earlier era—mail-order entrepreneurs—engaged in database marketing, although that wasn't what they called their *mailing lists*. Successful retailers, possibly the best model for face-to-face selling, have always kept track of the buying patterns, as well as the likes, dislikes, and special needs of their "regulars." And in the spirit of contemporary relationship or affinity marketing, they noted personal characteristics, such as birthdays and family members, often in as simple a form as notes on 3×5 index cards.

Database marketing is simply an extension of what direct marketers have been doing all along. A database needs *information*; in general, the more data the better. The difference between this kind of direct marketing and database marketing can be summed up in the saying "size matters." And so does cumulative effect because the impact of new technologies has been more than one-for-one proportional improvement. The improvements, in terms of both capacity and capability, have been exponential. Consider how far we have come. In the early years, during the 1950s, computers took up entire buildings, were enormously expensive, and complex, and could be used only by very large organizations. Today, many times that amount of computer capacity is available on a desktop costing less than two thousand dollars. In other words, most marketers can handle extremely large amounts of information about their customers and define smaller and smaller segments of those customers with the same interests at mere pennies when compared to the past.

A **database** is a customer list that has been enhanced with information about the geographic, demographic, and psychographic characteristics of these customers as well as a history of their transactions. Possessing this knowledge is the difference between having a customer *list* and having a customer *database*. It is also the difference between having relationships and customer retention and simply having buyers. The seller knows the customer and demonstrates that knowledge by sending only likely offers (no "junk"), and the customer responds with loyalty— thinking of the seller first and always willing to consider the seller's offers. That kind of relationship leads to affinity between seller and buyer. It becomes **interactive marketing**, with customers at its core.

This is the basis of CRM, **Customer Relationship Management**, and of success in the *e-commerce selling environment*. Sellers do more than "target" customers for messages. They concentrate on what these customers really need and want. When the customer "feels good" about a particular seller, that seller is able to keep his offers in the customer's "field of vision" or on his "radar," ahead of the other, almost limitless number of buying choices possible. The result is that the relationship makes it more efficient to make the sale.

As mentioned above, databases describe environments, such as ZIP Code areas, in which a high propensity of people in certain geographic areas to respond to an offer exists. In addition, the information in these databases can be further enhanced with data from other sources so that they become ever more descriptive—by describing different buyer types (demographics) and buying personalities (psychographics)—and, thus, be ever more predictive. As a result, fully enhanced databases provide the basis for increasingly sophisticated scientific analysis and statistical evaluation, leading to more accurate and profitable predictive modeling.

All of these improvements have meant exponential increases in productivity, not merely dollar-for-dollar increases. Thus, a business that invests in its database repeats a disproportionately high return in future productivity and profitability.

Database Productivity: Customer Loyalty and Retention and the Lifetime Value of a Customer

Direct marketers have always viewed customers as their organizations' most valuable assets. Like any productive asset, whether physical or intangible, a database of well-defined customers shares importance with a company's other revenue-generating assets because it has the ability to generate future revenues and future profits.

Direct marketers also have long known another important truth: It costs much less to retain customers than to obtain new ones. On an intuitive level alone, it makes excellent sense. If a customer makes one purchase from a seller and is satisfied, that individual is more likely to be open to hearing about other things the seller has for sale. Even if the buyer is a little bit skeptical, he is likely to give the seller the benefit of the doubt. And if he's satisfied again, he's really convinced. Two or three more satisfactory experiences and the seller will have to commit a really serious mistake to lose that customer. That sequence is how customer relationships are built and how customer loyalty and retention are developed—and how profitable transactions become profitable businesses.

The database and the information it provides are at the very core of every successful enterprise. Customer retention begins with a database. Careful analysis of the records of customers in a database helps the marketer identify repeat buyers and heavy users of the organization's products, and helps answer all the previously listed questions that establish and determine the value of a customer. A well-enhanced database also provides the key to current performance issues and predictive concerns: From what source(s) do desirable customers come? Which offer(s) activate them? What do they buy? How often do they buy and how much do they spend? And in conclusion, the magic question: Who will stay the longest and, over time, buy the most? That is *lifetime value.*

Thus, the ability to develop relationships and affinity with customers isn't just an abstraction. It means more efficient marketing because an intimate knowledge of customers as individuals means you are better able to send offers that will please them—and not annoy them even if they don't buy. But years and years of research demonstrate that such customers do buy more often from such marketers because the messages are about products and services that are relevant to them. It means customers will look for you from among throngs of competitors. A higher "hit rate" and, thus, more productive and more profitable marketing, are inevitable.

Direct marketers have long used calculations to reflect marketing productivity and to measure the lifetime value of customers. One well-known measure is Recency/Frequency/Monetary (RFM). Database technology now makes possible more sophisticated determinations of the Lifetime Value of a Customer (LTV). Such techniques are described and illustrated in Chapter 7.

The Direct Marketing Cycle

The direct marketing cycle is based on traditional scientific and business principles that sometimes get lost in the excitement of new ideas and developments. These are the basic stages of the direct marketing cycle:

1. Acquire and identify buyers and information about their demographic/psychographic characteristics as well as previous buying activities with you and others.

2. Organize (segment) these customers according to this data.

3. Establish patterns of sequencing and timing of sales. In other words, did one sale lead to a repeat sale of the same product (i.e., a continuity sale) or did it lead to purchase of a different (though probably related) item—a cross-sale?

4. Match customer characteristics with prospects that exhibit similar characteristics in order to acquire new customers.

5. Measure response of customer acquisition efforts relative to the historical record of ongoing cultivation of existing customers in order to determine what a new customer is worth over future time and then how much can be spent to acquire one.

6. Feed this information back into the system and experiment.

7. Begin again, with more insight than you had at the outset.

As mentioned previously, this list is a basic restatement of the scientific method. It also might be called the Direct Marketing Cycle. We also use it as the keystone of Full-Circle Marketing.

Full-Circle Marketing

The direct marketing cycle emphasizes a simple truth: all customers are not created equal and they must be interacted with on their own terms. One helpful way to express this is the notion of **Full-Circle**

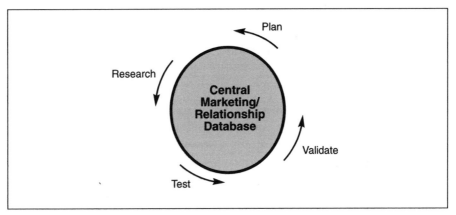

Exhibit 1-1: Full-Circle Marketing

Marketing, the framework for which is shown in Exhibit 1-1. The four steps of planning, research, testing, and validation are well-known in their own right. However, when driven by an enhanced database, the power of these disciplines is increased exponentially.

Step 1—Plan and Identify Objectives

A database marketing plan that includes clear objectives is an essential first step to avoiding problems. Such a plan measures progress, so you know when you have taken a wrong turn and when you have reached your final destination. Typical specific and measurable objectives might include the acquisition, retention, and development of specific numbers of customers.

Acquisition. By understanding previous customer acquisition sources and creative offers through the use of consumer and business data/information files, models can be built to simulate the buying process followed by a typical customer or category of customer. This knowledge makes it possible to develop a standardized approach to quickly identify which campaigns should go to which prospects.

Retention. Minimizing *customer attrition* is a significant challenge. One needs to understand why customers stop buying and terminate their relationship with the seller. Customers leave for all sorts of reasons, some that can be fixed (e.g., product or service problem) and others that can't (permanent change in life status). But, regardless, once you have identified and measured the reasons that cause some customers to leave and others to stay, you can create programs to regain some lost customers, better retain loyal customers for even longer periods of time, and recapture new customer acquisition costs more quickly. Thus, efficiency and profitability are improved. Another way to increase efficiency and profitability is to increase "share of customer" (i.e., increasing the total amount of business a customer does with you) by using information from previous transactions to identify the most likely continuity and cross-selling opportunities.

Develop the most profitable customers. Evaluate profit per transaction and determine potential lifetime value per customer in order to identify the most profitable customer segments, provide special treatment of them and thus increase penetration of those segments. By tracking every relevant transaction with each customer, you are building a foundation of knowledge for your future marketing strategy. Data is not to be tracked just for the sake of tracking it; it should be relevant to your marketing objectives.

Step 2—Research

In this step, segment and differentiate the customer database through detailed modeling and analysis, "mining" so-called data "warehouses." There are many tools available to help segment, profile and predict future response. Typical database analysis tools include Lifetime Value Calculation, Cluster Analysis, CHAID Analysis, Regression Analysis, and Correlation Analysis.

Research assists in determining segments that mean the most to your marketing efforts, allowing you to customize your approach to these customers. Likewise, it is the basis for attaining Step One objectives, such as increasing retention, locating new similar prospects, and identifying new continuity and cross-selling opportunities.

Step 3—Test

The ultimate goal of testing is to learn from success and failure. It is a continuous cyclical process critical to long-term success. The metrics and standards established during the planning stage are now put to the test.

A truly customer-driven organization views its products and services through the eyes of its customers and focuses on tests for developing and maintaining this process. Understanding customer needs, wants, motivations and, especially, disappointments, the marketer can customize promotional messages to respond to customers' serious concerns and motivations. Media analysis can reveal which marketing channels will be the most productive for communicating with customers and prospects.

Step 4—Validate

Testing and validation go hand in hand. The results of a test can validate that a particular segment has met expectations. Or, if a test segment's performance is marginally unproductive, relevant elements of the test can be recalibrated and the test can be conducted again. Of course, if a test's performance is dismal, the results can be examined, the reasons identified, and mistakes avoided in the future.

Many times the full-circle approach can be developed from prior campaign data. A model based on past information is tested in a small but statistically relevant sample, and the promotion, thus verified, can be rolled out to a larger market with a very high likelihood of success. Once such a model has been validated and proved successful, promotions can be calibrated and customized to match the most productive offer to prospects in specific segments.

The Uses and Users of Database Marketing

As anyone who has opened a mailbox, read a magazine or newspaper, answered a telephone, used the Internet, or watched television knows, the applications of database marketing are virtually endless. A few typical uses follow:

- **Traffic-building at the seller's location:** Retailers like Bloomingdale's, Neiman-Marcus, Macy's, Saks use direct mail, web sites and telemarketing—in addition to traditional print and broadcast media—to drive store traffic. They build databases in the process, as do the more successful specialty stores, such as Radio Shack. Countless manufacturers, Hewlett-Packard among them, do the same for their resellers all the way down the sales chain.

- **Lead-generation at the buyer's location:** Business-to-business marketers like IBM and Pepsi Cola Bottlers use direct mail, web sites, and telemarketing to generate leads and enhance the selling effectiveness of their personal sales forces.

- **Mail order (remote location):** The term *mail order* is a misnomer as both consumer and business-to-business organizations go beyond traditional direct mail and catalogs. They now use telephones, web sites, broadcast and print media. They solicit responses via the World Wide Web. Then, United Parcel Service and Federal Express, as well as the U.S. Postal Service, fulfill responses. "Mail" never enters the picture!

- **Multichannel distribution:** Williams-Sonoma, Sharper Image, Talbot's, Laura Ashley and Eddie Bauer are a few examples of enterprises whose roots are in mail order catalogs but who now populate shopping malls. Many have websites, too. From catalog shopping to buying via the Internet, from personal selling to telecommunication, channels have become blurred. The common denominator is their database.

- **Continuity Selling and Cross-Selling:** It has been mentioned numerous times in this chapter already, but it bears repeating one more time. Every airline, credit card company, and book/music CD club has had programs that encourage some form of automatic repeat buying (continuity) or of buying related goods and services (cross-selling) for years. Today, with more sophisticated technology, marketers are able to identify and learn about customers' needs and preferences and respond to them in ways that build strong relationships.

More Ways to Maximize Cross-Selling Opportunities

Hewlett-Packard, reacting to a warranty registration, mailed customers an offer of a "Support Agreement." To the same database, a publisher offered a training guide for the product.

This letter, inserted in a Lands' End mail-order brochure, provided a cross-sell offer from the Walt Disney World Resort:

Dear Lands' End Customer:

We've recently begun talking with Walt Disney World about partnering on some projects, both here in the USA and abroad. A relationship seemed a natural, in part because we share the same feelings you have about exceeding your expectations in everything we do.

Recently, we visited the Walt Disney World Resort in Florida and got a look at the Wilderness Lodge. It's pretty amazing. We said we'd tell you and other Lands' End customers about it in this brochure. And the Disney people reciprocated by putting together some customized vacation packages exclusively for our hardworking Lands' End employees and valued customers like you.

In the meantime, thanks for shopping with Lands' End!

The technology of the Internet and its possibilities have captivated many. While the failure rate has been high, there have been some noteworthy success stories. Sharper Image, with its considerable direct marketing experience, especially as a cataloger before it ventured into e-commerce, sent the following in advance of Mother's Day to a customer buying from its web site:

Dear Customer:

Still haven't found the perfect gift for Mom? It's not too late. We have a great gift collection to take care of just that. And you can save $10 at one of our stores on purchases over $50 now until Mother's Day, Sunday, May 14.

Here are a few suggestions...

Interactivity and the Convergence of Print, Broadcast, and Electronic Media

The rise of real-time interactivity between seller and customer is the next extension of direct marketing. Interactivity can be used to create and cultivate customers if it does so in conjunction with a database that tells the seller about both actual and potential customers. The crash of thousands of dot-coms at the turn of the century testified to the importance of database marketing as the keystone of the profitable use of all the new interactive technology available now and in the coming years.

Coupling new technology with the philosophy of direct marketing, reflected in the integration of direct mail, print, broadcast, telemarketing, and other forms of response media, will be necessary for success. Today's Internet-based electronic media have tremendously extended the opportunities for the acquisition and cultivation of customers through continuity- and cross-selling. Benefit-oriented promotion that is relevant to the recipient remains the key to developing profitable relationships with customers.

The range of interactive media is almost limitless, but the enduring idea is the use of all of these tools and processes as a direct medium and the development of and investment in the information in an enhanced database.

Personal Computers

PCs are the "old" technology of the new technology and thus in some respects the most developed. Still, their direct response potential has yet to be realized.

An endless number of on-line services offer consumer access to advertisers such as Lands' End, Barnes & Noble, Fidelity, Ford and American Express. They also provide access to travel bookings, investment transactions, automobiles, computers, and a host of other consumer purchases. So are the business-to-business applications.

Internet access, once confined to e-mail, special interest forums and service offers, now emphasizes electronic shopping. Even though the advertising pages of the Internet and the Web are information-laden, they are unorganized and unfriendly and not easy to use, though improvements are on the horizon. In the meantime articulated benefits to targeted prospects are hit-or-miss. Some have described the Internet as a classified directory badly in need of a Dewey Decimal System.

Television/Telephone Hookups

TV home shopping is the single most successful instance of interactive television in the U.S,, with the telephone serving as a response medium. Now a multi-billion-dollar enterprise, TV home shopping merchandise credibility has been enhanced with designer names and with trusted retailer names. Its most obvious shortcoming—lack of high-touch, direct contact with the merchandise—has been overcome by convenience and 24-hour availability.

Acceptance has been great, but it still represents, as do mail-order catalogs, a minuscule fraction of all general merchandise sales. Interactive technology, both fiber-optic transmission and wireless, is advancing rapidly. Cable TV home shopping, under these conditions, could one day become a video extension of direct mail, using the telephone or a cable network for near-immediate response. Still to come, of course, is customer acceptance of the process.

The Smart Card

Supermarket scanners have long tabulated customer purchases to regulate store inventories. Some retailers, like Wal-Mart, even profile typical market baskets as an aid to shelf location and product adjacency. A new wrinkle is created by the Smart Card, which looks like (and can be made to act like) an ordinary credit card. Embedded in it, however, is a small but powerful computer microchip that contains demographic and transaction data about the cardholder. Updated when it is inserted into a card reader during store checkout, the Smart Card can simultaneously record current transactions into the store's database and then profile the characteristics of specific product purchasers.

For both the store and the providers of products sold in the supermarket, the database identifies customers and their preferences for future direct-mail promotions. It also enables profiling of present customers so other prospects like them can be identified and solicited. Whereas supermarket advertisers have traditionally "broadcast" their messages to groups they think will come to their stores and buy their products, their new databases now allow them to "narrow cast" and even target customers individually.

The Smart Card, too, enables stores to trigger promotions geared to discount coupons, amount of transaction or purchaser demographics through scanning at the point of sale. (This capability has greatly reduced the historic 98 percent "wasted" distribution of coupons.) Shoppers who become members of an affinity group, through a buyer reward program, establish a relationship with the store. The expansion of the database allows verification of purchases and can even lead to the calculation of the lifetime value of a supermarket customer.

Privacy and Permission Marketing

The use of data culled from customers' transactions and lifestyles is the "lit fuse" of marketing. Many members of the general public, as well as privacy advocates in particular, are especially alarmed and alarming.

These concerns about privacy impact the future of direct marketing. Add to that an occasional tabloid "special report" about the invasive use of information garnered from "cookies" on the Internet, and it is easy to understand why it is in the interest of direct marketers to be responsible in both the acquisition and the use of data in order to avoid the imposition of regulations. In addition, and certainly not the least of the reasons for "enlightened self-interest," is that it is inefficient, as well as costly and counterproductive, to send irrelevant promotions to those not interested. That is an important reason why more and more attention is being given to market segmentation.

Some customers continue to view any promotion as an intrusion or a nuisance, feeling it is an invasion of their privacy.

Technology has developed, enabling the compilation of so-called "permission" lists of people accessing web sites who are agreeable to receiving relevant solicitations. Such technology permits virtually instant online access to data enhancement to augment that provided by the customer. In the long run, it is conceivable that consumers will receive fewer solicitations, but these will be more relevant. Database analysis pays dividends. As a result, less and less direct response advertising will be thrown away as "junk" because it was not properly directed.

Real-Time Database Marketing—with Permission!

Demand for and retrieval of data instantly is described as real time. Web sites are now able to capture registration data from visitors, along with permission for the use of such data in order to enhance service to them. And, in real time, with reference to external information sources, postal addresses can be standardized, address deliverability can be verified, and residency at that address can be confirmed.

Virtually instantaneously, too, the site can refer to its customer database for prior transactions with the visitor. From external data sources, it can enhance the visit with demographic and lifestyle variables not already known about the visitor.

Sites are thus able to use registration, prior transaction and enhancement information immediately. This enables the site to customize its banners, offers and promotions to the individual visitor. Cross-selling opportunities can be presented; customer relationships can be managed. Permission during registration not only builds a database for follow-up of customer transactions and profiling of prospective customers most like these, but it can alleviate privacy concerns in a palatable manner

The following are just a few of the means that Internet advertisers have to target their advertising messages:

- **Visit to a relevant site:** The time when a visitor is checking stock prices, for example, might be a relevant time to advertise a financial advisory service. Mail-order firms have applied this thinking historically in their directing messages to lists of buyers of related products.

- **Following surfing habits:** Keeping track of web-sites visited by IP addresses, as compiled by DoubleClick and others, can be a means of inferring interests. To minimize privacy concerns, this data may be stored in "cookies" on the individual's own computer. Browsing data, of course, is not necessarily as strong an indicator as trans-action data.

- **Web-site registration and/or transaction data:** This is comparable to a record of inquires or purchases at a retail store or from a mail-order catalog and could be a strong predictor of future buying behavior.

- **Knowledge gained from the Internet:** This might include the domain name of visitors, type of browser or computer and could be a good indicator of a consumer or industrial user.

- **Enhancement from off-line sources:** This could identify demographic and lifestyle characteristics as well as relevant transactions with others. Such enhancement can even be in real time, with a cluster code appended to a site visitor. An important element here is relating an e-mail address to postal (ZIP Code) address or GPS (Global Positioning System) location.

- **Permission List Identifiers:** OptinData (benefits2me.com) offers incentives for visiting a web site, registering, providing data, expressing interests and granting permission for relevant solicitations.

A recent article in *Fortune* magazine, headlined "How Much Are Your Eyeballs Worth?" related an Internet company's market valuation to what is in effect the Lifetime Value of a Customer. An executive at one such company was quoted: "The most interesting business models belong to companies that are able to sell their customer base." That is why the means of targeting enumerated here are so important to Internet organizations. While traditional advertisers seek out their prospects, Internet advertisers rely on prospects to seek them out. There must be an incentive and means for so doing. Database provides both.

Exhibit 1-2 illustrates how the Hewlett-Packard web site, from visitor-provided registration data and utilizing the global positioning system, determines location and directs the visitor to resellers, at the same time linking to its own on-line store.

Internet-related issues were the original impetus to the popularity of permission. In conjunction with the move to permission marketing, most smart direct marketers now publish privacy statements on their web sites and even in their catalogs and other direct mail.

The statements typically are one- or two-paragraphs on the order page of a catalog, although some are multiple-page documents linked to home pages. The former might simply provide assurance that no information will be accessed if the respondent so requests. The latter might provide this assurance in addition to stating the advantages of sharing information in order to provide added benefits and services to customers.

What about "Cookies?"

"Cookies" are bits of information provided by web sites to a browser and stored on an individual's personal computer in a Windows subdirec-

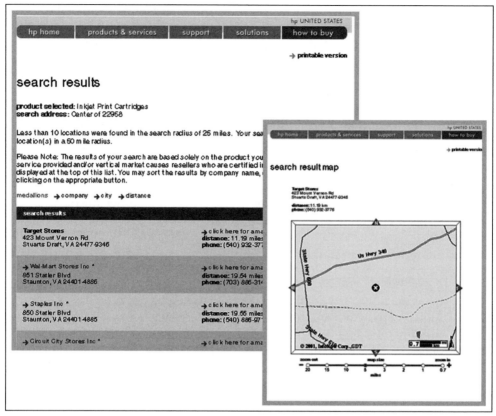

Exhibit 1-2: Utilizing Registration Information, a Web Site Directs a Visitor to a Reseller

tory of that name. They are most used to record site visits and surfing history. They may also be used to record the contents of a shopper's "cart" until ready to checkout. They can be valuable in greeting customers upon their return to a web site as well as identifying their past interests. Since some would prefer that others not know their visits, even though stored on their personal computers, rather than at a web site, browsers can be instructed not to accept them an inconvenience the next time the visitor chooses to engage a "shopping cart."

Workshop 1-1:

Turning Madame Tussaud's into a Strategy-Driven Direct Marketer

Strategy is possibly the most important of all business disciplines because it causes the questioning of the fundamental premises of the status quo. It also serves as a starting point for direct marketers seeking new directions. Introduction of strategic direct marketing, along with development and utilization of databased decision-making, into a traditional marketing environment takes a great deal of top-down long-range commitment.

This workshop is inspired by a 30-minute video titled "The Marketing Mix" that featured the famed London wax museum, Madame Tussaud's. Even though we do not have the video before us, let's see if we can apply the "SWOT" model of strategic planning (Strengths, Weaknesses, Opportunities, and Threats) to develop a direct marketing strategy that will enhance Madame Tussaud's. A SWOT analysis might also help answer the question that so often plagues would-be direct marketers: Where Do I Begin?

The video, produced by the British Broadcasting Corporation, describes some of Madame Tussaud's marketing challenges. We will use that information and come up with a strategy for using direct marketing to solve some of these problems.

In the video, Madame Tussaud's marketing director makes statements like "no customers ... no business" and "marketing is a philosophy ... with the customer at the core." He refers to FMCG—"fast-moving consumer goods" (package goods). He says that he wants to know why visitors come to the museum and exactly what happens during the visit. How might an awareness of database-driven direct marketing help him answer his questions?

Perhaps the marketing director should consider the lifetime value of a customer (LTV)? Its well-known brand name certainly opens the door to continuity and cross selling opportunities:

Continuity Selling Opportunities
■ Repeat visits to Madame Tussaud's
■ Additional visits to Madame Tussaud's wax museums located in other cities of the world
■ Visits to other London tourist attractions operated by the management of Madame Tussaud's, such as Windsor Castle and the Queen Victoria exhibit adjoining it

■ Referrals to others by more than 2,000,000 annual visitors to Madame Tussaud's in London.

Cross-Selling Opportunities

■ Kodak products already available include: disposable cameras, film, processing, slides
■ Why not a mail-order catalog offering artifacts, reproductions, related products appropriate for the image created by the Madame Tussaud's "experience?"

Before Madame Tussaud's can consider launching benefit-oriented direct-response advertising, it needs to clarify its identity. What, really, is Madame Tussaud's? Is it a museum? Is it an entertainment? Is it an experience? Is it a tourist destination? Is it habit-forming; i.e., is there a potential for repeat visits by those on a database?

The marketing director also needs to consider the relevance and importance, if any, of a database of customers. A carefully constructed database might help Madame Tussaud's calculate the value of a customer; profile customers, by product and by source; cross-sell other tourist destinations or other products; or plan, forecast, and predict customer behavior. Is one called for here?

SWOT Analysis Findings

Strengths as well as weaknesses are endogenous to the organization. That is, they can be controlled from within. Opportunities and threats are exogenous to the organization and are not easily controlled. Strengths can sometimes be used to exploit opportunities or to ward off threats. Opportunities can sometimes be exploited to overcome weaknesses, ward off threats.

Here is a summary of strengths and weaknesses, based on information revealed in the Madame Tussaud's video.

Strengths	
• 200+ years of history	• unique business
• world-wide reputation	• strong brand identity
• excellent location in the heart of London	• enormous customer base
• good transportation links	• established relations with affinity suppliers.
• close to other important attractions (Planetarium, Baker Street, Regent's Park)	• part of a bigger group
	• unlimited age appeal
• energetic, experienced marketing director	• appeals to all ethnic groups
	• enhanced fantasy
• high quality products	• variety, changing interaction
	• technical skill of staff
	• price reasonable to tourist

Weaknesses

- may still be perceived as old-fashioned
- possibly a lack of agreement on corporate objectives
- a specialized business with no clear product
- definition: is it a museum, an entertainment, an experience?
- no list of names, no database
- limited capacity to value customers, to profile these customers
- limited data in order to plan, forecast, predict, and explain sales.
- continuity and cross selling opportunities are also limited
- each member of the Madame Tussaud's group independent of others
- low repeat purchase
- reliance on one-time tourist
- queuing to get in, slow transaction
- crowded
- complex pricing
- poor accessibility
- perceived as dingy
- little integration in promotions
- relatively little promotion to locals
- waxworks don't translate to reality
- more topicality needed
- long distances for cross-selling other attractions

Opportunities and threats faced by Madame Tussaud's include:

Opportunities

- unlimited world market
- opportunities for continuity selling
- ditto for cross selling
- opportunities to up-sell
- opportunities to widen the product base
- database opportunities for segmentation, profiling
- opportunities in pricing thru estimations of demand elasticities
- price discrimination, e.g., premium prices, discounts
- place opportunities, e.g.,exhibitions to selected market segments
- joint ventures with other of their own tourist attractions
- increasing world-wide tourism
- capitalize on topical changes
- franchising
- market/product differentiation
- seasonal differences
- using the ever-present queue (line) to cross-sell
- package sales to tours
- cross sales of reproductions
- exhibit wax likenesses of famous cartoon characters
- direct response advertising placed in remote locations
- "Walkman" audio tours

Threats	
heavily reliant on tourists and thus...	• domestic visitors see Madame Tussaud's as expensive
• subject to exchange rates, terrorism, other exogenous factors	• inflation & reduction in living standard could further erode domestic business
• the "attractions" business in London is very competitive	• degeneration of London and bad press
	• competitive tourist destinations

Identification of the Issues

The SWOT analysis clearly identifies Madame Tussaud's strengths, weaknesses, opportunities, and threats. From these we can next identify the issues of concern to the organization:

Issues	
• service industry with typical service delivery problems	• customer acquisition
• smoothing demand (peak/off-peak)	• continuity selling ... repeat visits
• database development for promotion; for market research	• cross selling ... within Madame Tussaud's; within the group

There are two means through which direct marketing can begin to address these issues: product management and promotion.

Product Management. New product development might suggest these starting points to encourage customer continuity, especially by London residents:

- Special exhibitions, such as cartoon characters
- Group sales
- Season tickets
- Off-peak hours events
- Referrals, bring-a-friend
- Exhibits in other London locations.

To enhance customer cross-selling opportunities, consider the following as starting points:

- Visits to other attractions affiliated with Tussaud's
- Tie-ins with other local museums
- Mail-order catalog of reproductions of artifacts
- Video-tapes and audio-cassettes sales

- Adding value to the visit...developing a unique selling proposition (USP) for special groups.

Review of pricing strategy might be another starting point:

- Admission prices: individual, senior citizen, student, children, family, other "groups," season (high/low), overseas purchase; advance purchase
- Coupon tie-in with other product sales
- Premiums
- Gift book.

Promotion. In considering any promotion campaign, the direct marketer must live by these three rules:

1. Promotion must be measurable and accountable — where every cost is related to a result, often in the long-run (lifetime value of a customer)

2. Advertising must be benefit-oriented — it must tell prospects exactly what need or desire the product offered will satisfy

3. Promotion must use and build upon real information about customers to support decisions, to identify prospects, to acquire, and then to cultivate customers.

A major advertising medium for Madame Tussaud's, as demonstrated in the videotape, was television. The commercials were exceptionally well done and certainly conveyed a compelling image of the wax museum as an "experience." Measurement of these, however, could be difficult.

Limited attention was paid to either direct-response offers or other media. An exception was the "leaflets" (so called by the marketing director), which were distributed in hotels and other tourist spots in the United Kingdom and in other countries.

Do these leaflets present the seed for a customer-oriented promotion? How about expanding distribution of these, with a response device added, to niche markets ... to affinity groups ... or through wholesalers such as travel agents, airlines, hotels, car rentals, credit cards?

How about testing and integrating the media and techniques of direct marketing with current promotion efforts? There's no need to replace promotion strategy at the outset. Rather, augment it! New offers. New media. Niches. Timing. Increased coverage. Increased market pentration.

The Need for a Database

A database is, of course, most important. Although Madame Tussaud's marketing director admits to 2,000,000 visitors a year, there is no indication that any of these customer transactions, names or characteristics have been captured, analyzed, utilized.

Why record visitors? It is, after all, highly unlikely that direct mail promotion of another visit could pay for itself. But ... research of these names could pay off. Prospects could be identified for niche market promotions in media other than more-costly (per prospect) direct mail. Further, those who already have a customer relationship with Madame Tussaud's could be cultivated through mail-order cross-selling of reproductions of artifacts and even vicarious visits through books, video and/or audiocassettes, or a printed publication to subscribers.

The database provides the means of research to support decisions. It enables profiling of customers so as to direct the search among prospects for more like them. It provides the means for implementation of profitable programs of continuity selling and cross-selling. It aids scientific planning and forecasting.

When all is said and done, thinking like a direct marketer provides alternatives to the price competition that plagues so many in the tourism industry. *Non-price competition* is enhanced when offers and benefits are related to needs. It also is enhanced by a well-developed database and by relating costs to results.

Chapter 2

Basic Principles for Developing, Maintaining and Using a Database

Key Concepts
- Contents of a Database
- Demographic and Psychographic Data
- Buyer Behavior
- Customer Databases
- Prospect Databases
- Enhancement Databases
- Cluster Databases
- Analytical Databases
- Hierarchical Databases
- Relational Databases
- Normalization
- Merge/Purge and Duplication
- Nixies and NCOA

Applications
- Developing a Customer Database
- Using a Customer Database

What's the difference between a mailing list and a database? To be sure, the basic ingredient of both is a name and address record that is complete, accurate, and maintained (updated regularly). But a database goes much further: It incorporates the individual characteristics of customers and prospective customers as well as their prior transactions. This vital information drives the direct marketing process as it structures relationships and affinity.

Database Essentials

- A unique identifier such as an ID number or a match code
- Name and title of individual and/or organization
- Mailing address, including ZIP Code
- Telephone number
- Source of order, inquiry, or referral
- Data and purchase details of first transaction
- Recency/frequency/monetary transaction history by date, by amounts of purchases, by products (lines) purchased
- Credit history and rating

- Relevant individual data for consumer buyers, such as location, age, gender, marital status, family status, income, education, occupation; type of dwelling and its value, length of residence, geodemographic cluster data; lifestyle reflections of attitudes, opinions and interests.

- Relevant organization data for industrial buyers such as standard industrial classification (SIC), size, revenue, number of employees, length of time in business; perhaps information about the organization's economic/social location; and even information about the personality of individual buyers within the organization.

Exhibit 2-1 Database Essentials

Information a Database Should Contain

The key difference between mailing lists and databases lies in the greater analytical depth afforded by databases. The amount of computing power and analytical sophistication required very much depend on the needs of individual organizations as well as the potential usefulness (profitability) of acquired information. One must consider what's relevant to the future needs of the organization and what's attainable on a cost-effective basis. Most importantly, will the information, once compiled, be useful and will it, in fact, be used? Exhibit 2-1 presents a listing that can get a database off to a good start.

Information within a database can be categorized in the following way:

- **Geographic data** identifies whether a customer or prospect is located in an urban, suburban, urban fringe or rural area. It identifies a nation, region, state, county, or metropolitan area. It can identify smaller geographic units, including census tracts, block groups, Postal ZIP Codes and letter carrier routes. It can even pinpoint to latitude/longitude coordinates, utilizing the Global Positioning System (GPS).

- **Demographic data** can include such variables as age, gender, marital status, occupation and education. It can also include housing information such as owner or renter, type of structure, its value and its equipment. Often, change in demography is important. If a single person marries or if a baby is born, these events can have significance for certain marketers. So do population change or high mobility of residence.

- **Psychographic data** is associated with lifestyle. Knowing a customer's or prospect's personality, behaviors and "AIO's"—attitudes, interests and opinions—can help predict buying behavior. Psychographic and lifestyle information can be obtained from the interaction of geographic and demographic variables. It can also be determined from actions taken, such as subscribing to a certain publication, or buying a certain product. Survey research, including information provided on product warranty cards, can also demonstrate attitudes, interests and opinions as well as activities. (Lifestyle demand variables can also be built from thousands of product/service usage characteristics that represent propensity of demand for that specific lifestyle, i.e., propensity to play golf.)

- **Actions Taken** (Buyer Behaviors) have traditionally been identified by direct marketers through selections within their own customer lists or even those of other organizations. Such variables include buyers of all types of products, subscribers to highly specialized publications, members of differentiated book and record clubs, donors to causes, and supporters of organizations. Identification of the sequencing and timing of actions taken can be a basis for predictive modeling and determination of customer lifetime value.

Information is a perishable commodity. Customer activity fluctuates. Individuals and organizations comprising a database are not static. Their demographics change. They change jobs, within as well as between organizations. Their attitudes and preferences change. They die. They move. In 12 months, 20 percent of a customer list typically changes address.

Such volatility demonstrates the importance of proper mailing list maintenance. Lists that are solicited regularly and maintained current are more deliverable than are lists that are not qualified or are compiled from directories or rosters.

Kinds of Databases

A database can drive the entire operation of a marketing organization and an entire company. The following are five categories of database development and utilization.

The Customer Database

The simplest, yet most important, database may be little more than a collection of customer information. It can be used to identify the company's most valuable customers and communicate with them in ways that, based on their past preferences, are likely to elicit response. Purchase history can be combined with demographic and psychographic data to predict future purchases. This database can further categorize customers as:

- **Active Customers:** What actions have customers taken in the past? What products/services do they buy? Why do they buy? How recently have they purchased? How frequently have they purchased? How much did they spend? What are their product or service preferences? From what promotion source were they acquired? Identifying most active customers and most recent purchases helps to concentrate resources on most profitable segments of a customer list.

- **Inactive Customers:** How long have prior customers been inactive? How long had they been active? What was their buying pattern? How were they initially acquired? What offers have they received? This information can help design promotion that re-activates inactive customers.

- **Inquiries:** From what media source did inquirers come? What was the nature and seriousness of the inquiry? Is any demographic or psychographic data available?

- **Referrals:** Who recommended these? For what purpose? Can the name of the referrer be used in follow-up?

The Prospect Database

Databases of existing customers enable identification of prospects most likely to become customers:

- Profile customers in the customer database first.

- Then seek prospects like these.

- View such profiles in terms of *lists*—of readers of publications, viewers of television programs, listeners to radio, those responsive to electronic communication, and/or visitors to websites—in order to effectively use all advertising media, not just direct mail.

- Think in terms of *market segmentation and product differentiation.* Then, position differentiated products (such as recordings of rock music) to market segments (high school students, for example).

- Employ a *rifle* rather than a shotgun approach to prospecting. Aim for *individuals* with characteristics similar to those of existing customers.

- Experiment with prospect lists and test them.

The Enhancement Database

This is where the more contemporary ideas of databases go well beyond mailing lists. Sophisticated technology can overlay multiple databases to transfer information. This can substantially increase the quantity and quality of information about each customer or prospect.

In it simplest form, an enhancement might be the addition of age from a driver's license record or a telephone number from a directory record. Other possibilities include past transactions; demographic and psychographic data; credit experience, if pertinent; people on the move, evidenced by an address change; significant characteristics of a business; and a multitude of customer behavior and "actions taken" data.

By overlaying multiple databases, duplications between and among these can be eliminated. "Hotline names" (those who responded most recently) and "multibuyers" (those who appear on more than one response list) can be identified.

Negative screening, such as a credit check, can be used to remove a record from a solicitation database.

The Cluster Database

Databases can be further enhanced using publicly available information on people, groups, and businesses. Certainly a major database for direct marketers is that of the decennial Census of Population and Housing. The Census is particularly useful in explaining the characteristics of a small geographic cluster (such as a ZIP Code area) and, from this, evaluating a buying environment in order to predict response. Look also at:

- Affinity groups: clubs, associations, neighborhoods where people with like interests tend to cluster. Behavior within such clusters, including buying habits and attitudes, tends to be influenced by peer groups.

- Geographic reference groups small enough to facilitate prediction through environmental demographic databases such as census tracts, block groups, ZIP Code areas, postal carrier routes and GPS clusters.

- Lifestyle (psychographic) reference groups, having common activities, attitudes, interests, and opinions.

- Industrial data for business purchasers, including such variables as size, revenues, capitalization, number of employees, standard industrial classification (SIC) and business clusters derived from socioeconomic data.

The Analytical Database

Databases should be utilized not just to collect transaction and other relevant information about customers but also to aid decision-making. Use a database as an analytical tool; employ statistical techniques and findings of survey research as well as results of experimentation (testing). Be aware of the predictive models and simulations used to support decision making:

- Measure response and keep records for accountability purposes: which lists and media are most productive?

- Analyze, interpret results, and evaluate the effect of marketing decisions.

- Predict future response.

Designing a Database

The two broad categories of databases to consider when thinking in terms of reference and retrieval of relevant data are hierarchical and relational databases.

Hierarchical Databases are built around a single, central record. All information relative to an individual customer is contained therein. There is no need in such a system to cross-refer to other data sources. Airline and hotel reservation systems have been developed in this way. While hierarchical databases provide high-volume access and ease of use, their analytical capabilities can be limited by the extent of the data available.

Relational Databases are a more recent approach to database development and utilization. They provide the advantages of simplicity and flexibility, minimizing redundancy. Related information is drawn from different, independent database sources as needed. A product database can be linked to a customer name/address database to direct promotion to specific product buyers. The separate product file enables analysis of a product line regardless of customer. Links can be established, too, with billing and/or shipping and inventory records.

How a Relational Database Is Built

A customer table can be built by using database software such as Microsoft Access. This Database Management System (DBMS) is one of many applications that allow creation, modification, and access via other applications for record manipulation. A data dictionary contains descriptions of the data within the database and allows flexibility in layout and formatting of files. Data is stored in tables having rows and columns linked together with a common key, such as a unique customer ID number. One column in a table could represent a customer name and each row an individual customer. Another could contain the unique customer number that would allow a reporting system to link this table to another table that contains historical transaction data by customer number. Yet another table could be linked with information pertaining to the promotional efforts to that customer.

A primary key of Customer Number links a "parent" table with a "child" table. This unique field will not contain duplicate values and can link one table to another in a one-to-many relationship. It is one-to-many because each customer can relate to many orders or promotional efforts.

The database wizard within Microsoft Access can be used to build a contact management system with predefined templates. The wizard leads the user through a series of design steps that provide several functions, including the ability to add optional and suggested fields, select a screen display, select a report style, and enter a title or name for a new database. Once the application is complete, the user can enter and modify data and develop new tables that link to keys within the customer file in order to expanding the use of the database.

Relational databases are especially useful in tracking customer data because they have the flexibility needed to track this data, which often changes frequently. Because of table-driven features, relational technology also is more scalable and portable.

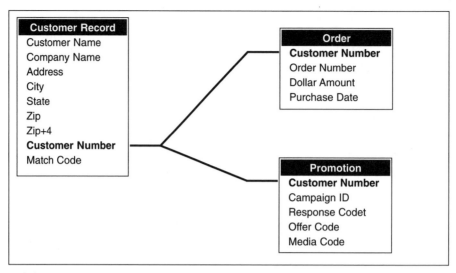

Exhibit 2-2: Example of Tables Linked in a Relational Database

One of the more powerful functions of a relational database is the ability to query associate records from multiple related tables and join them together. When relations are joined on a given data item, only records that share the same value of the query will appear in the result. Defining the relationship(s) enables the marketer to specify the type of connection ("join") wanted for the tables. For example, does the marketer want customer records to appear *only* if there are corresponding order *and* promotional records or does the user want to see *all* customer records regardless of the presence of child records. See Exhibit 2.2

File **normalization** is an important part of the database building process and is by definition the restructuring of data files with the goal being to reduce the data to its simplest structure and minimize redundancy of data. Ultimately, it is desirable to organize data fields in a way that will achieve the most efficient yet most flexible way to store data. There are several forms of normalization:

- **1st normal form:** Eliminate duplication, records and fields
- **2nd normal form:** Organize all data in a table to relate to one subject, usually a primary key.
- **3rd normal form:** eliminate fields derived from other fields, for example total cost can be calculated in a report.

Using the database wizard within Microsoft Access, a contact management system can be built with predefined templates. The wizard will lead you through a series of design steps including adding optional and suggested fields, selecting a screen display, selecting a report style, and entering a title for the new database. Once the application is complete, data can be entered and modified and new tables developed that link to keys within the customer file for expanding the use of the database.

Relational databases offer the most flexibility in working with customer data as information to track may change frequently. Because of the table driven features, relational technology is also more scalable and portable.

Using Merge/Purge and Match Codes to Eliminate Duplication

A database must be designed to eliminate duplicated information and, thus, wasted effort. The more external lists are used to supplement a house list, the more complex this becomes. Customer lists from different sources may duplicate each other; compiled lists may contain duplications *within, between, and among* lists; and, many names may already be on a house list. The solution: use merge/purge match codes to eliminate duplication.

The merge/purge process extracts information from each record in the form of a match code, constructed so that each record can be compared with every other record in the database, without need for exact matching. For example, look at the two surnames below. It is likely that this is the same person:

Melinda Barton   Melinda Burton
5410 Salisbury Drive   5410 Salisbury Drive
Lexington, MA 02173   Lexington, MA 02173

An example of a simple 18-digit match code derived from the two preceding records is shown in Exhibit 2-3. Other data might be added to the match code such as a Social Security number or a birth date. Through match codes, millions of records can be compared within and between lists. Exhibit 2-4, for example, displays multiple appearances on two or more mailing lists, with variations of duplicate names/addresses.

As Exhibit 2-5 shows, even a 5 percent "hit" rate can result in substantial cost savings, as 5 percent fewer pieces need to be mailed. Identification of potential duplication of 15 percent, when one million names on various databases are merged and purged, would result in a reduction of 150,000 pieces of mail. At an assumed cost of $500 per thousand names mailed, this results in a mailing cost savings of $75,000. Offsetting this saving would be the cost of the merge/purge process itself that, at $10 per thousand names examined, would amount to $10,000 for a one million name/address input.

Position	Item	Description
1	State	A unique alpha-numeric code assigned to each state
2-5	ZIP Code	Last 4 numbers of 5-digit ZIP Code
6-8	Surname	1st, 3rd and 4th alpha characters of surname or business name
9-12	Address	House or business street number
13-15	Address	1st, 3rd and 4th alpha characters of street name
16	Surname	Alpha-numeric count of characters in surname
17	Given Name	Alpha initial of first name
18	Given Name	Alpha-numeric count of characters in first name

Example Address

Melinda Barton
5410 Salisbury Drive
Lexington, MA 02173

Derived Match Code

92173BRT5410SLI6M7

Exhibit 2-3: Mailing List Match Code

Using Merge/Purge to Find Multibuyers

Besides eliminating duplicate names/addresses, saving money, and sparing customers the irritation of receiving redundant mailings, the merge/purge process offers another, possibly even greater advantage. If the same name/address is found on two or more customer lists simultaneously, it is conceivable that the multibuyer is an above-average prospect. Experimentation has shown, in fact, that the expectation of a higher rate of response from those names appearing on three lists is greater than the expectation from those names on two lists. The merge/purge process can identify these multibuyers for special handling.

Other Uses of Merge/Purge

The merge/purge process can also effectively remove names of individuals who have expressed a desire not to receive particular solicitations as well as those who have been poor credit risks or are otherwise potentially undesirable customers.

Maintaining a Database

A database is a perishable commodity. Unless it is kept up to date, information is suspect. When incorrect addresses or telephone numbers result in misdirected advertising promotions, the cost is twofold: (1) the cost of the wasted contact, and (2) the sacrifice of potential response.

Name	Address	City	State	Zip
Debra Simpson	948 S Ruby Ave	Sober	NJ	08106
Debra Simpson	948 S Ruby Ave	Sober	NJ	08106
Safiyya Sobell	107 Alexander St	Sober	NJ	08106
S Sobell	107 Alexander St	Sober	NJ	08106
R Peters	Apt 902 797 N 6th	Sober	NJ	08106
R Peters	789 N 6th St 63	Sober	NJ	08106
John Ziebart	44 Marsac Pl	Sober	NJ	08106
Walter Ziebart	44 Marsac Pl	Sober	NJ	08106
Horace Roberts	253 N Sixth St	Sober	NJ	08107
Horace Roberts	253 N 6th Apt 2	Sober	NJ	08107
Susie Martin	49 Hawthorne Ln S	Sober	NJ	08107
Susie Martin	49 Hawthorne Ln S	Sober	NJ	08107

Exhibit 2-4: Merge/Purge Duplication Listing

A database should be designed so as to make it easy to maintain. Information needs to be compiled in a uniform manner. Only when such uniformity exists is it possible to use merge/purge or match codes with any assurance of reliability.

These tasks need to be performed on a regular basis:

1. Nixie removal
2. National Change of Address (NCOA)
3. Transactions status update.

Nixie Removal

The term **nixie** refers to mail that has been returned because it is undeliverable as addressed and no forwarding address has been provided.

	Total Number of Names/Addresses Merged		
% Duplication	100,000	500,000	1,000,000
5%	$ 2,500	$12,500	$ 25,000
10%	$ 5,000	$25,000	$ 50,000
15%	$ 7,500	$37,500	$ 75,000
20%	$10,000	$50,000	$100,000
25%	$12,500	$62,500	$125,000
30%	$15,000	$75,000	$150,000

Assumes Mailing Cost of $500 per Thousand Pieces Mailed

Exhibit 2-5: Economic Value of Merge/Purge of Mailing Lists Utilizing Match Codes to Identify Duplication and Multibuyers

This might result from a simple error in the street address or ZIP Code. If such an error can be traced, the address can be corrected.

Other possible reasons for undelivered mail are that the person to whom mail is addressed is deceased or has moved and left no forwarding address. In such cases, the name should be removed from the mailing list portion of the database, leaving other records intact until and if a correct address is known.

Often, mail addressed to a deceased person will continue to be delivered to a survivor. Or, mail to an individual who has changed positions or even left an organization will be received by the replacement in that position. Although the Postal Service will not send notifications in such instances, experienced direct marketers obtain list corrections through special mailings. Also, when a salesperson from the firm calls on the customer, corrected information can be obtained.

Other ways in which mailing lists can be updated to avoid "nixies" include references to news items as well as references to public records such as births, deaths, marriages and divorces.On the Internet, similar issues arise due to invalid or inactive email addresses.

Change of Address Update

Whenever possible, address corrections should be requested through the U.S. Postal Service. Mail prepaid with first class postage is automatically returned if undeliverable or forwarded without charge if the new address is known. For a fee, the sender will be notified of the new address as well.

The Postal Service offers a variety of address correction procedures for advertising mail. Most notable is the National Change of Address (NCOA) file that virtually all major mailers, and a goodly number of minor ones, use regularly.

Direct marketers often encourage those on their databases to inform them of any change of address or telephone number, and provide the means for doing so.

Transactions Status Update

It is of vital importance to keep the transactions status of customers always up to date. New transactions from customers should be entered into the database promptly because they have a major impact on customer evaluation. They also exert a major influence on the performance of future solicitations.

Above all, direct marketers do not want to distribute their direct response advertising indiscriminately. They want to make sure not only that their messages are delivered but that they are delivered to the right prospects at the right time.

Database Security

Like buildings, equipment and inventories, databases are assets. Unlike tangible assets, they are somewhat more portable. Millions of records can be packed on CDs or pocket-sized cassettes. Loss or misuse of these records through falling into the wrong hands can be highly detrimental to the organization. But unfortunately, because their value is intangible, they are not easily insurable, except for replacement and duplication costs.

For these reasons, special precautions must be taken to prevent destruction, loss, theft, or unauthorized use. Attention should be given to:

- Proper program administration and assigning responsibility for development, modification, and utilization.

- Limiting exposures through secured location, proper storage, controlled access, cryptographic techniques, adequate erasure, and destruction.

- Marking the list, to discourage unauthorized use.

- Discouraging theft through visible security, awareness of misuse precautions, and apprehension of violators.

- Maintaining accountability for systems and documents.

The logical first step is to make sure the database is stored in a manner that protects it against natural hazards of fire and water damage, as well as theft or unauthorized use. To discourage theft, access to list files should be limited and controlled at all times. Should a list be lost, either inadvertently or through improper handling, duplicate records should be available at a remote location.

A variety of marking techniques has been developed for "seeding" mailing lists. In the event a list is misappropriated or misused, such decoys—which are either invalid spellings or fictitious names that are known and appear nowhere else— can identify misuse. Still, these do not always lead to the culprit! Certain mechanical or cryptographic precautions can be taken to discourage theft, such as passwords or a connecting procedure from the end of one storage device to the beginning of the next.

Any storage or list marking efforts should be known to all involved in database handling.

Workshop 2-1:

Developing and Using a Customer Database

This workshop is inspired by a declining birth rate that has resulted in a declining market demand. This stimulated a British baby shoe manufacturer to develop a direct-marketing strategy that would influence buyer behavior toward its product line.

The British shoe manufacturer, C&J Clarks, Ltd., faced a difficult sales problem. A declining birthrate caused a 13.1 percent decline in market demand for children's shoes.

As a result, retailers were carrying less stock and thus restricting consumer choice. Salespeople for C&J Clarks, Ltd., who called on some 2,000 retailers every 6 to 8 weeks, found it increasingly difficult to maintain retailer interest in carrying a full range of styles and colors, in spite of a schedule of advertising that the firm was running in specialized media.

As an alternative to this general magazine advertising, executives of the firm decided to contact new mothers in another way and to measure specific results from that contact. The new promotional strategy involved use of The Bounty Box, a gift pack containing advertising and product samples given to new mothers while still in the hospital. About 280,000 new mothers were reached through this medium every year.

A mailing piece with a special offer was also designed. The package contained a letter, a four-color brochure, and a reply card, low-key in nature and designed to position Clarks as a company that knows about babies. The letter offered a handsome color poster, 16×20 inches, which could be hung in the new infant's room at home. The poster depicted toy blocks, each containing copy describing "stepping stones" the infant would pass: crawling, sitting, speaking, standing, teething, and, of course, getting the first pair of shoes from Clarks.

This offer from Clarks, distributed within The Bounty Box, resulted in a 15 percent response. Clarks thus generated its own database of new mothers, about 42,000 annually. When it was time for the baby's first shoes, the mothers received a letter giving valuable guidance in buying the child's first shoes.

Clarks' salespeople presented to each retailer an outline of the program and a sample of The Bounty Box. They gave the retailer, too, a 5-by-7-inch bound presentation, printed on heavy paper stock. Each page described a typical fitting situation. The Clarks salespeople also left a window decal, a die-cut illustrating the baby's block idea, and, as an in-store display, a building block box stand on which to display their First Shoes.

It was suggested that the fitter ask for the name of the family making a purchase as a result of this program in order to contact them when the baby would be ready for another pair, size.

Dear Mrs. Jones:

During the next nine months or so your baby's going to start to walk. And although one of the healthiest things in the world is for him (her) to run around in bare feet, sooner or later he's (she's) going to need shoes.

Obviously, you're going to want good-looking shoes. But there are more serious considerations that should affect your choice. That's why we've sent you this leaflet explaining what you should be looking for in a child's first shoes and, more importantly, why you should take so much trouble over them.

When you've read the facts in the leaflet, we believe you'll decide to buy Clarks First Shoes. So at the bottom of this letter, we've listed your nearest First Shoes stockists.

Every one of them has a trained fitter on the staff who'll be able to give you all the help you need in choosing the most important shoes you'll ever buy.

C&J Clarks, Ltd.

The Bottom Line

What were the results? Against a 13.1 percent decline in the overall market, the company's volume increased 4 percent. Retailers upped stock orders 8 percent. After testing, the program became a continuing one.

The real learning experience here, however, may well be that of breaking with traditional ways of doing business, of seeking and experimenting with new and different ways of achieving results, relative to costs. The basis for such action is typically research and accumulation of facts by testing alternative strategies.

What does this case tell us about creating and then cultivating customers with an appropriate and relevant database?

Referring to the contents of this chapter, how might C&J Clarks have enhanced this customer database, beyond recording the first sale, from either internal or external sources?

How might they go about determining the lifetime value of a new customer acquired from The Bounty Box new mothers promotion?

Chapter 3
Data Enhancements

Key Concepts
- Data Sources and Collection
- Data Mining
- Data Warehousing
- Online Analytical Processing (OLAP)
- Balanced Scorecard Dashboard
- Drill Up and Drill Down
- Application Service Provider (ASP)
- Viral Marketing

Applications
- Using a Balanced Scorecard Dashboard
- Mining Information from a Data Warehouse
- Developing a Customer Profile
- Using a Customer Profile to Identify New Customers

Data Sources and Collection Methods

Exhibit 2-1 in the preceding chapter listed the kinds of information that might be included in the typical consumer database, such as name/address, transactions and relevant demographics data. For business-to-business organizations, typical information, such as the names of buyers, decision-makers, as well as influencers (gatekeepers), is often augmented with transaction data and relevant information about the organization as a whole as well as the individual buyers.

Other information may be appropriate for a supplemental database, such as information about undesirable prospects, credit risks, or those who don't want to be solicited. Another related database might categorize and identify ZIP Codes or other cluster areas in which response from prospects is more likely to occur, or even other data such as climactic regions most suitable for particular clothing or plant varieties.

To identify prospects with the greatest potential to become customers, many enterprises rely on outsourcing and external databases. Paying to use this kind of data as needed is probably wiser than bringing it in-house where maintenance can be a problem and a considerable expense. Another option is outsourcing to a database marketing service bureau that can append thousands of variables to your file and then allow customized access and "what if" views via the Internet, charging on a per-use basis. Compiled lists are an example of data sources that can be "rented" for specified usages without the cost of acquiring and maintaining data referenced infrequently.

Information costs money, but so do bad decisions. Building a database invariably represents a considerable investment of both time and money. It is, therefore, important to consider just what will be done with data once it is collected. Here is a list of key questions:

- How will the data be stored and accessed?

- How will it be maintained and kept current?

- Will it provide benefits at least equal to its cost?

- Will it aid in decision-making?

- Will the database be used for analysis and evaluation in ways that lower ultimate costs by increasing efficiency, productivity, and revenues?

Data Warehousing

Historically, marketers have complained about the need for more information. In recent years, that complaint has changed: Keeping up with information has become an overwhelming task. As a result, many organizations are resorting to **data warehouses**, whether in-house or out-sourced to a service bureau. Such a marketing data warehouse is simply a central repository of customer transactions and relevant demographic data that serves as a tool for analytical and strategic decision-making. The typical data warehouse generates historical trends.

A key benefit of a data warehouse is that it integrates data across the organization into a standard unified format. Its historical nature enables "mining" for trends to predict the future. The warehouse also allows a combination of detailed and summarized data for both micro and macro intelligence.

For most companies the initial steps to building a data warehouse are already in place with current data collection and recording systems. Building a logical model that incorporates a high-level view of the data and its interrelationships can be time consuming. Regularly scheduled maintenance of the data warehouse—often with a daily, weekly, monthly, quarterly, or even real-time data feed—is absolutely critical.

Organizations can no longer put off the centralization of marketing data as a tool for executive decision-making. The job of database

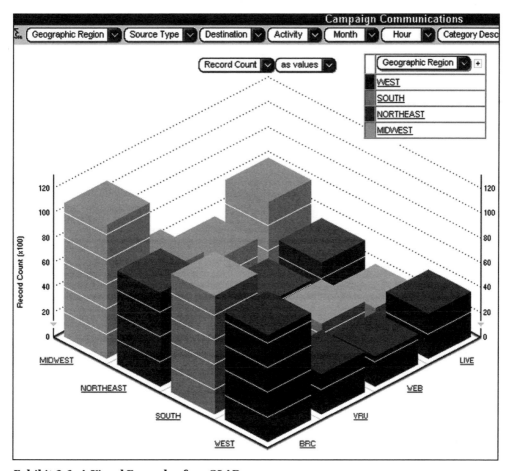

Exhibit 3-1: A Visual Example of an OLAP

managers is becoming one of knowledge management that revolves around the enterprise's data warehouse.

Data Mining

The true value of the integrated data warehouse can be found by leveraging decision support tools, such as OLAP (on-line analytical processing) to mine the data for hidden patterns. OLAP has long been the domain of business analysts and statisticians, but sophisticated new tools now provide business analysis capabilities via the data warehouse available throughout an organization. Previous tools provided only static reports, offering little flexibility in terms of what a user could glean or screen from the warehouse.

With OLAP, users can slice and dice the data from a summary level down into the detail of the data record. They can get information on customers by region or by revenue and do it all from the desktop. Exhibit 3-1 provides an OLAP illustration, and the accompanying CD provides a demonstration.

Balanced Scorecard Dashboard

A Balanced Scorecard Dashboard is another management tool many organizations are now using to measure performance and enable strategic decision-making. Such a scorecard uses metrics to measure financial performance like earnings and growth, but it can also incorporate an enterprise's measurements of customers and marketing processes.

Linking the scorecard to business strategy and integrating it into overall management processes enables organizations to become more effective in planning, budgeting, resource allocation and measuring

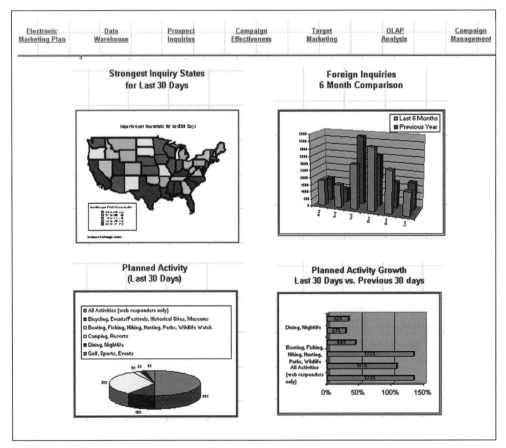

Exhibit 3-2: A Balanced Scorecard Dashboard

return on investment. Once a company has determined the marketing performance metrics needed, such as rates of responses to promotion efforts or revenues by source, an aggregate summary can be displayed in monthly, daily, or real-time visual graphic reports via a web portal to the customer data warehouse. Many systems permit the measurement of a multitude of metrics and drill down into underlying levels where applicable. Graphical, intuitive reporting formats, such as those in Exhibit 3-2, make it easy for managers to analyze data and see where specific efforts are in relation to others.

A typical starting point is to build a mission control dashboard, similar to that in a car that gives critical information on amount of fuel and speed. Such a corporate dashboard, however, is built with graphs, maps, and statistics gauging progress to benchmarks that define success.

Drill Down and Drill Up to Intelligence

When a direct marketer is looking for a new dimension, such as sales by store site, a "drill down" into the particular region will provide a graphic display or report of the sales by store by region. A further drill down can look at an individual store and summarize product category sales. Further drilling down can show which individual customer has purchased at a higher rate than another with related demographic and lifestyle attributes. Enhanced statistical data on the file can also allow drilling up to predictive variables that define future marketing campaigns.

Outsource Vs. In-House

The data warehouse is an advanced source of dynamic and vital marketing information. For years the benefits of data warehousing have been unavailable to middle-tier businesses due to the high costs of hardware, software, and limited access to skilled people to design and run tools on a daily basis. A typical home-grown data warehouse could take an internal team six months or more to implement and might cost anywhere from $750,000 to $3 million to launch and operate. Now, with the emergence of web-enabled application service providers (ASPs), organizations can utilize service bureaus to manage and maintain their CRM applications and data warehouses with minimal upfront investment and a monthly subscription fee. Access to the data center is done seamlessly via a private virtual network that allows the service bureau ASP to serve as your strategic outsource while you focus on your core business. Key advantages include access to massive databanks of demographic and lifestyle data that can be linked to your marketing file so as to determine which variables correlate to your market.

Outsourcing data warehousing processes can be a win/win business strategy with these advantages:

- Enables limited technology risk, since much of the hardware and software could be obsolete within a short time.

- Maintains management focus on core initiatives—to focus on customers and fulfillment.

- Reduces cash flow challenges—by adding flexibility and not tying up cash up-front.

- Alleviates the competition for skilled talent.

- Increases speed to market and usability.

- Allows scalability—your vendor will have systems in place to allow you to grow faster.

- Allows control of a critical process and reduces the high risks of internal empire building.

Enhancing a Database

A customer list becomes a database when it is enhanced to include more than a name, an address, and a telephone number. It is enhanced when it records relevant information about each customer's transactions. It is enhanced further when demographic and/or psychographic information is appended for each consumer or industrial buyer. Enhancement of a database can also include environmental information about ZIP code areas for consumers or about standard industrial classification codes for businesses.

In essence, enhancing a database provides more information about customers and why they buy so that relationships and affinity with them can be nurtured.

Any organization must first know about its own customers. This knowledge opens up the opportunities for continuity selling and cross selling. It also is the prelude to pinpointing prospects most likely to become customers in the future.

A simple five-step sequence can help an organization profit from an enhanced database:

1. Identify current customers.

2. Enhance that database with external data.

3. Overlay environmental data.

4. Use the tools of prediction.

5. Use analytical tools and techniques.

These five steps can mean the difference between profit and loss. Note that these steps reflect the Full-Circle concept described in Chapter 1.

Step One: Identify Current Customers

Many well-intended marketers spend considerable time and money on seeking new customers without first learning about the characteristics of their present customers.

By answering some basic questions about current customers, a marketer can more easily (and less expensively) find others like them. Who are these customers? Where are more like them to be found? How were these customers obtained? Which offer the most opportunity for continuity sales and cross sales? How much can be spent to acquire them; what is their lifetime value? These are questions that an enhanced customer database answers.

Step Two: Enhance That Database with External Data

First of all, make sure to have a proper mechanism for the development and maintenance of the customer database. Then, capture customer information that is relevant for pinpointing future revenues. This includes products purchased as well as recency/frequency/monetary value and other transaction data. It also might include significant demographic and psychographic data derived from databases external to the organization.

Step Three: Overlay Environmental Data

Certain kinds of environmental data can help predict future purchasing behavior. Perhaps the characteristics and variables found within ZIP Code areas influence response. Characteristics of a firm or industry may impact response. Environmental data can be geographic, demographic or psychographic. It can be a predictor of lifestyle and buying behavior.

Step Four: Use the Tools of Prediction

Develop high regard for and a comfort level with numbers and statistics. Not every technique is complicated. At the low end, a simple response percentage can highlight the most productive segment of a response list. At the high end, a complex, multivariate regression analysis can correlate response variances with behavioral variables found within a cluster of ZIP Code areas.

Step Five: Use Analytical Tools and Techniques

Most direct marketers test often, and they collect a great deal of data. Properly analyzed, such data can provide much guidance for future actions. A validation of a direct marketing test should enable the marketer to verify that the assumptions built into the profile or predictive model are correct. The resulting information should identify the best customers, locate them, and show how to cultivate them. Such analytical databases also should track the lifetime value of a customer because this is the best way there to set promotion budgets for new customer acquisition.

A Guide to an Endless Array of Enhancements

A customer database usually contains proprietary information, such as actions taken, product preferences, and credit worthiness. It may be beneficial, however, to add information such as age (from a public record of drivers' licenses), a mobility indicator such as length of residence (from a telephone directory compilation) or a credit rating (from a credit bureau).

An external database can also be used as a *negative* screen to suppress promotion to those desiring not to be solicited (from the Direct Marketing Association's mail and telephone preference compilations) or an address where a prospect no longer resides (from the Postal Service's NCOA file).

All of this information is available from compiled lists, response lists, and credit reporting databases. But before turning to external data sources, take a second look at what already exists in-house. Believe it or not, a life insurance company once surveyed its policyholders to determine their ages, overlooking that it already had this information in its underwriting database and the fact that this sensitive information could have been easily overlaid.

Compiled Lists: The Range of Public Records

Carefully developed and maintained name/address compilations can be a key source of data. This information can be transferred to customer or other response lists to segment and qualify them.

There are a great many compilations available, ranging from those owned by list compilers, who collect data on millions of households and residents, to smaller lists of individuals or organizations within trade, professional or membership rosters.

While such information—directory listings and license registrations, for example—are matters of public record, often clearly visible, there is a great deal of concern by privacy advocates over the potential harm from the transfer of such data. This concern, even a breach of confidentiality, can override the need for targeting relevant messages to likely prospects and thus minimizing the potential for intrusion and nuisance from "junk" advertising.

It behooves those accessing information to be responsible in its acquisition and use. It helps to think about data as a means to define market segments, rather than as a way to single out an individual. For example, knowledge of age of a cluster of individuals can be a legitimate means to direct advertising for certain offers, thus minimizing waste as well as avoiding intrusion of those to whom the message is not relevant. On the other hand, specific reference to an individual's age on a direct mail envelope, where it is visible to others, could result in resentment and be seen as an "invasion of privacy."

Telephone Directory Compilations. Drawn from white pages (individuals) or yellow pages (organizations), these enormous databases yield a treasure trove of information. For households, mobility can be estimated, multi-unit buildings can be identified or an address can be associated with a ZIP Code or other small geographic area for which census data is obtainable.

For businesses and other organizations, Standard Industrial Classification codes can be determined by cross-referencing Yellow Page listing categories. The year the organization first appeared can be determined, or a franchise such as McDonald's can be identified, as can a brand affiliation such as General Electric, or membership in a professional society. As with households, telephone or FAX numbers can be appended. The extent of Yellow Page advertising can be identified, too, if relevant.

Telephone directory compilations can themselves be enhanced from other databases and usually are. Gender can be approximated from first-name tables; ethnicity can be approximated from surname tables. Telephone surveys of directory listings of organizations provide names/titles of decision-makers, number of employees, and sales volume. First-time listings—of households on the move or of business start-ups—can be isolated as well.

City (and/or Criss-Cross) Directories. Where available, these household compilations can augment telephone directories, which omit both those who lack telephone service and those who, through their own choice, prefer not to be listed. City directories are typically compiled through mail surveys or house-to-house canvasses. They often list all persons in the household, along with age, marital status and family relationships. Children are included as are senior citizens living with their children. City directories are readily obtainable for manual perusal, and they are often incorporated into databases offered by list compilers.

Voter Registration Files. Like city directories, county election boards or commissions typically compile these locally. Like city directories, they include many individuals who may not appear in telephone directories. But, they are far from comprehensive. Not all U.S. residents are citizens and, of those who are, not all are registered voters.

Voter lists may show party affiliation, an important qualifier for political candidates, although affiliation may not be current. Addresses may also be out of date if the voter has not voted recently. For these reasons, voter lists are probably most effectively used when they are joined with other databases by a professional compiler.

Real Estate Records. Information derived from public real estate records can provide considerable enhancement to a customer database, especially when offers relate to home furnishings, maintenance, gardening and/or landscaping.

Available data, for either customer enhancement or prospect qualification, includes: type of dwelling unit (single or multi-family, condominium), month and/or year purchased, market value, and residence of owner.

Rosters. Membership rosters of local PTAs, service clubs, neighborhood and trade associations, professional societies, and special interest groups may be a useful source of customer and prospect information. The key qualification is the nature of the group with which an individual or organization is affiliated.

Since rosters are typically in hard copy, working with them can be cumbersome. Duplication may result when an automated means for merge/purge is unavailable. Roster data may not always be current, and many groups frown on their use as mailing lists.

Still, the information in rosters, especially evidence of affinity with a particular group and its interests, can be a worthwhile enhancement to a customer database. Collections of rosters, drawing together local groups, may be available.

Automobile and Drivers' License Registrations. When these are available from the various state motor vehicle departments, registration records can provide year, make and model for each automobile in a household. They can also identify new vehicle purchasers, and, because certain vehicles—sports utilities, vans, and pickup trucks—can be associated with certain lifestyles, offer clues about a customer's lifestyle. The number of vehicles owned in a household, as well as their combined market value, can also be discriminate variables.

When automobile registrations are recompiled annually, they can be used to update mailing addresses. Drivers' license registrations, however, may be issued for as many as five years.

Still, driver's license registrations can be a good source of age and gender as well as height and weight information that can be important predictors of interest in products such as large or tall clothing sizes. A driver's license record can also indicate some degree of physical mobility and acuteness, important qualifiers for products such as insurance.

Lifestyle Compilations. Generally derived from warranty registrations returned to manufacturers or survey responses by consumers themselves, these provide a variety of demographic data about individuals and households. Psychographic data volunteered by respondents also provide indicators of attitudes, interests and opinions. Coupled with environmental data obtainable for ZIP Code areas, such databases become valid lifestyle measurements.

Tens of millions of records, compiled month-to-month and regularly maintained through address correction procedures, comprise these lifestyle databases. Dozens of activities and interests from antique collecting to wildlife/environmental issues can be identified. Included are such diverse indicators as bible/devotional reading, casino gambling, snow skiing, gardening, motorcycling, and watching TV sports.

Demographic selections from such databases often include gender, title, age, home ownership, marital status, income, occupation, children at home, education, religion, ethnicity.

Directed marketers effectively using lifestyle compilations often transfer relevant information from these databases to their own customer records. They can model customer penetration correlated with these variables so as to predict likelihood of response to their offers from segments of a large compilation. These segments become key sources of new customer acquisition.

Cooperative Databases. These are another information source where several organizations fund the development of jointly shared databases. Each contributes its own customer names and information records. In many cases, the use of such a database is restricted to the contributors who can have access to other contributors' names without knowing the source of those names. This system works well in the publication and catalog arena in which many participants have up-sell opportunities and uses include screening for multiple buyers, RFM, etc. Cooperative databases can be difficult to implement in an industry with overlapping competitors.

Credit Reporting Databases

Major credit reporting organizations offer a broad array of enhancements and qualification screens, negative as well as positive. Their databases let an organization suppress promotion to those with poor credit records, and direct promotion to those qualified for and likely interested in an offer. They are also excellent sources of up-to-date, deliverable addresses, because these are corrected as consumers and businesses pay their bills.

A great deal of the demographic data offered as mailing lists by credit reporting organizations is derived from sources external to them. For consumer records, this includes a variety of information about those in the household as well as the housing itself. For business records, primary and secondary industry classifications are shown, as are other nonconfidential data derived from survey or observation.

The use of information from credit-reporting databases is, in the eyes of consumers and consumer advocates, controversial—especially when it is used for offers that do not grant a credit privilege. That is why highly personal and confidential information obtained in the process of credit checking and reporting is available to credit grantors only.

On the other hand, credit organizations have modeled the likelihood of bankruptcy without individually identifying those bankrupts. This kind of modeling with predictive averages is a useful enhancement for a customer database as well as an important qualifier for offers to be directed to prospect lists.

Respondents to Direct Offers

Experienced direct marketers know that the most important qualification of a mailing list is a history of response. Actions taken can be predictive. These can help a direct marketer predict whether a prospect might make similar or related purchases in the future. A purchaser of a travel cruise to Alaska, for example, might be a more likely prospect for a world cruise than one who had bought a weekend Caribbean cruise. Enhancing a database with information from other response lists can provide a great deal of information about customers.

Conducting a merge/purge of several response lists against each other as well as a current customer list can offer further predictive likelihood by identifying multibuyers. Large database compilers have facilitated this by marking mail-order buyers from many, many individual response lists and identifying them by purchase dollar range and purchase method. In doing so, they have coupled the typically larger numbers of records available in compiled lists with qualifications of mail responsiveness, recency of purchase (hotline buyers) and frequency of purchase (multibuyers). The result is the best of both worlds: high volume and great qualification.

Viral marketing—a virus-like proliferation of messages—is another approach to create awareness and adoption of a product/service by employing word of mouth or referral networks. Hotmail, an e-mail service which signed up millions of subscribers with the help of a link at the bottom of every message its users sent, provides an example of viral marketing. The benefits are a combination of speed to market, economy of marketing dollars, and the effectiveness of referral all into one package.

Compiling a Customer Profile

The primary reason for enhancing a database is to develop an accurate profile of current customers that can be used to identify prospects whose important characteristics are like those of the most profitable current customers.

Organizations have sometimes developed cursory profiles of their customers through primary research, surveying a sampling of them in order to determine their key characteristics. Today's database and analysis technology, however, provides opportunities for statistical modeling that can embrace not just a sampling but an entire customer file. Further, it can categorize these customers by product(s) purchased, by recency/frequency/monetary analysis, by credit experience and a host of transaction variables. Then, it can relate its findings to an infinite array of enhancements: geographic, demographic and psychographic.

Because today's organizations—their product and promotion strategies, their databases, their markets—are dynamic, customer profiling through statistical modeling needs to be a never-ending process.

A starting point for developing such profiles is through the calculation of market penetration. This, in its simplest form, is a percentage relationship of customers to some benchmark universe. It tells what percentage of the total universe of potential buyers are customers. To be even more predictive, such arithmetic should be performed on customer segments: R/F/M categories, product lines, and specific demographics.

The benchmark universe can be as broad as a total population or a count of all households or of all families. It may be as narrow as a count of mailings of a particular promotional effort to a particular list. Industrial organizations might view their prospect universe as all firms within a standard industrial classification (SIC), within a size category or within a geographic area. The universe could be even further refined by demographics such as age, marital status, occupation, educational level, or by numerous other restrictions.

When determining penetration of customers in a market it is well to keep in mind the "equal effort over time" dilemma. There may be higher concentration of customers in a particular segment, high-income households, for example, simply because prior marketing efforts, for a good many years, have been directed to that segment. Without objective guidance, one may have unintentionally bypassed even more productive, lesser-income segments.

A solution to this dilemma is to measure a controlled universe such as a direct-mail effort across all household income segments with response key-coded by income category.

Suppose an organization mails an offer to 19,600 households, each identified as falling into one of four low-to-high income ranges: A, B, C and D. A total of 350 responses to the offer is received, an average of 1.79 percent response. When the response is tabulated by household income range, market penetration is shown to increase as household income increases:

Income Segment	Total Mailed	Total Responses	% Response to Mailing
A	5,793	60	1.04
B	2,735	33	1.21
C	6,731	138	2.05
D	4,341	119	2.74

From this table, it is apparent that the response rate from the offer is positively correlated with household income. The response rate increases along with household income. Since the market potential has been defined with a direct-mail effort sent to all available households irrespective of income, the market penetration, viewed as a series of response rates, is controlled. Thus, we are not faced with the "equal effort over time" dilemma.

Now, let's assume that we have a list of 350 customers, who were acquired over a period of time from a market potential universe consisting of 19,600 households. Let's change only the column headings on the preceding table to look like this:

ZIP Code Cluster	Total Households	Total Customers	%Customers/ Households
A	5,793	60	1.04
B	2,735	33	1.21
C	6,731	138	2.05
D	4,341	119	2.74

What we are showing here is a clustering of 350 customers according to their ZIP Code locations and calculating the percentage of customers we have among all households in those ZIP Code clusters. Once again we see that market penetration increases from A to B to C to D. What we don't know in this instance, however, is *why!*

If we had the means to correlate our customer penetration of the market potential of the four ZIP Code clusters, we ought to be able to seek prospects and more readily convert these to customers in cluster D than in cluster A. The trick is to know what independent variables distinguish D from A demographically, psychographically, and geographically.

Try eyeballing the ZIP Codes in which the greatest market penetration occurs. What is *different* about each ZIP area? Are they rural or urban? Are the housing structures multi-family? Are the neighborhoods "new" or "old?" Are the household heads young or old, college postgraduates or high school dropouts? We might even look at a census of population and housing. From all of this data, it may be possible to discover what distinguishes the high penetration areas from those with low penetration?

Using Customer Profiles to Find New Customers

A customer profile—real or estimated—is the starting point in seeking out new prospects or prospect lists. Consider generating an indexed market penetration analysis of customers against a compiled list. A customers/households indexing might look like the one below. Length-of-residence of a household is estimated by the number of years a telephone directory listing has appeared at its current address:

Length of Residence	Number of Households	%	Number of Customers	%	Customer%/ Household%
1 Year	10,000	32.26	100	10.00	31.00%
2 Years	9,000	29.03	150	15.00	51,67%
3 Years	7,000	22.58	200	20.00	88.57%
4 Years	4,000	12.90	250	25.00	193.80%
5 Years	1,000	3.23	300	30.00	928.79%
Totals:	31,000	100.00	1,000	100.00	

From this analysis, it is apparent that customer penetration is positively correlated with length-of-residence at an address. Similar market penetration analyses might be drawn from other compiled lists; e.g.:

- Make, model and year of automobile registered
- Age as given on a driver's license
- Assessed valuation, as shown on a property tax record
- Political affiliation, as shown on a voter registration
- Standard industrial classification
- Yellow Pages advertising and listing classification(s)

Frequently, too, warranty card disclosures that include lifestyle indicators can be used for segmentation purposes.

The Customer Database and the 80/20 Principle

Simply put, the 80/20 principle means that eight out of ten new things we try fail. This means that 80% of the new lists, alternative copy platforms, or other variables tested are less effective than current efforts. A marketer's current program is the best cumulative effort, the best result of all our prior experiences and tests. It takes a lot of "test" efforts to beat an established "control" effort that has evolved over time.

The 80/20 principle demonstrates the relationship between marketing effort and result. While the actual percentage will vary among different organizations, it can be shown that 80 percent of a firm's customers do not contribute as much profit as the other 20 percent. Put another way, 80 percent of the profit in an organization comes from 20 percent of its customers.

Forward-looking organizations understanding this principle seek out the 20 percent of their customers (or prospective customers) who will contribute the highest returns and direct 80 percent of their marketing effort towards them. Marketing costs can thus be targeted in order to maximize profit. Because it can identify both profitable customers and wasted effort, a database—properly developed, maintained, and utilized— is the means through which this can be achieved.

Traditionally, marketing costs—and advertising costs in particular— have been viewed as an expense. Typically, marketers have used sales history from prior or current sales periods in order to set the marketing budget for the next period. The fallacy of this method of budgeting is that marketing effort comes only as a result of sales; i.e., "the more we sell, the more we can spend on marketing."

In direct marketing, where acquiring that 20 percent of customers that brings in 80 percent of the profits is paramount, it makes sense to view the cost of acquisition—the marketing effort—as a cause of sales, and therefore as an investment.

It is evident that if the marketer who focuses on those customers that provide 80 percent of revenues will be successful. Using modeling tools, the marketer can clone those best customers and find others in the customer file and in the surrounding universe that will behave just like the best in order to maximize future revenue streams. With the knowledge that 20 percent of sales effort provides 80 percent of sales revenue, the marketer can know that it is vital to keep these individuals happy and focus on those core customers.

Interactive Workshop 3-1:
Using a Balanced Scorecard Dashboard to Mine for Information

(For demonstration, go to the CD-Rom accompanying this book.)

USA800 is a telemarketing firm in Kansas City that provides inbound inquiry call support for large clients, including many state tourism departments. USA800 contracted with Ruf Strategic Solutions to develop data warehouse and analytical services so they could provide a private-label value-added service for their clients. After some client survey work, it was determined that many state tourism departments were requiring a higher-level knowledge and service for managing their customer relationship process. A product, named Evaluate, was developed with the state of Arizona cooperating to develop the initial prototype.

Evaluate, developed in 5 weeks, incorporated a personalized dashboard of key metrics that defined success for the state's tourism department. Included were: inquiry activity for the past 6 months; inquiry activity for the past 30 days; communication media used during the past 30 days; inquiry average cost, by activity planned; strongest inquiry states for the past 30 days; foreign inquiries; 6-months comparisons; planned activity; and, planned activity growth.

This produces the "customer" component of the balanced scorecard. Future development will integrate corporate strategy in four dimensions: financial, customer, internal, and innovation. Applying these simple metrics will modify the organization's behavior from event-driven to strategy-driven—a coherent, targeted, strategy-focused organization capable of managing rapid market response and sustained growth.

Exercise:

Accessing the CD-ROM accompanying this book, enter the balanced scorecard dashboard in Interactive Workshop 3-1. Evaluate the current published information. Glance at the average inquiry cost by activity planned. Gauge and get a directional reading of the up-to-the-minute status of the current inquiries by activities desired. In this instance, it costs $21.28 per lead for a golf, sports, and events inquiry based on the source of the lead. The cost of each advertising source and the number of respondents also can be seen. (Inquiry cost is the number of inquiries/ad cost.)

Based on all tourism events possible, which one might lead that activity to be more costly per inquiry? Why?

Now, double-click on the dashboard gauge in order to drill into "Average Cost per Inquiry by Region." Notice how the interest in specific activities is spread throughout regions.

Next, click on the "West" region to drill deeper into this Census region and a breakdown of its "Pacific" and "Mountain" areas. Notice how, with each drill-down, the relative average cost per inquiry changes. Drilling into the "Mountain" region will bring up DMA's in Arizona that have high call volumes. DMA (Dominant Marketing Area) is a media area commonly used for advertising via radio and TV. By clicking the "Phoenix DMA" we drill another level into the 10 counties within the Phoenix DMA. Clicking on "Maricopa County," we can examine the activities planned by inquirers in the 11 cities represented by the data. Selecting "Phoenix" we find 12 ZIP Codes from which to select, after using an 80/20 suppression which isolates 20% of the ZIPs that have 80% of the inquiries. With review of this information, it is evident that "Resorts to Ranches," a promotion for a country bed and breakfast escape, is of great interest to inquirers from this area. Click on ZIP Code "85018" and you're able to drill right down to the individual inquiry record and a wealth of data, including not only name, address, city, state and ZIP code but also, inquiry date and time, inquiry ID, and inquiry cost. What ways might you utilize such a drill-down approach to provide more effective communications?

As a further exercise, enter your web browser and type www.ruf.com to reach the Ruf Strategic Solutions website. Go to "Customers Only" and enter, as your account name: "onlinedemo." Then repeat, as your password: "onlinedemo." You can explore an endless array of segmentation and analysis possibilities.

II
The Essential Tools of Information Gathering and Analysis

Chapter 4

Information Gathering: Sources and Uses of Data

Key Concepts
- Surveys and Experiments
- Quantitative Uses
- Qualitative Uses
- Exploratory Research
- Descriptive Research
- Causal Research
- Primary Data
- Secondary Data

Applications
- Sources of data
- Copy Testing
- Survey Design

All sound business decisions turn on two components: facts or information and judgment. That means research, and it means determining one's information needs and then the sources of information available to meet those needs. Direct marketers have always operated this way, and the rest of the marketing community and business in general are following.

The purpose of research is to make better decisions that enable executives to manage risk better and to solve problems more effectively.

Most direct marketers work with vast amounts of data. Intelligent decision making demands that they know how such data are gathered, synthesized, and analyzed in order to make the best decisions for segmenting markets and constructing offers that have the highest appeal and thus success.

The research that this process is based on focuses on fact-finding and information gathering. It is also concerned with analytically solving problems and recommending action. Today, increasingly sophisticated information-gathering and analysis tools are needed for handling both surveys and experiments due to:

- The complexity and scope of marketing activities.
- The vast amount of information available.
- The shortening of time allotted for decision-making.

Research has two basic outcomes: *quantitative* (such as summary numbers used to describe demographic variables in a house file, or numbers describing recency, frequency and monetary value of customer transactions) and *qualitative* (such as the reasons for buyer behavior, rather than who, where or how many buy).

Surveys and Experiments

Different methods of research can produce quantitative outcomes. Two broad methods are surveys and experiments. A *survey* looks at things the way they are. A mailed questionnaire, for example, may attempt to profile respondents' reactions to a product offer or a promotional campaign. It may seek to anticipate future buying intentions; to determine product or service preferences; to guide pricing decisions; or to measure attitudes, interests, opinions.

An *experiment* is designed to measure the effect of a change. What is the effect of adding a new feature to a product? What happens when the price for a product is raised or lowered? What is the result of specific promotion in specific market segments? What is the response influence of one promotion strategy relative to others?

In collecting primary data, as with surveys, what respondents *say* and what they *do* are, unfortunately, often quite different. The more valid and projectable research, therefore, may be that which measures actions rather than opinions.

For example, a survey of magazine readership among a broad-based sample concluded that twenty times as many respondents stated they read *Atlantic Monthly* as stated they read *Readers' Digest*. The researcher questioned the potential conclusion—that more people read *Atlantic Monthly* than *Readers' Digest*—because at the time of the survey the circulation of the *Digest* was a hundred times greater than the *Atlantic Monthly*. One more example drives the point home. In a survey by a mail-order insurance company, in which the company remained anonymous during interviewing, a large majority of the respondents replied "No" to this question: "Would you purchase life insurance by mail without guidance of an agent?" Yet, it was known that all of these respondents had purchased life insurance by mail from the company conducting the survey!

A better alternative, albeit probably more costly, might be to offer a product or service for sale and then measure those who actually respond, not simply those who say they would if given the opportunity. In other words, test the hypothesis.

Uses of Research: Identifying Problems and Objectives

Research is useful whenever managers seek solutions to problems or need to become more knowledgeable about the options facing them. It can help relate risks to rewards and, thus, is especially valuable for estimating the impact of making the wrong decision.

Research can be used to fulfill one of three objectives:

1. Preliminary exploration of problem and solution alternatives. *Exploratory research* seeks to develop better understanding of a problem and to identify relevant alternatives.

2. Describe an existing market situation or condition. *Descriptive research*, as the name implies, describes market, customer, and prospect characteristics or functions. It often provides a snapshot of some aspect of the market environment using census data, surveys and polls.

3. Demonstrate a "cause and effect" relationship between two or more situations, condition or factors in a market. Descriptive research can often show that two variables are related; *causal research* can show how those variables are related or the extent or nature of their relationship.

Because research itself is an expense, it must provide benefits that justify its costs. Potential risk must be related to potential reward. Three criteria can determine whether research information is valuable to a business decision:

1. The degree of uncertainty regarding the outcome of various courses of action

2. The economic consequences of making a wrong decision

3. The amount by which the information, if obtained, is expected to reduce the initial uncertainty.

The term uncertainty is used here, in a statistical sense, to describe a lack of advance knowledge of the outcome of some action. Uncertainty is, thus, itself a risk. Research attempts to reduce uncertainty to a manageable risk in order to eliminate undesirable alternatives, such as unprofitable market segments, from all those being considered.

Research can help answer managerially relevant questions. In deciding the extent of advertising effort, research can help establish how both the message and media aspects of the advertising budget are to be determined. Should the budget be a result (based on actual past or expected current sales) or a cause (based on objective future sales)? Do the expected results warrant the estimated costs? Do the anticipated rewards outweigh the potential risks?

Research can help decide how a budget will be allocated, too. Which products will be offered? At what prices? Which market segments will be targeted? And, what blend of offer, copy, graphics, and media will generate the best results?

In short, research testing can help make decisions based on facts, not hunches. While it is not a substitute for sound executive judgment, experimentation is a great decision-making aid. Knowing how to use the tools of research can foster improved decision-making, thereby producing more efficient use of time and money.

Sources of Data

A basic problem for contemporary database marketers isn't availability of data. Many marketers feel there is an overload of data. The problem involves determining what data is needed, where and how to obtain it, how to interpret it and get useful insights on which to base decisions, and then what to do with it.

Types of data are usually categorized into two broad groups. **Primary data** is new to the world and did not previously exist. It usually is collected for a specific research need through any of the available and appropriate media, including personal (face-to-face), telephone, mail, e-mail, fax, web-based surveys, observation, or experimentation. Primary data collection is expensive and usually is conducted when secondary data is not available.

Secondary data is data that has originally been collected for another purpose by someone other than the researcher but which are relevant and available to the researcher. Secondary data is available from many sources, including an organization's own house file; government organizations; trade, business, and professional associations; public and private libraries; research and data banks and the World Wide Web; financial institutions and public utilities; and foundations and nonprofit organizations. Exhibit 4-1 lists some sources of secondary data. Before using any

A. The Organization's Own Internal Records

B. Government Sources: Federal, State, Local

    1. U. S. Department of Commerce
       — Bureau of the Census

    2. U. S. Department of Labor
       — Bureau of Labor Statistics

    3. U. S. Department of Agriculture

    4. Other U. S. Government Sources
       — President's Office
       — Congress
       — Treasury Department
       — Interior Department
       — Health & Human Services Department

    5. State and Local Governments
       — Economic Surveys
       — License Registrations
       — Tax Records

C. Trade, Technical, Professional and Business Associations

D. Private Research Organizations

E. Foundations, Universities and Other Nonprofits

F. Libraries, Public and Private

G. Advertising Media

H. Financial Institutions and Utilities

Exhibit 4-1: Some Sources of Secondary Data

secondary data, the researcher needs to ensure the validity of data. There are no hard-and-fast rules for ensuring secondary data validity, but the researcher should carefully consider the credibility of the source organization providing the data and assess the rigor of the method of data collection.

Before investing in collection of primary data, a marketer should look to one's own organization, which might have already traveled the proposed research road and collected data that could be used for solving the problem at hand. While most secondary data is usually less costly and can be obtained more quickly than primary data, a major disadvantage of

Primary Data Collection Methods			
Format	**Advantages**	**Disadvantages**	**Applications**
Personal Interview	Provides a complete and accurate sample and complete information. Allows questions to be structured to fit the situation; high response is virtually assured.	Expensive and the interviewer may create bias that can influence the subject. Interviewers require supervision and control to standardize handling, and avoid cheating. Not statistically quantifiable; projections are subjective.	Used to ascertain attitudes and motivations, on a one-to-one controlled basis, for background information and for generation of ideas about future actions.
Telephone Interview	Fast, economical, can easily reach a representative sample; non-response is low; easy to get respondent's participation; can coincide with other activities, such as TV viewing.	Excludes unlisted numbers except in random-digit dialing. Information may be limited and certain types of questions cannot be used.	Used to increase number of one-to-one interviews when in-depth research is not necessary.
Focus Group Interview (Unstructured small group of subjects converse in a relaxed environment)	Great sounding board for product benefits and promotion features. Good for idea generation and creative evaluation.	Cannot be scientifically controlled and findings cannot be measured or projected. Interaction can sometimes influence participants.	Used chiefly as a sounding board, to obtain reactions; to generate ideas.
Mail Questionnaire	Provides great versatility at relatively low cost. No interviewer bias; no field staff required. Respondents may remain anonymous and replies can be confidential; response can be timed to the respondent's convenience.	High rate of non-response; often requires follow-up. Results may show bias. Surveys can take a long time to develop and even the best questions may be misunderstood when interviewer is not present.	Used to maximize number of observations and to provide more valid basis for projection.
Observation (In-store, in-home audits, recording devices, and direct observation at point of sale)	Removes respondent bias.	Opportunities to use this technique are limited.	Used to obtain objective findings, even though opportunities for use are limited.
Dry Testing (Sending out promotions for a product being contemplated, but not yet available)	May help measure potential interest in a product yet to be introduced.	Product may be misrepresented, need to promptly return remittances. More costly than a survey.	Used as a test, with the inherent advantages of an experiment, yet in the guise of a survey.

Exhibit 4-2: Primary Data Collection Methods

secondary data is that the researcher lacks control over how the data was collected.

Primary data are collected through the survey methods shown in Exhibit 4-2. Surveys can yield valuable information about:

- **Actions:** What respondents have done or are doing

- **Intentions:** What respondents expect to do in the future

- **Motivations:** What reasons respondents give for acting

- **Attitudes, Interests, Opinions:** Respondents' views

- **Psychological Traits:** Respondents' state of mind

- **Knowledge:** How respondents perceive specific offerings

- **Socioeconomic Factors:** Age, income, education, etc.

A survey that asks prospects if they *intend to buy* can also be translated into an offer and tested with a prospect list where a prospect is *asked to buy*. Direct marketers tend to favor the latter kind of experimentation (testing), which focuses on results (**behavioral data**) rather than opinions (**attitudinal data**). However, most direct marketers also realize that surveys have the ability to uncover certain "unseen" attitudinal or motivational factors that cannot be ascertained from just the behavioral responses. For example, whether a person responds favorably to a direct mail offer or not does not tell the marketer why the person has responded the way he did. By asking questions in survey format, a marketer may be able to discern what motivated a person to respond favorably or unfavorably. Workshop 4-2 provides a brief overview of the critical issues in survey design and an example of a survey.

In an experiment, one or more controllable factors (called independent variables) are manipulated to determine their influence on various events or outcomes (called dependent variables) such as the response to an advertised offer. The results are measured in an environment that the experimenter creates and in which controls serve to pinpoint the cause of behavior differences among respondents. Issues in experimentation are discussed in more depth in a later chapter.

Workshop 4-1:

Experimentation (Testing) of Copy Approach in Fund Raising[1]

In the sale of intangible services and especially in fund raising, the directed marketer needs a keen awareness of what motivates response. Donors to worthy causes often contribute for reasons of their own and these reasons may not have anything to do with the cause itself. The potential benefits received are not readily apparent. This presents a real challenge to the direct marketer engaged in fund raising.

The experiment (test) presented here was structured to determine which teaser copy appeal generated the most response. Measurement was not of what respondents *said* they would do . . . but of what they actually *did*. The mechanics of structuring and evaluating experiments is dealt with in Chapter 10. Herein, we simply want to demonstrate the value of research.

The American Heart Association needed to raise more funds for its health improvement activities at a lower cost. Direct mail had historically been the most important medium for the organization's fund raising and an effort was to needed to improve on the current response.

Several copy approaches were developed. Through scientific experimentation involving test mailings in excess of 200,000 pieces and confirmation with another 200,000 pieces, these copy approaches were tested against each other and also against the "control" that currently was being used. With experimentation, of course, it is necessary to have all aspects of the mailing remain the same except for one variable within each text segment. In this way, the change in response can be attributed to the change in that variable.

The decision was made to test six copy approaches in the form of "teasers" displayed on the outside of mailing envelopes. Six such "teasers" would be tested against each other and also against the control, the envelope that the fundraiser had been using successfully in the past, but which did not have any "teaser" at all.

A letter, contribution form and reply envelope were enclosed in each mailing envelope. These forms were essentially the same for all mailing packages except for the beginning of the letter. This emphasized the particular copy approach that was featured on the mailing envelope. The response from each group and for each copy approach was tabulated separately through key codes appearing on the contribution form.

---

[1] This case was developed by Freeman F. Gosden, Jr., who conducted the experiment from which it was derived.

The following copy approaches were tested:

Effort	Copy Approaches
1	"Use the enclosed FREE GIFT"
2	"Emergency Heart Attack Card Enclosed"
3	"4 years ago Billy Thompson's dad would have died ..."
4	"If you have ever worried about having a heart attack – "
5	"You hold lives in your hands TODAY ... THAT'S IMPORTANT"
6	"We'd like to show you how you can save a life. YOURS"
7	(Control) No teaser copy

Which copy approach do you think generated the most response? What are your reasons for your belief?

Here are the rank-ordered actual results:

    6 (best); 4 (good); 3 (good); 1 (poor); 5 (poor); 7 (poor); 2 (poor).

Workshop 4-2:

A Primer on Survey Design

The first step in designing a survey is to decide on what information is needed to adequately answer the problem faced by the marketer. Without a clear problem definition and a good understanding of the environmental context of the problem, it is simply not possible to design a good survey. Often, exploratory research techniques, including focus groups with customers and prospects, in-depth interviews with experts (including the decision makers who will use the data collected through the survey) are needed to clearly define the problem and the many factors that can impact the decision. This is one of the most important steps, but frequently researchers tend to spend less time in carefully going through this step.

The second step involves deciding on the method of administration of the survey - that is, personal, telephone, mail, e-mail, fax or web-based administration. Many issues including complexity of the information, whether visual cues are needed or not, amount of intended data collection, cost and time of data collection, provision of anonymity of responses etc. can influence the choice of method of administration. Some of these issues are described in Exhibit 4-2.

The third step involves deciding about the exact wording and format of response for each question. The basic principle of good wording is to write a question that can be easily and unambiguously understood by the intended recipients of the survey. To do this right, some of the issues to consider are as follows. Is the question really necessary? That is, avoid asking "it is nice-to-know" questions. Are several questions needed instead of one? That is, avoid asking more than one issue in the same question. Use simple and unambiguous wording in question design. Avoid leading questions, such as "Excessive time spent on surfing the Internet is *bad* for kids. Don't you agree?" Avoid loaded questions such as "Do you believe that private citizens have the right to bear concealed weapons to protect themselves and their families from *violent* criminal attack?"

With respect to format of response, the possible options are open-ended (no categories of response given), dichotomous (two categories such as yes or no), multiple choice (multiple categories that respondent can choose from). Although responses to open-ended questions often provide valuable qualitative insights, these should be used sparingly in a survey for the following reasons. First, answering these questions takes longer time and often subjects are not motivated to write answers to many open-ended questions. Too many open-ended questions in surveys usually result in low **response rates** (the percentage of people who respond to a survey) and lot of missing data (unanswered questions). Second, interpretation of data collected through open-ended questions is often hard to analyze.

Our recommendation is that you provide response categories to questions to the extent possible. Use open-ended questions when you may have no idea about what the response categories might be to a question. Ensure that the response categories given in a multiple-choice question are **mutually exclusive** and **collectively exhaustive** (that is, no overlap between categories and taken together the categories must cover all possible responses). For questions related to attitude, interest, opinion, buying intention, satisfaction, importance, etc., try to use response formats that have been used by past researchers. Many of these concepts have been researched extensively and very good measurement scales already exist in numerous published articles and books that specify the exact wording as well as the format of response.

In the fourth step, decide on the question sequence, that is, how the questions are arranged in a survey. The standard practice is to use general questions at the beginning and more specific questions later. Demographic or background information type questions are often included at the end of the survey.

The fifth step involves deciding on the actual look of the survey including the layout. Good practices include separating questions by logically ordered sections in the survey, making sure the actual survey is visually appealing etc. Also, to avoid boredom of respondents, to the extent possible use different types of scales and response formats in the survey. The final and perhaps the most important step is to pretest the survey with a few members from the intended recipient group. Pretesting helps to identify and eliminate any potential problem in the survey including obvious errors (such as typos) and not-so-obvious errors (such as unclear terms or questions or difficulty in answering questions).

Other pragmatic issues with respect to survey design are these: A cover letter, often sent with a mail survey, describes its purpose, anonymity, how long the survey will take to complete, who is the intended respondent, offer of any incentive to respond, and how the data will be used. Incentives, both financial and nonfinacial (such as sharing results from a survey) are used frequently to increase survey response rate.

An example of a mail-survey for a company that wishes to remain anonymous (called CFX here) is shown below. The survey was developed after extensive, in-depth, one-on-one interviews with key decision-makers of the company and a few customers. There were multiple goals for the survey including the issues customers consider important in choosing suppliers in this industry, customer perceptions of satisfaction with the company, Internet-readiness of customers, etc. It took two months and six revisions to generate the pretest version of the survey. The pretest version was tested with five customers and modified again based on their feedback. The survey was sent to CFX's customers with a cover letter from the president of CFX.

Customer Opinion Survey

How important are the following issues to you in choosing a supplier for hydraulic products?	Not at all important								Extremely important
1. The reliability of the supplier	1	2	3	4	5	6	7	8	9
2. The timeliness of the deliveries by the supplier	1	2	3	4	5	6	7	8	9
3. The availability of a large breadth of products to choose from	1	2	3	4	5	6	7	8	9
4. The availability of well documented technical specification	1	2	3	4	5	6	7	8	9
5. The price of products	1	2	3	4	5	6	7	8	9
6. The credit policy of the supplier	1	2	3	4	5	6	7	8	9
7. The availability of electronic payment/debit option	1	2	3	4	5	6	7	8	9
8. The return policy of the supplier	1	2	3	4	5	6	7	8	9
9. The warranty coverage provided by the supplier	1	2	3	4	5	6	7	8	9
10 The ability to talk directly to a salesperson about your needs	1	2	3	4	5	6	7	8	9

Please indicate your <u>perceptions</u> of Company CFX as a supplier of hydraulic products:	Strongly Disagree								Strongly Agree
1. CFX is a reliable supplier	1	2	3	4	5	6	7	8	9
2. CFX provides timely delivery	1	2	3	4	5	6	7	8	9
3. CFX offers a large breadth of products to choose from	1	2	3	4	5	6	7	8	9
4. CFX provides well-documented technical specifications for its products	1	2	3	4	5	6	7	8	9
5. CFX's products are competitively priced	1	2	3	4	5	6	7	8	9
6. CFX offers a good credit policy	1	2	3	4	5	6	7	8	9
7. CFX offers a good return policy	1	2	3	4	5	6	7	8	9
8. CFX has good warranty coverage on its products	1	2	3	4	5	6	7	8	9

1. *Overall, how satisfied are you with CFX's products and services?*

0%	10%	20%	30%	40%	50%	60%	70%	80%	90%	100%

Not at all satisfied   Completely satisfied

2. *Overall, how would you rate CFX as a supplier?*

1	2	3	4	5	6	7	8	9

Much worse than suppliers in the hydraulic industry   Much better than suppliers in the hydraulic industry

3. *Approximately what percentages of your purchases at this location are supplied by CFX?*

☐ 0-2%   ☐ 3-5%   ☐ 6-10%   ☐ 11-20%   ☐ More than 20

4. *In your opinion what is the most valuable service provided by CFX?*

_____

_____

Exhibit 4-3: Example of Primary Data Collection Survey   *continued on next page*

Exhibit 4-3: Example of Primary Data Collection Survey *(continued)*

1. Do you currently have access to the Internet at this location? ☐ Yes ☐ No

2. Do you currently purchase any of your supplies over the Internet? ☐ Yes ☐ No

3. Do you currently purchase any of your hydraulic or pneumatic supplies over the Internet? ☐ Yes ☐ No

4. Do you currently purchase from purchasing groups or consortiums? ☐ Yes ☐ No

5. For your hydraulic and pneumatic needs, how often do you like to see a salesperson?

   ☐ Never ☐ Once a year ☐ 2-4 times/year
   ☐ 5-6 times/year ☐ More than 6 times/year

6. For routine services (such as inquiry, follow-up, checking on order status, delivery schedule etc.) with regards to hydraulic and pneumatic supplies, what would you prefer to use?

   ☐ Internet ☐ Supplier's call center
   ☐ Supplier's sales person ☐ No preference

7. In your opinion, what is the most valuable function of a supplier's salesperson?

   ☐ Technical Assistance ☐ New Product Information ☐ Needs Assessment
   ☐ Order Expediting ☐ Pricing Considerations ☐ Other (please write)

Your title/position?

☐ Technical Assistant ☐ New Product Information ☐ Owner/President
☐ Purchase Manager ☐ General Manager ☐ Parts Manager
☐ Technician ☐ Other (please specify): _____

Your annual sales (revenue) at this location is:

☐ $0 - $499,999 ☐ $500,000 - $999,999 ☐ $1M - $5M
☐ $5M - $15M ☐ More than $15M

The number of full-time employees at this location is:

☐ Less than 10 ☐ 11-29 ☐ 30-59
☐ 60-99 ☐ 100-249 ☐ More than 250

What is the primary industry that your business falls under? (Please indicate by checking the appropriate 2-digit SIC code)

☐ 16 (Heavy Construction) ☐ 33 (Primary Metal Industries)
☐ 37 (Transportation Equipment) ☐ 24 (Lumber & Wood Products)
☐ 34 (Fabricated Metal Products) ☐ 50 (Wholesale Trade)
☐ 26 (Paper & Allied Products) ☐ 35 (Industrial Machinery & Equip.)
☐ 76 (Repair Services) ☐ 30 (Rubber & Plastic Products)
☐ Other (please write): : _____

Please comment on any issues that you **feel are important** but are not included in this survey:

_____
_____
_____
_____

Chapter 5

Using Basic Statistical Concepts

Key Concepts
- Descriptive Statistics
- Population
- Sample
- Measures of Central Tendency
- Measures of Variability
- Frequency Distribution
- Normal Distribution
- Inferential Statistics
- The Law of Large Numbers
- Confidence Intervals
- Statistical Significance
- Null Hypothesis

Applications
- Finding Confidence Levels
- Testing Hypotheses

Numbers are the bread-and-butter of direct marketers and are the basis of every business decision. But numbers by themselves are virtually meaningless. The real meaning of numbers comes from understanding the relationships between and among them. That is why statistical techniques are so important. They are the basic tools of interpretation and decision making. This chapter provides an overview of the key statistical rules and terms for understanding, manipulating, and interpreting numbers and numerical relationships effectively. A summary of more common statistics terms is given in Exhibit 5-5 at the end of this chapter for your reference.

Basic Working Concepts: Population and Sample

First, the most basic statistical concepts used in direct marketing are population and sample. An example of a direct marketer using these concepts to market a computer game will show these concepts in action. The direct marketer has identified an organization that has a list of 100,000 customer names and addresses available for rent. All of the people on that mailing list comprise the direct marketer's **population** for her marketing effort. That is, a population is the entire group of individuals who share some common set of characteristics, in this case membership in the mailing list. In this example, the population size, often denoted as N, is 100,000. Clearly, the direct marketer wants to minimize the risk of mailing to the wrong people (maybe most of these people on the list are not interested in computer games). Instead, a smart direct marketer will test the list by renting a **sample** of names (a subgroup) chosen randomly from the list (population) and making her offer only to the members in this sample.

If she rents 5,000 names (i.e., sample size, often denoted as *n*, is 5,000), sends an offer to these 5,000 people, and 100 people accept the offer, the sample response rate is 2%. This number is called a **sample statistic** (a summary description of a characteristic of the sample). The direct marketer has found a valuable piece of information from making the offer to the sample. However, her real goal is to know how close this sample statistic may be to the **population parameter** (the response rate that she would obtain had she mailed to all 100,000 members in the list) so that she can decide whether to rent the names from the entire list. In other words, she wants to be able to predict the behavior of the entire list from this sample.

This process of guessing the population parameters based on sample statistics is called **inferential statistics**, a topic that will be revisited later. In traditional statistical notations, Greek symbols such as μ, σ are used to represent population parameters (mean and standard deviations) and English symbols such as $\bar{x}$ (pronounced as x-bar) and s are used to represent corresponding sample statistics.

Descriptive Statistics

Direct marketers use **descriptive statistics** to describe the characteristics of a sample and to generate some feel for a group of data. While many different measures are used, the common ones can be broadly classified as measures of central tendency and measures of variability in the data.

Measures of Central Tendency

Measures of Central Tendency try to describe the "typical" sample member based on a set of characteristics such as age, income etc. Three commonly used measures of central tendency are mode, median, and mean.

Mode is a value in a string of numbers that occurs most frequently. For instance, if a house file contains 1,000 customers and 500 of them made one purchase last year, 300 made two purchases last year, and 200 made three or more purchases last year, then the mode for number of purchases made last year is one.

Median expresses the value that lies in the middle of a set of ordered values. For example, if the house file is sorted by revenues generated from each customer, then the revenue value for the customer in the middle of the sorted file is the median (also called the 50th percentile).

Mean is the arithmetic average of a set of numbers. Continuing with the same example, the mean is simply the average revenue from all customers in the house file.

Using Central Tendency Measures

Clearly, the type of data plays a role in a marketer's choice of central tendency measures. Typically, for data that are categorical (such as gender of a customer or marital status of a prospect), mode is the appropriate measure for central tendency. If data are continuous (such as income of a prospect, or the monetary amount of an order placed by a customer), it is appropriate to report median and mean.

Note that there is no reason to expect that the mean and the median will be the same for a set of numbers. In fact, for most data sets, these will be somewhat different because any extreme value (large or small) in the data will have a disproportionate effect on the calculation of mean rather than median. For example, if a few customers in the house file made a large number of purchases, the mean number of purchases will be pulled more than the median number towards the higher value.

Although not considered as a traditional central tendency measure, direct marketers are often interested in a sample statistic called proportion. **Proportion** is simply the percentage of a sample belonging to a group. For example, if a direct marketer mails 5,000 offers and receives 100 orders, the proportion of the sample responding favorably to the offer (often called response rate) is 2%. The similarity of proportion and sample mean can be illustrated as follows. The response data could be coded in the following way: For each person responding to an offer, the data value entered for response is 1, and for each person not responding to the offer, the data value entered for response is 0. In that case, the numerical average (or, **sample mean**) of the response will be equal to the "proportion of those who responded favorably to the offer."

Measures of Variability

Measures of Variability describe the degree of dispersion (i.e., how spread out the values are) in the data. The typical measures of variability include range, variance, and standard deviation. **Range** identifies the difference between the maximum and the minimum value in a data set. The **variance** is the average squared deviation from the mean, with the exception that for all practical purposes, the divisor used in calculating this average is (n-1) instead of n. The **standard deviation** is simply the square root of variance. Note that all three measures are indices that provide direct marketers an idea about the degree of spread in the data values. These three indices are appropriate to use only when data are continuous.

The formulas as well as definitions of the measures are summarized in Exhibit 5-5. Most spreadsheet packages today will easily calculate these statistics.

Frequency Distribution

To make sense of a data set, direct marketers often create a **frequency distribution**, which is an organized set of data created by summarizing the number of times a particular value of a variable occurs. Although frequency distribution typically shows the number of times (count) each value occurs in a sample, direct marketers also create percentages based on these numbers and graph these percentages using a bar chart to create a **histogram**. The percentages or the relative counts are called **probabilities**. Exhibit 5-1 provides a frequency distribution and histogram for age distribution in the "Mountain & Valley Resort Property Owners Data" that will be used later in this book.

A frequency distribution and a histogram offer meaningful ways to understand data. In the data set in Exhibit 5-1, there are few members in the lowest age group (18-35 years). The most common value for age groups (i.e., the mode) is 36-49 years. The median age group is 50-64 years. This age group already sorts the horizontal axis in the histogram and the 50th percentile falls in the 50-64 age group. The percentages show that if a member is selected at random, there is 28.43% chance that the person's age is 65+ years. Also, if a member is chosen at random there is a 38.65% (4.15%+34.50%) chance that his/her age is less than

Age Group	Frequency (Count)	Percentage
18-35 years	13	4.15%
36-49 years	108	34.50%
50-64 years	103	32.91%
65 plus years	89	28.43%
Total	313	100%

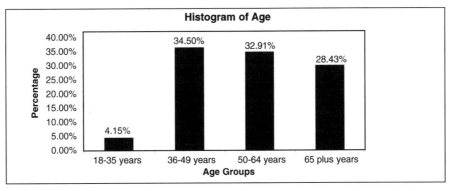

Exibit 5-1: Example of a Frequency Distribution

or equal to 49 years. This last calculation illustrates the cumulative probability of belonging to a group (its percentage plus the percentages of all other groups before it).

Although frequency distributions and/or histograms are usually employed for categorical data, these tools can also be used for continuous data. In order to use a frequency histogram for continuous data, a marketer must first choose appropriate categories to convert the continuous data. It is customary to choose **equal interval** (width) categories. For instance, if a marketer has information about the actual age of customers in the house file showing the minimum age is 18 years and maximum age is 84 years, appropriate categories may be: 20 or less, 21-30, 31-40, 41-50, 51-60, 61-70, 71-80, 81 or more. Today, most spreadsheet programs will create a histogram automatically for data and even choose equal interval categories for displaying continuous data.

Normal Distribution

The best known probability distribution in statistics is the **normal distribution** that looks like a bell-shaped curve. Probabilities from normal distribution are completely determined by two parameters: mean and standard deviation. A normal distribution is shown in Exhibit 5-2. The area under the curve represents the probability of occurrence for a normally distributed variable. The total area under the curve is 100%. A

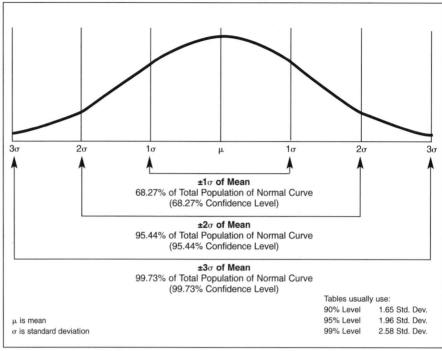

Exhibit 5-2: A Normal Distribution

normal distribution is symmetric around its mean. Therefore, the area under the curve from either the extreme left or the extreme right up to the mean is 50%.

Some of the important aspects of a normal distribution are as follows. If the data are normally distributed, 90% of data values will lie within 1.65 standard deviations from the mean, 95% of data values will lie within 1.96 standard deviations from the mean, and 99% of data values will lie within 2.58 standard deviations from the mean.

For example, if the distribution of income in a city is normal with a mean of $50,000 and a standard deviation of $10,000, then there is a 95% chance (probability) that a person chosen at random from this city will have income between $31,400 and $69,600 (50,000 ± 1.96 × 10,000). Also, it can be expected that 97.5% of people in the city will have incomes below $69,600 (i.e., the cumulative probability for mean plus 1.96 standard deviation above the mean). This is the total area under the curve from the extreme left up to the mean (50%) plus the area from the mean up to 1.96 standard deviation (½ of 95%).

A special form of the normal distribution is called the standard normal distribution that has a zero mean and a standard deviation of one. The table of probabilities for a standard normal distribution is widely available and used for calculation of probabilities for a normal distribution with any mean and standard deviation by using a conversion.

Any normal variable, X, with a mean of μ and a standard deviation of σ, can be converted to standard normal variable, Z, by using the conversion, $Z = (X-\mu)/\sigma$. Fortunately, most direct marketing applications do not require cumbersome calculations by hand to get exact probabilities using normal distribution tables. Today, most common spreadsheet packages will automatically calculate these probabilities. The CD-ROM accompanying this text demonstrates probability calculation using the normal distribution.

Inferential Statistics

As described earlier, direct marketers are often interested in estimating–inferring–population parameters using sample statistics. Intuitively, one would expect that the sample statistic (for example, the response rate in the sample) should be a good estimate (guess) for the unknown population parameter (response rate in the population). However, the sample statistic is rarely exactly equal to the population parameter. To appreciate this issue further, consider a simple example.

Think of the city of your residence. Suppose we are interested in estimating the average dollar amount spent by each adult citizen in your city on direct order from apparel catalogues. The population is all the adult citizens in your city. If we had access to purchase data from all of these people, we could calculate the population average (μ) of the dollar amount spent on direct order from apparel catalogues. We could also draw a histogram of these numbers to get the population distribution and even calculate the population standard deviation, σ. Unfortunately, in most cases such specific data do not exist. That is, in reality all such population parameters and distribution are unknown.

Suppose, we choose 100 names at random (a sample) from the city telephone directory and ask them the question, "How much do you spend on direct order from apparel catalogues?" Based on the data collected from this telephone survey, we can calculate the sample statistics such as the sample average ($\bar{x}$) or the sample standard deviation (σ). We could also draw a histogram using these data to obtain the sample distribution. If another person chooses 100 names at random from the same telephone directory, chances are the average and standard deviation in that sample will be different from those obtained in the first sample because different members from the population are likely to be included in the second sample. In other words, the values for the sample statistics will be different from sample to sample. Note that the population parameters (had these been known) do not change, but the sample statistics change from one sample to another. Due to the very nature of randomness in the sampling process, the value of a sample statistic may be either close to or far from the unknown population parameter. The fundamental problem in inferential statistics deals with how to use the sample statistic, a variable, to estimate the population parameter, a fixed value.

The Law of Large Numbers

The law of large numbers (or the central limit theorem) solves the fundamental problem described above by stipulating the distribution of the sample statistic. Because a sample statistic is a variable (changes from sample to sample), there must be a distribution for a sample statistic. The theoretical distribution of a sample statistic (such as the sample mean, $\bar{x}$) is called a **sampling distribution**. The law of large numbers posits that as long as a sample was drawn at random and there was a reasonably large sample size (more than 30), the sampling distribution of sample mean will be approximately normal. The sampling distribution of the sample mean will have the same mean as the population mean (μ). The standard deviation (also called standard error and denoted as $s_{\bar{x}}$) of the sampling distribution of sample mean will be approximately equal to the standard deviation in the population (σ) divided by the square root of the sample size. In practice, the population standard deviation (σ) is unknown and is replaced by the sample standard deviation.

The beauty of this law is that in one stroke it solves the fundamental problem by allowing us to calculate the probability (a measure of our confidence) of how close a sample statistic will be to an unknown population parameter by using the tables of normal distribution. In other words, it allows us to ascertain the degree to which the sample results are "true" in the sense of being "representative of the population."

Confidence Intervals

A confidence interval denotes a range prediction for a population parameter with a certain degree of confidence (probability). Let's revisit the direct marketer (sent an offer to a sample of 5,000 from a list of 100,000 and got 100 orders) introduced at the beginning of this chapter.

Suppose the data are coded for the variable "response" as "1" for those who placed an order and "0" for those who did not. Calculating descriptive statistics on the response variable will produce a sample average of 0.02 (i.e., 2% response rate) and a sample standard deviation of 0.14. The 2% response rate is a sample statistic. The direct marketer is really interested in predicting the response rate in the population. Using the law of large numbers, the sampling distribution of the response rate will be approximately normal and this distribution will have a mean equal to the unknown population response rate. The standard deviation (standard error) for this distribution will be equal to 0.00198 $(0.14/\sqrt{4,999}\,)$.

Using some algebraic manipulations and using properties of normal distribution, it is easy to show that the 95% of times the population response rate will be in the range defined by sample response rate ± 1.96 times the standard error. That is, the 95% confidence interval for the population response rate is (0.161, 0.239) or 1.61% to 2.39%. In other words, there is a 95% chance that if the direct marketer mails to the entire list, the actual response rate will be somewhere between 1.61% and 2.39%. Of course, the flip side is that there is a 5% chance that the response rate may fall beyond the range—either less than 1.61% or more than 2.39%.

Direct marketers often work with 90%, 95%, or 99% confidence intervals. The formulas for the confidence intervals differ only in the multiplier of the standard error (1.65, 1.96, or 2.58 respectively). The CD-ROM accompanying this book demonstrates calculations of these as well as other non-standard (such as 92%) confidence intervals.

Hypothesis Testing, Statistical Significance, and P-Value

A hypothesis is a statement by the direct marketer about the value of a population parameter (such as response rate). Hypothesis testing is a statistical procedure designed to accept or reject the statement based on sample information. Unfortunately, the logic behind the rule of hypothesis testing is somewhat convoluted and often difficult for marketers to understand. That's the bad news. The good news is that the actual procedure for testing and rules of acceptance/rejection are straightforward. Thus, once you understand the logic of hypothesis testing for a simple situation, you can easily apply the procedure and rule for any complicated situation.

The hypothesis testing procedure involves assuming a value for a population parameter (such as population response rate), getting sample data from the population, calculating the sample statistic (such as sample response rate), and then calculating a probability of getting the sample statistic if the assumption is correct. This probability is called the p-value. The exact calculations for getting the p-value depends on many issues including the type of hypothesis, the sample size, the sampling distribution, the value of the sample statistic, etc. Most computer programs handle the mechanics and produce the p-value for the marketer. This discussion will concentrate on using and understanding this p-value, assuming it is produced by a computer program.

The rule for using the p-value is that if the p-value turns out to be smaller than a prespecified level (often 0.05 or 5%), the assumption made about the value for the population parameter is rejected. The prespecified level is called the α-level or the **level of significance**. The logic behind this rule is that when the p-value is small, the chance of getting the sample response (if the assumption about the population response is correct) is also small. Since in reality we know little about the population response rate and we actually obtained the sample response rate, we question and reject the assumption that we made about the population response rate.

Let's illustrate this concept with the direct marketer and her computer game. Suppose, the direct marketer wants to test the hypothesis that the population response rate equals 1.5%. The p-value (produced by a computer) for testing this hypothesis works out to 0.012 (or 1.2%). If the direct marketer uses the traditional α-level of 5%, using the rule, she will reject the hypothesis that the population response rate equals 1.5% because the p-value is less than the α-level. The α-level, or the significance, indicates the direct marketer's tolerance for making an error. That is, in this example, the direct marketer is willing to accept a chance of error of up to 5% in her decision about rejecting the hypothesis. The p-value indicates the chance of error that the direct marketer will incur if she decides to reject the hypothesis. When the chance of making an error is less than the prespecified level of tolerance for error, the hypothesis is rejected.

At this point a question arises: Is there some relationship between confidence interval and hypothesis testing? The answer is yes. For example, the 95% confidence interval for this example is 1.61% to 2.39%. That is, there is a 95% chance that the population response rate is within this interval and only a 5% chance that the population response rate is outside this interval. The hypothesized value, 1.5%, lies beyond this confidence interval. Because the 95% confidence interval does not include the hypothesized value, then at most we will make a 5% error in concluding that the hypothesized value must be incorrect. In other words, if we are willing to tolerate an error of up to 5% (the significance level), we should reject the hypothesis based on the fact that the hypothesized value is not within the 95% confidence interval. This is the reason why the confidence interval is often denoted as $(1-\alpha)*100\%$, where α is the significance level. Thus, there is an exact correspondence between confidence intervals and hypothesis testing.

Why is it necessary to use the p-value approach to hypothesis testing at all if the situation can be handled using confidence intervals, which are much easier to understand? The reason is while the confidence intervals are more intuitive and easier to understand, these are ideally suited for a simplistic hypothesis like the example above. When one wants to test more complicated statements (such as "there is a positive linear relationship between a person's income and his propensity to order from a catalog"), it is much easier computationally to use the p-value approach to hypothesis testing.

Types of Hypothesis Testing

The next step in this discussion is to distinguish the types of hypotheses (null versus alternative), the type of testing (one-sided or two-sided) and the types of errors in testing (Type I and Type II).

As indicated earlier, hypotheses are always formed using population parameters, but tested with sample statistics. A **null hypothesis** (denoted as H_0) is usually a statement of status quo, one of no difference or no effect. Usually if the null hypothesis is not rejected, no changes will be made or no action will be taken. An **alternative hypothesis** (denoted as H_1 or H_a) is one in which a difference or effect is expected. Thus, the alternative hypothesis is the opposite of the null hypothesis. The null hypothesis is the assumption that is tested using the p-value approach described earlier. The rejection of the null leads to the acceptance of the alternative hypothesis. It is customary to formulate the null hypothesis in such a way that the rejection of the null leads to the desired conclusion.

Assume that unless the population response rate is at least 1.5% or more, the direct marketer is not really interested in renting the whole list. In other words, no action will be required if the marketer cannot reject the statement that the population response rate is less than or equal to 1.5%. In that case, the set of null and alternative hypothesis will be written as:

- H_0: Response rate from the population (the entire list) is less than or equal to 1.5%.
- H_a: Response rate from the population (the entire list) is more than 1.5%

The test of the above null hypothesis is one-tailed (or, one-sided) because of the one-sided directionality stated in the alternative hypothesis.

On the other hand, suppose that the direct marketer is only interested in understanding whether the response rate from the list is different (better or worse) from the historic response rate that she gets from mailing to her house file (say 1.5%). Then, a two-tailed (or, two-sided) test will be needed and the set of hypotheses would be expressed as:

- H_0: Response rate from the population (the entire list) is equal to 1.5%.
- H_a: Response rate from the population (the entire list) is different (more or less than) 1.5%.

The p-value of 0.012 reported earlier was based on a two-tailed test. Most computer programs automatically report the two-tailed p-value for hypothesis tests. However, in practical applications, one-sided hypothesis tests are used more often. Therefore, a rule is needed to convert any two-tailed p-value to one-tailed p-value. Fortunately, an easy conversion rule exists.

The **conversion rule** states that if the value of the sample statistic is consistent with the direction of the value in the alternative hypothesis, then p-value for one-tailed test is one-half of the p-value for the two-tailed test. If the value of the sample statistic is inconsistent with the direction of the value in the alternative hypothesis, then the p-value for the one-tailed test equals one minus one-half of the p-value for the two-tailed test. This one-tailed p-value is then compared to the α-level, and as before, the null hypothesis is rejected if the one-tailed p-value is less than the α-level.

Let's see how we can apply this conversion rule for the direct marketer who wants to test the following hypotheses using a 5% α-level:

- H_0: Response rate from the population (the entire list) is less than or equal to 1.5%.
- H_a: Response rate from the population (the entire list) is more than 1.5%.

The alternative hypothesis specifies the direction for the response rate to be greater than 1.5%. The actual response rate obtained in the sample is 2%, which is greater than 1.5% and, thus, is consistent with the direction specified in the alternative hypothesis. Therefore, the one-sided p-value equals one-half of two-sided p-value (0.012). Thus, the one-sided p-value is 0.006 (or, 0.6%). Because this one-sided p-value is less than the α-level, the direct marketer rejects the null hypothesis and accepts the alternative hypothesis. In other words, based on the results of this test, the direct marketer will decide to rent all the names from the list.

A word of caution is in order here. The conversion rule (from two-sided to one-sided p-value) and the rejection/acceptance rule (reject null if p-value is less than the α-level) are predicated on the assumption that the marketer specifies the type of hypothesis (one-sided or two-sided) and the α-level before looking at the sample data. In other words, marketers should not first run an analysis and then choose either the type of

Decision	H₀ is	
	True	False
Reject H₀	Type I error	No error
Do not reject H₀	No error	Type II error

Exhibit 5-3: Two Types of Errors in Hypothesis Testing

hypothesis (one-sided or two-sided) or the α-level. Doing so will invalidate and critically undermine the statistical properties of hypothesis testing.

Two types of error can occur in tests of hypotheses. A Type I error results when the decision maker rejects the null hypothesis even though it is, in fact, true. In this instance, the wrong decision involves taking an action when one shouldn't, influenced by a chance occurrence. A Type II error occurs when the decision maker does not reject (accepts) the null hypothesis when it is, in fact, not true. In this instance, the wrong decision is to not do something when one should. This, too, is a chance occurrence in statistical terms. These two types of errors in hypothesis testing are summarized in Exhibit 5-3.

In the p-value approach to hypothesis testing, the focus is solely on controlling the probability of Type I error. When a direct marketer chooses a α-level (level of significance) of 5% for a hypothesis test, he is setting his tolerance limit for incurring Type I error at 5%. It would be nice if we could control the chance of both types of errors. Unfortunately, the chance of type II error is mathematically related to the chance of Type I error. As chance of Type I error decreases, the chance of Type II error increases. Thus, statistical hypothesis testing helps decision makers avoid making wrong decisions in terms of doing something when they should not (i.e., reject a null and take an action) and incur needless costs. But, there is also a lost opportunity cost (revenue foregone) associated with not doing something when one should (i.e., not rejecting the null when in fact it should be rejected). This second category of cost relates to making Type II errors, which is typically left somewhat uncontrolled in hypothesis testing.

Needless to say, statistical and probability theories are ways of measuring risk and assessing, but not eliminating, uncertainty. To make an intelligent decision, the marketer must sample from a population, measure relevant variables, compute sample statistics for these relevant variables, infer the values for population parameters of those relevant variables and, finally, make a decision mindful of the chance of incurring either a Type I or a Type II error.

Interactive Workshop 5-1:
Using EXCEL for Confidence Intervals and Hypothesis Testing

(For demonstration, go to the CD-Rom accompanying this book.)

This workshop demonstrates how to use a spreadsheet package such as Microsoft EXCEL® for calculation of confidence interval (CI) and for hypothesis testing.

In order for you to use the data set in the accompanying CD-ROM, you must have EXCEL installed on your computer. Also, you should make sure that the "Analysis ToolPak" (an add-in module that comes with EXCEL) is loaded into your EXCEL program. To test if "Analysis ToolPak" is already loaded, open any EXCEL file, click the Tools menu, and then click on "Data Analysis."

If you find many options starting with ANOVA, then "Analysis ToolPak" is already loaded. If you do not find "Data Analysis" under the tools menu, or if under the "Data Analysis" you do not see ANOVA options, you will need to add the "Analysis ToolPak."

To add the "Analysis ToolPak" to EXCEL, click Tools, click Add-Ins, check "Analysis ToolPak" among the options, and click OK.

Return to the confidence interval and hypothesis-testing problem described in this chapter. The direct marketer sent an offer to 5,000 prospects drawn at random from a list, and obtained 100 orders (or positive responses). This data set is labeled as "workshop5.1.xls" on the CD-ROM. The data set has two columns (A and B). The first column (A) contains subject ID (numbers ranging from 1 through 5000), and the second column (B) contains values for a variable labeled OFFER. This variable takes two values (1 = responded favorably, 0 = did not respond).

To produce a 95% CI for the variable OFFER (as described in the text), please complete the following procedure:

- Open the data set using EXCEL
- Click on Tools in the EXCEL menu
- Click on Data Analysis
- Select Descriptive Statistics in pop-up window, click OK
- Type in "B1:B5001" in the Input Range box
- Make sure the Labels in First Row box is checked
- Click New Worksheet Ply and type in "New1" in the box
- Check Summary Statistics
- Check confidence level for mean; Click OK

Offer	
Mean	0.02
Standard Error	0.001980097
Median	0
Mode	0
Standard Deviation	0.140014002
Sample Variance	0.019603921
Kurtosis	45.06666197
Skewness	6.859200789
Range	1
Minimum	0
Maximum	1
Sum	100
Count	5000
Confidence Level (95.0%)	0.003881859

Exhibit 5-4: Utilizing EXCEL for Confidence Intervals and Hypothesis Testing

If you followed the above procedure correctly, EXCEL should produce a worksheet labeled "New1" as shown in Exhibit 5-4.

Note that the value of the mean in the table shows the proportion of positive responses, 100 out of 5,000, or 2%. The standard deviation and the standard error values in the table match the numbers reported in the text. The confidence level in this table refers to the half-width of the 95% CI. That is, to get the upper (lower) bound of exact CI, you need to add (subtract) this half-width to the mean. Thus, the 95% CI for this problem is 0.02 ± 0.00388, which works out to be between 1.61% and 2.39% as mentioned in the text.

Unfortunately, there is no convenient way to get a p-value from EXCEL for testing a hypothesis such as the population proportion equals 1.5%. However, as described in the text, the 95% CI can be used to test any such hypothesis about proportion of positive responses using 5% level of significance.

Frequency Distribution: A summary table that shows the number (or, percentages) of observations belonging to each category of a variable.

Histogram: A bar chart of a frequency distribution, where the height of the bars represent the percentage of observations in each category of a variable.

Mean: The average of all values of a variable.

Median: The middle value in a set of ordered values of a variable.

Mode: The value that occurs the most for a variable.

Population: An entire group of individuals who share some common set of characteristics.

Population Distribution: The frequency distribution of a variable in a population.

Population Parameter: A summary measure that describes a characteristic of a population, such as a variable's mean.

Range: The difference between the highest and the lowest values of a variable.

Sample: A subset of members from a population.

Sample Distribution: The frequency distribution of a variable in a sample.

Sampling Distribution: The theoretical frequency distribution of a sample statistic.

Sample Statistic: A summary measure that describes some characteristic of a sample, such as average age.

Standard Deviation: The square root of variance.

Standard Error: The standard deviation of the sampling distribution of a statistic.

Variance: The average squared deviation from the mean for all values of a variable.

Exhibit 5-5: Summary of Terms

Chapter 6

Data Analysis Tools and Techniques

Key Concepts
- Bivariate Analysis
- Cross-Tab and Chi-Square Analysis
- T-Tests
- Correlation Analysis
- Simple Regression
- Multivariate Analysis
- Multiple Regression
- Logistic Regression
- Aid/Chaid Analysis
- Principal Components Analysis
- Cluster Analysis

Applications
- Using Excel for Cross-Tab Analysis
- Using Exel for Independent Sample T-Test for Means
- Using Excel for Independent Sample T-Test for Response Rate
- Using Excel for Correlation Analysis
- Using Excel for Simple Regression Analysis
- Using Excel for Multiple Regression Analysis

Focus in this chapter is on understanding the data analysis tools and techniques available to direct marketers, what each does, and how each can be used in the managerial decision-making process.

Some of the techniques (albeit less sophisticated ones) are available in spreadsheet programs such as Excel. However, we recommend you use statistical software such as SPSS, Statistica, or SAS to apply these techniques for analyzing your data set. Many statistical programs use point-and-click interfaces that make them relatively painless to use. For direct marketers, the critical issues are to be able to understand what each technique is capable of doing and then to be able to interpret the results from running an analysis. Consequently, we are mainly concerned in this chapter with user-related issues.

For most of the techniques covered in this chapter, we will illustrate a direct marketing relevant application using a data set. Whenever possible, we will provide actual computer output to show you what to expect when you run such analysis. Although we use SPSS for all of these analyses, you could use other statistical packages to do the same. We will start with simple two variable (Bivariate) analyses and gradually build up to more complicated analysis using multiple variables (Multivariate).

Bivariate Analysis

This section covers these types of two-variable analysis: cross-tabulation and chi-square, independent sample t-test, correlation and simple regression.

Cross-Tab and Chi-Square Analysis

The cross-tab (also called cross-classification table or pivot-table) is simply a summary table that classifies each observation in a data set with respect to two or more categorical variables. The entries in the cross-tab are typically counts that may be easily converted to percentages or probabilities.

Cross-tab is a great tool for getting a feel of the data and exploring general relationships between variables. For instance, consider the following question posed by a direct marketer of a credit card. This card issuer usually makes more money when card users carry a balance at the end of the month (i.e., do not pay in full). The marketer suspects that whether or not a person pays the credit card balance in full is related to the gender of the user of the credit card. He looks through his house file and creates a new categorical variable (called credit card balance) that takes a value of "yes" if the user has carried a monthly balance forward

Count

| | | GENDER | | Total |
		Female	Male	
Credit card balance	Yes	152	325	477
	No	248	275	523
Total		400	600	1000

Exhibit 6-1: Example of a Cross-Tab Relating Credit Card Balance to Gender

Chi-Square Tests

	Value	df	Sig. (2-sided)
Pearson Chi-Square	25.144	1	.000

Exhibit 6-2: Example of a Chi-Square Test of the Relationship of Credit Card Balance to Gender

at least once in the past year and "no" if not. A cross-tab using this variable relative to gender is shown in Exhibit 6-1.

The cross-tab in Exhibit 6-1 shows that, of the total 1,000 users in the house file, 600 are males and 400 are females. Of the 600 males, 325 (or 54.2% of males) have carried a credit card balance. Of the 400 females, 152 (or 38% of females) have carried a credit card balance. Clearly, the relationship between the two variables (Gender and Credit Card Balance) appears to be that males are more likely to carry a balance than females. Before jumping to this conclusion, however, the marketer needs to recognize that these 1,000 users in the house file are only a sample from a population of all potential credit card owners that the firm might target in the future. Is there in fact a relationship between the two variables in the population? A Chi-square test can provide the answer this question.

The principle behind the Chi-square test is that the variables in the test are assumed to be independent (not related) in a cross-tab and the p-value (probability) of obtaining the sample result is calculated accordingly. If the p-value is lower than the predetermined (usually 5%) α-level, we reject the independence assumption and conclude the two variables in the cross-tab are indeed related. Using the notation introduced in the preceding chapter, the set of hypotheses that will be tested by this direct marketer, using a 5% α-level, is:

- H_0: There is no relationship between gender of a person and whether the person carries a credit card balance in the population.
- H_a: There is a relationship between gender of a person and whether the person carries a credit card balance in the population.

Note that the alternative hypothesis is two-sided. Chi-square tests do not allow for a one-sided hypothesis test. The result of the Chi-square test is shown in Exhibit 6-2.

The last column of the table (labeled "Sig.") gives the -two-sided p-value for testing the null hypothesis. Using the rule (p-value less than the α-level), the marketer will reject the null hypothesis at a 5% level. Often this is stated, "Results are statistically significant at a 5% level." This means that the marketer will conclude there is a relation between gender of a person and whether the person carries a credit card balance. Moreover, going back to the results from the cross-tab, the marketer will conclude that males are more likely to carry a balance than females. Thus, perhaps, in future direct offers, the marketer will likely target males more than females.

A word of caution is in order. The p-value from Chi-square tests, similar to all other statistical tests, is sensitive to sample size. That is, in a large sample size (a common occurrence for direct marketers), even very small differences in the cross-tab may result in rejecting the null hypothesis (i.e., produce a statistically significant result). Direct marketers will be wise to carefully investigate if the actual difference in the cross-tab is large enough to warrant managerial action—in this case targeting more males than females in future offers. In this example, the probability difference of carrying a balance (between males and females) is 16.2% (54%-38.2%). Whether this difference is manageri-ally significant or not, and thus warrant further action, has to be decided by the marketer.

Thus far, a 2×2 cross-tab—two variable, each having two cate-gories—has been used. However, cross-tabs also can be used for three or more variables as long as there are enough observations in each cell of the cross-tab. For example, the direct marketer may want to further slice and dice his house file based on a member's marital status (single, married, widowed/divorced) along with the two variables used earlier. Of course, it gets more complicated (and expensive) to do such analysis, but the pay-off in terms of marketing insights generated may be worth the cost.

Independent Sample T-Test

Direct marketers typically use t-tests to answer questions like these:

- Is the average dollar amount of orders from males greater than that from females?
- Is the response to an offer from prospects in List A equal to the response to the same offer from prospects in List B?

The test is applicable where data is available from prospects belonging to two non-overlapping groups (such as males versus females, or prospects from list A versus prospects from list B) and where an average for the variable of interest (such as the response rate or the dollar revenue generated) can be meaningfully computed.

Return to the credit card issuer. The card issuer makes a small amount of money (not as much as he can make if people carry balances on their card) based on how much a card user charges to the card. The

	Gender	N	Mean	Std. Deviation
Amount charged	Male	600	2629.4717	793.7728
	Female	400	1796.8900	901.1177

Exhibit 6-3: Group Statistics Relating Amount Charged to Gender

marketer suspects that the average dollar amount charged on the card is higher for males than females. In the house file, he creates a new variable (calling it amount charged) which is the total amount charged by each user during the past year. He then calculates the average dollar amounts charged, separately for males and females, and records these results as shown in Exhibit 6-3.

It seems from the numbers reported above that males, on average, charge more ($832.58) than females. But before concluding such is the case, the card issuer needs to recognize that these 1000 members in the house file are really a sample from a population of all potential credit card users that the firm might target in the future. Is there in fact a relationship between the average amount charged by males and the average amount charged by females in the population? To answer this question, the marketer needs to conduct an independent-sample t-test.

The logic underlying the t-test is similar to that for hypothesis testing. The hypotheses are set up, the null hypothesis is assumed true, and the p-value of obtaining the sample result based on the assumption is calculated. If the p-value is lower than the predetermined (usually 5%) α-level, the null hypothesis is rejected and the alternative hypothesis is assumed to be correct. Using the notation introduced in the preceding chapter, the set of hypotheses that will be tested, using a 5% α-level, is:

- **H_0:** The average amount charged by males is lower than or equal to the average amount charged by females in the population.
- **H_a:** The average amount charged by males is higher than the average amount charged by females in the population.

Note that the alternative hypothesis is one-sided because at the start of this example it is stated that the marketer expected males to charge more than females. Also, recall that the computer output will produce a two-sided p-value and the conversion rule must be used to get the one-sided p-value and then compared it to the desired α-level. The result from conducting the t-test is shown in Exhibit 6-4.

It is a bit difficult to understand this output because it really contains results from three tests (done automatically by the program).

Independent Sample T-Test

		Levene's Test for Equality of Variances		T-test for Equality of Means			
		F	Sig.	t	df	Sig. (2-tailed)	Mean Difference
Amount charged	Equal variances assumed	40.688	.000	15.386	998	.000	832.5817
	Equal variances not assumed			15.002	779.608	.000	832.5817

Exhibit 6-4: Example of an Independent Sample T-Test of the Relationship of Amount Charged to Gender

The next-to-last column labeled "Sig. (2-tailed)" contains the two-sided p-value for the t-test. However, there are two p-values in that column of this table because there are two different ways of calculating the p-value, depending on whether one thinks the variances in the two groups are equal or not. The first number reflects the p-value assuming the variances are equal, and the second number reflects the p-value assuming that variances are not equal. In most practical applications, the marketer does not really know if variances are equal or not between the groups. Thus, it is recommended to use the p-value in the second row in the column labeled "Sig. (2-tailed)."

The two-sided p-value is 0.00. The conversion rule states that if the sample values are consistent with the direction predicted in the alternative hypothesis, then the one-sided p-value is one-half of the two-sided p-value. In this case, the sample averages are consistent with the direction specified in the alternative hypothesis; therefore the one-sided p-value is 0.00 (one-half of 0.00). Comparing this one-sided p-value to the pre-specified α-level of 5% leads to rejection of the null hypothesis. Again, some marketers/consultants will report this analysis as having a result that is statistically significant at 5% level. But the basic idea remains the same: Acceptance of the alternative hypothesis that males, on average, charge more than the females in the population of credit card users.

As indicated earlier, p-values are sensitive to sample size. That is, a marketer can get a low p-value and thereby obtain a statistically significant result even if the actual difference is small. So, the marketer must

Group Statistics

	LIST	N	Mean	Std. Deviation
RESPONSE	1.00	500	4.800E-02	.2140
	2.oo	750	7.200E-02	.2587

Exhibit 6-5: Group Statistics Example Relating Response to Lists

Independent Sample T-Test

		Levene's Test for Equality of Variances		T-test for Equality of Means			
		F	Sig.	t	df	Sig. (2-tailed)	Mean Difference
Amount charged	Equal variances assumed	12.060	.001	-1.719	1248	.086	-2.400E-02
	Equal variances not assumed			-1.785	1191.462	.075	-2.400E-02

Exhibit 6-6: Example of Independent Sample T-Test Relating Response to List

decide if the observed difference in amount charged ($832.58) between males and females in the sample is worth pursuing for future targeting actions. In other words, we have demonstrated statistically significant difference. Whether this difference is managerially significant can only be answered by using sound executive judgement.

One more example to demonstrate the independent samples T-test follows. Suppose the credit card marketer is trying to decide whether to obtain names and addresses from two different lists (list 1 and list 2). Both lists contain 100,000 names and addresses. The cost for renting the names is $40 CPM (cost per thousand names) for list 1 and $50 CPM from list 2. The credit card marketer asks the list broker for a sample of names from both lists. He gets names and addresses for 500 prospects from list 1 and 750 prospects from list 2. The marketer sends a credit card offer to prospects from both lists and tracks the responses to this offer. How should the direct marketer proceed?

First, although the marketer observed sample response rates, he is really interested in knowing whether the observed differences in sample response rates will hold when he mails to all prospects on the lists. A logical way to approach this decision is to conduct an independent sample t-test using the response rate variable. The hypotheses the marketer wants to test at 5% level are:

- **H₀:** The response rates from both lists are equal in the population.
- **Hₐ:** The response rates from both lists are different in the population.

The alternative hypothesis is two-sided because the marketer has no idea what to expect from the lists. The marketer enters data for the variable response as "1" if a person takes the credit card offer, "0" otherwise. The result of the independent sample t-test is shown in Exhibits 6-5 and 6-6.

The response rate from list 1 is 4.8% and the response rate from list 2 is 7.2% (shown in Exhibit 6-5). The two-sided p-value for the test of hypotheses is in the last row of the column labeled "Sig." in the table of independent sample t-test (Exhibit 6-6).

Because the p-value of 0.075 (i.e., 7.5%) is more than the pre-specified 5% level of significance, the null hypothesis cannot be rejected. In other words, the difference in the response rates from list 1 and list 2, as observed in the test, is due to chance variations induced by the sampling process; in theory words, statistically insignificant. Therefore, if the marketer has a limited budget and has to choose one list or the other, he might as well go for the low cost one, i.e., list 1.

Correlation

Marketers use correlation analysis to answer questions such as:

- Is there an association between age of a person and the amount that that person orders from a catalogue?
- Is there an association between income of a person and the number of times the person ordered from a catalogue in the last year?
- Is there an association between how long a person has been in the database and the amount that the person orders?

For each of these questions, if an association exists between the variables, marketers also want to know how strong is that association?

Correlation coefficient is a summary index that captures both the strength and the direction of association between two continuous variables. The value of a correlation coefficient can range from -1 to +1. The strength of association between two variables is communicated by the absolute value of the correlation coefficient. For example, correlation coefficients near -1 or +1 indicate a near perfect or very strong association between two variables. Coefficients near 0 indicate a lack of association. The sign of the correlation coefficient indicates the direction of the association. A positive coefficient indicates that higher values of one variable tend to be associated with higher values of the other variable. A negative coefficient indicates that the higher values of one variable tend to be associated with lower values of the other variable.

Let's illustrate correlation analysis using data from the credit card marketer. The marketer has information on each card user's age in the house file and suspects that the higher a person's age, the higher the average amount such a person is likely to charge on a credit card. In other words, the marketer expects a positive association (correlation)

Correlations

		Amount Charged	AGE
Amount charged	Pearson Correlation	1.000	.319 **
	Sig. (2-tailed)		.000
	N	1000	1000
AGE	Pearson Correlation	.319 **	1.000
	Sig. (2-tailed)	.000	
	N	1000	1000

**Correlation is significant at the 0.01 level (2-tailed)

Exhibit 6-7: Correlation Analysis to Show the Relationship between the Age of a Credit Card User and the Amount Charged

between age and amount charged (the variable we created in the earlier example). As in earlier examples, the marketer recognizes that the house file data is a sample from a population of all possible future credit card users; therefore, he wants to test the following hypotheses at the 5% α-level:

- **H_0:** There is a negative or zero correlation between age and amount charged in the population.
- **H_a:** There is a positive correlation between age and amount charged in the population.

The alternative hypothesis is one-sided because the marketer expected a directional relationship between the variables. The output from running a correlation analysis is reported in Exhibit 6-7.

The output is in the form of a matrix of numbers. The correlation coefficient (the number corresponding to Pearson correlation) is 0.319 and the p-value (the number corresponding to Sig. [2-tailed]) is 0.000. Of course, the p-value reported is for a two-sided test. Using the conversion rule, the p-value for the one-sided test is also 0.000 (one-half of two-sided p-value because the correlation coefficient is positive and thus consistent with the direction in the alternative hypothesis). The one-sided p-value is less than the 5% α-level. Therefore, the marketer rejects the null hypothesis and accepts the alternative hypothesis that there is a positive association between age and amount charged. As discussed previously, some analysts will explain this result as "the correlation is statistically significant at a 5% level." What it implies for the marketer is that as a customer's age increases, he is likely to charge more on the credit card.

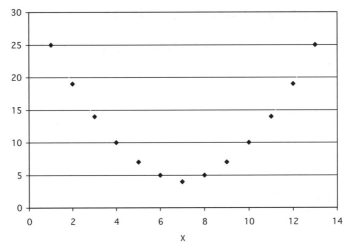

Exhibit 6-8: Scatter Diagram Visualizing Non-Linear Correlation

Once an association has been established (i.e., the correlation is statistically significant), the next logical question is how strong is the association? Because correlation coefficient values are constrained between -1 to +1, there are rules of thumb available to make broad judgments about the strength of the association. Many direct marketers use the "rule of thumb" that correlation in the range of -0.3 to +0.3 represents a weak association, correlation in the range of -0.7 to -0.3 or +0.3 to +0.7 represents a moderate association, and correlation in the range of -0.7 to -1 or +0.7 to +1 represents a strong association. Using this rule of thumb for this example, the association between age and amount charged on the credit card is at best moderate.

Correlation analysis suffers from one significant limitation. Correlation only measures a special type of association, called linear (straight-line) relation, between variables. That is, a correlation coefficient captures how well a straight line may represent the relationship between two variables. In many data sets, variables are related in a way that cannot be represented well by a straight-line approach. For example, in the scatter plot shown in Exhibit 6-8, there is a perfect, albeit non-linear, relationship between the two variables X and Y, but the correlation coefficient is 0 because the relationship cannot be represented by a straight-line.

Thus, a near-zero correlation coefficient does not imply no association between the two variables; it means there is no linear association between the two variables. Therefore, direct marketers will be wise to use correlation coefficient along with a graphical representation of data points as in a scatter plot.

Simple Regression

Simple regression is often used by direct marketers primarily to predict the value for one variable using the value of another variable. For instance, our credit card marketer might be interested in predicting the dollar amount a person is expected to charge on the card relative to the person's age. A secondary benefit of simple regression is its ability to provide an explanation of the nature and strength of relationship between the two variables. In statistics, the variable one wants to predict or forecast is called the **dependent** or **criterion** variable (typically denoted by Y). The variable used to make the prediction is called the independent or predictor variable (typically denoted by X). In the previous example, the dollar amount a person is expected to charge is the dependent variable and the person's age is the independent variable.

The mechanics behind a regression involve finding a "best fitting line" in a scatter plot of data of Y and X. Put simply, it means regression attempts to find a line such that all the points taken together in the plot of Y and X fits this line the best. The method for determining the best fit is called "least-squares." In this method, the regression line is found such that the sum of squared deviations of all points from the regression line is minimized. The regression line is expressed in the following form:

$$Y = b_0 + b_1 X$$

In this equation, the b_0 is called the intercept and b_1 is called the coefficient of X. Note that, once the values for b_0 and b_1 are known, marketers can use the equation to predict or forecast values for Y for any known value of X. The value of the intercept is the predicted value for Y, when X equals 0. The coefficient of X, b_1, is the slope (rise over the run) of the regression line. It represents how much Y will change if X is changed by one unit. A positive coefficient implies that as X increases, Y will also increase. A negative coefficient indicates that when X increases, Y decreases.

The credit card marketer who wants to predict and explain the dollar amount charged on a credit card using a person's age might run a simple regression. The output is shown in Exhibit 6-9.

In this example, the credit card issuer's house file constitutes the sample. The population consists of all potential users of the issuer's credit cards.

We start with the part of the regression output labeled ANOVA (an acronym for analysis of variance). The ANOVA table shows a test of hypotheses for the overall regression equation. The set of hypotheses being tested in this part is:

Model Summary				
Model	**R**	**R Square**	**Adjusted R Square**	**Std. Error of the Estimate**
1	.319a	.102	.101	833.6663

a Predictors: (Constant), Age

ANOVAb

Model		**Sum of Squares**	**df**	**Mean Square**	**F**	**Sig.**
1	Regression	88470052	1	88470052	113.297	.000a
	Residual	7.79E+08	998	780866.117		
	Total	8.68E+08	999			

a Predictors: (Constant), Age
b Dependent Variable: Amount Charged

Coefficientsa

Model		**Unstandardized Coefficients**		**Standardized Coefficients**		
		B	**Std. Error**	**Beta**	**t**	**Sig.**
1	(Constant)	1436.690	85.469		16.809	.000
	AGE	17.217	1.618	.319	10.644	.000

a Dependent Variable: Amount Charged

Exhibit 6-9: Output of a Simple Regression Analysis

- H_0: The regression model does not explain the relationship between the dependent and the independent variable in the population.
- H_a: H_0 is not true.

If this null hypothesis is not rejected, there is not much point in proceeding to interpret the rest of the output. The p-value for testing this hypothesis is shown under the column labeled "Sig." in the ANOVA table. The p-value is 0.000. Thus, the H_0 is rejected at 5% α-level. Many analysts will explain this result as: "The overall regression is statistically significant at 5% level." In other words, the marketer can conclude that there is indeed a relationship in the population between the amount charged and a person's age.

Next, the part of the output table labeled "Coefficients" contains values for intercept and slope as well as tests of significance for these items. The unstandardized coefficient (B) corresponding to a constant is the value of the intercept, and the unstandardized coefficient (B), corresponding to age, is the value of the slope. The last column in this table contains the two-sided p-values for testing whether the values for intercept and slope are 0. Since both p-values for intercept and slope are 0.000, the marketer can conclude that these values are statistically significant. Having established the statistical significance of the overall regression and the coefficients, the marketer can now write out the regression (or, prediction) equation as:

$$\text{Amount charged} = 1436.69 + 17.217 * \text{Age}$$

What does this equation really mean for the marketer? For starters, it means that as a person's age increases by one year, the amount charged on the credit card increases by seventeen dollars and twenty-two cents. That is the interpretation of the slope of the regression line. The interpretation of the intercept is meaningless for this (and many other) problems. Literally, it means if a person's age is 0, that person is expected to charge $1,436.69 on the credit card! Our recommendation for direct marketers is not to worry too much about the value or the test of significance for the intercept.

The equation is also useful for prediction purposes. For example, if the marketer knows the age of a list of prospects, it is possible to forecast the amount that will be charged by each person on the prospect list. For instance, a prospect who is 45 years of age is expected to charge $2,211.46 (1,436.69 + [17.217 * 45]) on the credit card. Thus, the direct marketer can use the equation to forecast the amount that is expected to be charged by each prospect, sort the prospect file using this forecasted variable, and then pick the top 10% or 20% of the sorted file for sending offers. This method is called scoring and is frequently used by direct marketers.

The table from the regression output titled "Model Summary" also provides useful information for marketers. The column labeled "R" shows the correlation between the dependent and the independent variable. Note that R has the same value in the correlation example described earlier. The term "R Square" (R^2) is the square of the correlation coefficient. R^2 indicates the amount of common (shared) variance between the dependent and the independent variable. The variance is a measure of variability (or degree of uncertainty) in a variable. Therefore, high values of R^2 indicate that the regression model explains a lot of uncertainty in the values of the dependent variable. The value for R^2 goes from 0 to 1, with 0 indicating that the regression model explains no uncertainty in the values of the dependent variable and 1 indicating perfect explanation of uncertainty in the values of the dependent variable.

It is a common practice in regression to use the value of R^2 to make managerial judgments with respect to the explanatory power of the regression model. Rules of thumb for R^2 are: 0-10% is low, 10-50% is moderate, and more than 50% is high. In this example, the value of R^2 is in the borderline of low to moderate. That is, the model is not doing a great job in explaining the variance in the dependent variable, the amount charged on the credit card. That is not surprising; given that the marketer has used only one independent variable, age, in the regression model.

There are some critical issues for using regression analysis correctly. First, there are certain assumptions that, if violated, can undermine the validity of statistical significance tests in regression. Fortunately, regression models are fairly robust to violations of such assumptions. (Such assumptions are covered in our discussion of multiple regression that follows.)

Second, marketers need to be careful in using the regression model for predicting Y using values of X that are far away from the observed X-values in the data set. For example, in the credit card marketer's house file, the values of age range from 18 to 85 years. The credit card marketer will be wise not to make a prediction for amount charged using the regression equation for a 100-year old person.

Third, in practical direct marketing applications of regression, one often finds very low values of R^2 or variance explained. A low R^2 value often discourages novice users. However, for practical direct marketing applications, the more important criteria is how well the model can forecast in a prospect file rather than how much variance the model can explain in the house file.

Multivariate Analysis

The term **multivariate analysis** refers to statistical techniques that use multiple variables *simultaneously* to get a feel for data, *make predictions*, and *explain relationships* among variables. This section will cover these types of multivariate analysis: multiple regression, logistic regression, AID/CHAID analysis, principal component analysis, and cluster analysis. As in the case of bivariate analysis, the focus will be on user-related issues rather than the mechanics of each technique. The use of multiple regression, logistic regression, and AID/CHAID analysis will be demonstrated by using a data set. For the other two techniques (principal component analysis and cluster analysis), descriptions of how and where these techniques are used by direct marketers will be provided.

Multiple Regression

The best way to understand multiple regression is to consider it an extension of the simple regression technique, with the exception that there are multiple independent variables. Suppose the credit card marketer has obtained additional demographic data—value of a person's home (homeval) and the person's annual income (income)—for each member of his house file. The credit card marketer still wants to predict the amount a person is expected to charge (the dependent variable). However, now he has three independent variables (age, income, and homeval) to help him make such predictions. The mechanics of multiple regression involve finding the best-fitting plane such that the sum of squared deviations of all points from this plane is minimized. Formally, the multiple regression equation (with one dependent variable, y, and n independent variables, X_1, X_2, ... X_n) is expressed in this form:

$$Y = b_0 + b_1 X_1 + b_2 X_2 + b_3 X_3 ....+ b_n X_n.$$

In this equation, the b_0 is still called the intercept and b_1, b_2 ... b_n are called the coefficients of X_1, X_2 ... X_n. Note that, once the values for b_0, b_1 and b_2 are known, marketers can use the equation to predict or forecast values for Y for any known values of the independent variables (X's). The value of the intercept is the predicted value for Y when all independent variables equal 0. The coefficient b_1, represents how much Y will change if X_1 is changed by one unit, provided all other X-variables are held constant. As in the case of simple regression, the sign of a coefficient represents the direction of relationship between the dependent and independent variable.

Let's revisit the example of the credit card marketer who wants to predict and explain the dollar amount charged on a credit card using a person's age, income and value of home. Suppose the credit card marketer ran multiple regression and obtained output shown in Exhibit 6-10.

As in the case of simple regression, start with the ANOVA table. The ANOVA table shows a test of hypothesis for the overall regression equation. The set of hypotheses being tested in this part are:

- H_0: The regression model does not explain the relationship between the dependent and all the independent variables (considered together) in the population.
- H_a: H_0 is not true.

If this null hypothesis is not rejected, there is not much point in proceeding to interpret the rest of the output. The p-value for testing this hypothesis is shown under the column labeled "Sig." in the ANOVA table. The p-value is 0.000. Thus, the H_0 is rejected at 5% α-level. Many

Model Summary				
Model	R	R Square	Adjusted R Square	Std. Error of the Estimate
1	.579a	.335	.333	761.0816

a Predictors: (Constant), Income, Age, Homeval

ANOVAb						
Model		Sum of Squares	df	Mean Square	F	Sig.
1	Regression	2.91E+08	3	96948753	167.371	.000a
	Residual	5.77E+08	996	5792745.158		
	Total	8.68E+08	999			

a Predictors: (Constant), Income, Age, Homeval
b Dependent Variable: Amount Charged

Coefficientsa						
Model		Unstandardized Coefficients		Standardized Coefficients		
		B	Std. Error	Beta	t	Sig.
1	(Constant)	191.245	99.500		1.922	.055
	AGE	12.695	1.414	.235	8.977	.000
	HOMEVAL	1.429E-03	.000	.198	7.476	.000
	INCOME	1.207E-02	.001	.412	15.497	.000

a Dependent Variable: Amount Charged

Exhibit 6-10: Output of a Multiple Regression Analysis

analysts will explain this result as: "The multiple regression model is statistically significant at 5% level." In other words, the marketer can conclude that there is indeed a relationship in the population between the amount charged and, simultaneously, a person's age, income and home value.

Next, the part of the output table labeled "Coefficients" contains values for the intercept and coefficients as well as tests of significance for these items. The values for the unstandardized coefficients (B) and the two-sided p-values for testing whether these coefficients equal 0 are shown in this table. Since p-values for all coefficients (except the intercept) are 0.000, the marketer can conclude that these coefficients are statistically significant. Although the p-value for the intercept is 0.055, as we explained earlier in the context of simple regression, the interpretation of the intercept is often meaningless for direct marketers, and it is a commonly accepted practice to leave the intercept in the regression model regardless of whether or not the coefficient is significant. Having established the statistical significance of the overall regression and the coefficients, the marketer can now write out the regression (or, prediction) equation as:

*Amount charged = 191.245 + (12.695 * Age) + (0.001429 ** *Homeval) + (0.01207 * Income)*

How should a marketer interpret the numbers in this equation? Consider the coefficient for age as an example. It means that as a person's age increases by one year, the amount charged on the credit card increases by $12.69 provided the other variables (homeval and income) are held constant. To understand this further, suppose that two persons (A and B) in the database have identical homeval and income, but person A is 30 years old and person B is 31 years old. Then, the coefficient of age indicates that person B is expected to charge $12.69 more than person A. The coefficients for homeval and income can be explained in a similar manner.

A natural question to ask at this point is: What is the importance of ranking these three independent variables for predicting the amount a person is expected to charge on the credit card? Looking at the magnitude of the values of the unstandardized coefficients, one may be tempted to conclude that age is the most important variable, followed by income and homeval. Such a conclusion would be wrong because the scales used to measure the independent variables heavily influence the unstandardized coefficients. To take the effect of scales out and to make a proper comparison, direct marketers should look at the values of the standardized coefficients. These values, shown in the table labeled coefficients, show that income is the most important variable, followed by age and homeval.

As before, the regression equation is also useful for prediction purposes. For example, if the marketer knows the age, income, and homeval for a list of prospects, it is possible to forecast the amount that will be charged by each person on the prospect list. For instance, a prospect who is 45 years of age, has annual income of $100,000, and has a home valued at $150,000 is expected to charge this amount on the credit card:

$2,183.87 = 191.245 + (12.695 * 45) + (0.001429 * 150,000) + (0.01207 * 100,000)

Thus, the direct marketer can use the equation to forecast the amount that is expected to be charged by each prospect (i.e., score the prospect file), sort the prospect file using this forecasted variable, and then send credit card offers to only the top 10% or 20% of the sorted file.

The table from the regression output titled "Model Summary" also provides useful information for marketers. The column labeled "R" shows the multiple correlations between the dependent and all the independent variables. The term R Square (R^2) is the square of the multiple correlation coefficient. R^2 indicates the amount of common (shared) variance between the dependent and all the independent variables. In multiple regression, it is customary to look at the value of "adjusted R Square" (instead of R^2) to make managerial judgments with respect to the explanatory power of the regression model. The value for "adjusted R Square" goes from 0 to 1, with 0 indicating that the regression model explains no uncertainty in the values of the dependent variable and 1 indicating perfect explanation of uncertainty in the values of the dependent variable. Rules of thumb for adjusted R^2 are: 0-10% is low, 10-50% is moderate, and more than 50% is high. In this example, the value of adjusted R^2 is moderate (33.5%). Astute readers will notice that the variance explained has increased from 10.2% in the simple regression (with only age as the independent variable) to 33.5% in the multiple regression (with age, income, and homeval as multiple independent variables).

Multiple regression is a complex and a powerful tool. We have only provided a very brief overview of this tool. Many excellent textbooks focus on this topic alone and most universities have semester-long courses devoted to this topic. Used properly, this tool can benefit direct marketers tremendously. However, it is also easy to abuse this technique! We want to point out a few user-related issues with respect to multiple regression. First, all of the concerns expressed in discussing simple regression (such as satisfying statistical assumptions, predicting Y values using X values that are far away from the observed X values in the data sets, etc.) are equally important for multiple regression as well.

Second, in practical applications, direct marketers often have a large number of independent variables to choose from. It is tempting to run a multiple regression model with all independent variables, look at the statistical significance of the coefficients for each variable, throw out the ones that are not significant, and rerun the multiple regression with only those variables that had statistically significant coefficients. While this approach may seem logical, there is a danger that following such procedure will result in a model that is sub-optimal. Without going into the statistical reasoning behind this danger, we want to make a few broad recommendations as listed below:

■ Although this example has used continuous independent variables such as age, multiple regression can also use dichotomous categorical variables such as gender. In using categorical variables, it is customary to code the two categories as 1 and 0. If there are more than two categories in a variable, direct marketers are advised to create "dummy variables" to handle such situations. If a categorical variable has three categories (say red, yellow, and blue), two dummy variables are needed to effectively represent the values of the original variable. Here is an example of how to code such dummy variables:

Original Variable	Dummy Variable 1	Dummy Variable 2
Red	1	0
Yellow	0	1
Blue	0	0

■ If managers believe that certain independent variables should impact the dependent variable, those independent variables must be retained in the multiple regression regardless of the statistical significance of their coefficients.

■ It is possible to choose a "best" subset of independent variables using variations of multiple regression techniques such as employing a forward, backward, or stepwise selection method. These methods work in an incremental fashion. For example, in the forward selection method, the first independent variable to enter the model is the one that has the highest bivariate correlation with the dependent variable. Once the first variable has entered the model, the method then looks for the next best variable given that the first variable is already in the model. The method keeps finding each additional variable until the added variable is no longer statistically significant.

Clearly, these methods are better than putting all variables in the model, estimating the model coefficients, and then throwing out all the nonsignificant variables. However, the chance of finding a suboptimal model is not eliminated completely by following any such methods.

■ There are several ways to increase the usefulness of multiple regression as both a predictive and explanatory technique. One popular technique is transformation of the dependent and independent variables such that the relationship between these transformed variables is more linear than was the relationship among the original (untransformed) variables. Another technique is to use square or cubic terms of the independent variables in the equation to capture non-linear relationships. One can also use interaction terms to capture the effect of specific combinations of the independent variables on the dependent variables.

■ Direct marketers should consider splitting their data into two sets randomly. Then, they should use one set (called calibration or estimation sample) to estimate their model coefficients. The multiple regression equation based on the calibration sample can then be used to predict the value for the dependent variable in the other data set (called validation or hold-out sample). The predicted values of the dependent variable can be compared with actual values of the dependent variable to get an idea of forecasting error. Many indices of forecasting error can be calculated, the common ones being MAPE (mean absolute percentage error) and RMSE (root mean square error). If the multiple regression model chosen based on the calibration sample performs well in predicting in the validation sample (i.e., generates low MAPE or RMSE), direct marketers will have more faith in their model.

Logistic Regression

Logistic regression is ideal for predicting and explaining a dependent variable that has only two categories. Often direct marketers are faced with such dependent variables. Examples include whether a person responds to a direct promotional offer (two categories of response, yes/no). While many direct marketers continue to use multiple regression models for such categorical dependent variables, there are compelling theoretical and practical reasons to consider using a logistic regression in such situations. First, use of multiple regression for a categorical dependent variable almost always violates the statistical assumptions of multiple regression models. Second, the predictions based on multiple regression models often are inferior to predictions based on logistic regression models for categorical variables.

In logistic regression, the categorical dependent variable is transformed, and this transformed variable is modeled as a linear function of the independent variables. For example, if a dependent variable, Y, is categorical and can take only two values (yes = 1; no = 0), then instead of modeling Y, logistic regression will model G, called logit of a yes response, as given here:

$$G = b_0 + b_1 X_1 + b_2 X_2 + b_3 X_3 \ldots\ldots\ldots\ldots + b_n X_n.$$

In this equation, G equals $\ln(p/(1-p))$, where ln is the natural log; p is the probability of a yes response (i.e., probability Y equals 1); $X_1, X_2, \ldots X_n$ are independent variables. Although this may look somewhat complicated, the actual use and interpretation of the output from the logistic regression will be very similar to that of multiple regression.

```
Dependent Variable:    OFFER (Offer of Balance Transfer Check)
Values for OFFER are: 1 = responded favorably
                      0 = did not respond favorably

                   Chi-Square       df       Significance

Model                251.009         3          .0000


Cox & SnellR2          .222
Nagelkerke R2          .296


Classification Table for OFFER
The Cut Value assumed is .50

                       Predicted Based on the Logistic Model
                                        Percent Correctly
                         0   I   1          predicted
Observed Values    +------+------+
     .00           I  412  I  112  I          78.63%
                   +------+------+
    1.00           I  160  I  316  I          66.39%
                   +------+------+
                   Overall hit rate            72.80%


———————————Independent Variables in the Model ——————————-

Variable    B          S.E.       Wald    df   Sig.     R        Exp(B)

AGE         .0128       .0043     9.0520   1   .0026   .0714    1.0129
HOMEVAL     3.25E-06   5.798E-07 31.3894   1   .0000   .1457    1.0000
INCOME      3.11E-05   2.734E-06 129.2043  1   .0000   .3032    1.0000
Constant   -4.4159      .3511    158.1818  1   .0000
```

Exhibit 6-11: Output of a Logistic Regression Analysis

Suppose that the credit card marketer sent an offer of a balance transfer check (i.e., using this check consumers can transfer balances from other credit cards to this credit card) to his house file. Suppose he created a new variable (call it offer), which takes a value of 1 for those who responded positively to this offer and 0 for those who did not. The marketer wants to predict and explain this dependent variable (offer) using the three independent variables: age, income, and homeval. Suppose he ran a logistic regression and obtained the output shown in Exhibit 6-11 from a computer program.

In interpreting the output, start with the overall significance of the logistic model shown at the top of the output. The p-value for testing the overall model significance is 0.000 (under the column labeled Significance). Thus, the overall model is significant at the 5% level. As in the case of multiple regression, if this test of the overall model is non-significant, there may not be much point in interpreting the rest of the output.

The two different R^2 values (Cox and Snell, and Nagelkerke) can be interpreted similarly to the adjusted R2 in multiple regression for making managerial judgements with respect to the model. In this case, the values indicate a moderately strong relationship between the dependent and all the independent variables (considered together). A better managerial tool, the hit-ratio, is explained later.

Next, the numbers in that part of the output labeled "Independent Variables in the Model" shows the coefficients for each independent variable (under the column labeled B) and the p-value for testing each coefficient (under the column labeled Sig.) For example, the coefficient for age is 0.0128, and the p-value for testing whether this coefficient is 0 equals 0.0026. Because the p-value is less than 0.05, the marketer concludes that the coefficient for age is statistically significant at the 5% level. The interpretation of this coefficient is that, if a person's age is increased by 1 year, the logit of yes response to the offer (G), goes up by 0.0128 units, provided the other two independent variables are held constant.

This interpretation may seem highly unappealing. A more intuitive explanation of how to interpret the coefficients will follow.

Using the coefficient values in this table, the prediction equation of the logistic regression model can be written as:

G (logit of yes response) = - 4.4519 + (0.0128 * age) + (0.00000326 * homeval) + (0.0000311 * income)

To use this equation for prediction, consider person A, who is 49 years old, has a homeval of $100,000, and an income of $162,589. Plugging these numbers in the above equation results in a predicted value of G as 1.5583. Using the formula for G, we can solve for p; the probability of a favorable response for this person is:

Logit of yes response (G), ln(p/(1-p)) = 1.5583
Odds of yes response, p/(1-p) = Exp (1.5583) = 4.75
Probability of yes response, p = 4.75 (1+4.75) = 0.826

In other words, there is an 82.6% chance that this person will respond favorably to the offer of a balance transfer check. Thus, the direct marketer can use the equation to forecast the probability of a favorable response in a prospect file (assuming the prospect file has the values for the three independent variables). The marketer can then sort the prospect file, using this forecasted probability of favorable response, and send balance transfer check offers to the top 10% or 20% of the file.

Returning to the explanation of the coefficients, suppose that the prediction equation and the subsequent calculation are used to figure out the probability of a favorable response for person B, who is 50 years old, has a homeval of $100,000, and an income of $162,589. The only difference between person A and person B is in their ages. Using the same method described above, the odds of yes response and probability of yes response for person B will work out to 4.847 and 0.829 respectively. In other words, as age increases by 1 year but the other independent variables remain constant, the probability of responding favorably to the balance transfer check offer increases from 82.6% to 82.9%.

Finally, the table labeled "Predicted Based on the Logistic Model" is a classification table for all 1,000 observations produced automatically by the program. As explained earlier, a logistic regression prediction model can be used to predict the probability of a yes response for each observation. Then each observation is classified as yes/no depending on whether the probability of response was greater than 0.5 (identified in computer output as "cut value assumed is 0.5"). That is, the program classified each observation as "yes" if the predicted probability of response for that observation was higher than 50%. These predictions were crossed against observed responses (yes/no) to create the table. The numbers in this table can be interpreted as follows.

Of the 1,000 members in the house file, 476 responded favorably and 524 responded unfavorably to the offer. Of those who responded favorably, the model correctly predicted the outcome for 316 members (66.39% correctly predicted). Of those who responded negatively, the model correctly predicted the outcome for 412 members (78.63% correctly predicted). The diagonal elements in this table represent the correct predictions and the off-diagonal elements represent the incorrect predictions by the model. Thus, of the total 1,000 members, the model correctly predicted the outcome for 728 members (412+316). This resulted in an overall 72.8% of correct prediction. This overall percent of correct prediction is called the hit-ratio, and direct marketers often use this index to judge the usefulness of predictive models.

All of the broad recommendations made for multiple regression apply to logistic regression as well. These include using categorical independent variables, retaining theoretically or managerially important independent variables in the model even if their coefficients are not statistically significant, using stepwise variable selection techniques, and using calibration/validation samples for evaluating predictive accuracy of models. The caveats mentioned for the proper use of multiple regression are also applicable for logistic regression.

Aid/CHAID Analysis

AID is an acronym for Automatic Interaction Detector. CHAID is an acronym for Chi-squared Automatic Interaction Detector. AID/CHAID analysis can be used as a stand-alone tool or in conjunction with multiple and logistic regression. Predictive results from multiple and logistic regression models often can be improved by the addition of specific combinations of independent variables (called interactions). In this context,

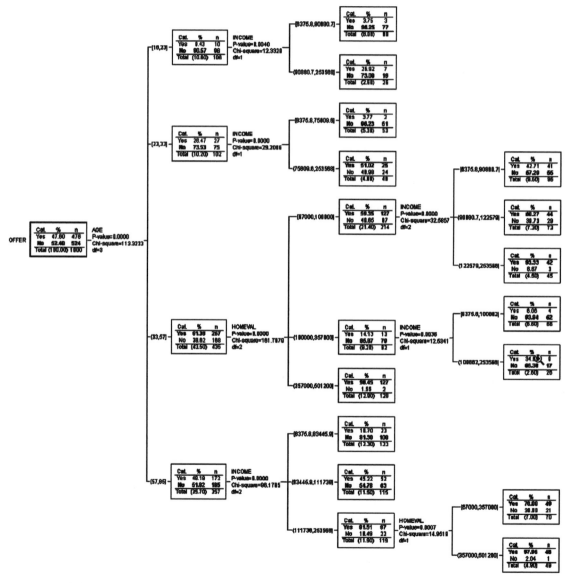

Exhibit 6-12: Example of a CHAID Analysis

Observed	Predicted		% Correctly Predicted
	Yes	No	
Yes	335	141	70.37
No	80	444	84.73
Overall hit-ratio is 77.90%			

Exhibit 6-13: CHAID Classification Table

AID/CHAID can be used to find those specific combinations that have the potential for increasing the predictive ability of the multiple or logistic regression models. Used as a stand-alone tool, AID/CHAID analysis is often used to predict membership of cases or objects in the classes of a categorical dependent variable based on one or more predictor variables.

In general, the procedure involves progressively splitting the data set into multiple segments in an effort to maximize the difference between the percent of observations that belong to each category of the dependent variable. AID/CHAID output often resembles a decision tree. It begins with one root node that contains all the observations, and the data then branch into mutually exclusive subsets of data. At each node of this decision tree, important statistics are provided to help managers make decisions.

In the credit card marketer's data used in the logistics regression example, there is one categorical dependent variable (offer) and three independent variables (age, homeval, and income).The output from running a CHAID analysis on this data set is shown in Exhibit 6-12. The root node (beginning of the decision tree) shows that the data set has 476 "yes" responses and 524 "no" responses.

The next branch of the decision tree varies depending on which node is being examined. For instance, at the 57-85 years age node, the next split identifies three subsets based on a person's income. Of these three subsets, the most promising segment (81.5% of yes response) is the highest income segment, those with annual income between $111,738 and $253,568. As attractive as this segment appears, it is further split by CHAID into two subsets based on a person's homeval. This final split identifies a sub-segment where probability of yes response is a whopping 97.96%. The characteristics of this segment is age group 33-57 years, income $111,738-$253,568, and homeval of $357,000-$501,200.

Similar to logistic regression, CHAID analysis also produces an overall classification table. This classification table is shown in Exhibit 6-13. The hit-ratio (or, overall correct prediction percentage) is 77.9%, which is higher than the overall hit-ratio obtained in the logistic regression. However, another interesting point to note is that the percent of correct prediction in the "yes" response group is also lower in the logistic regression (66.39%) than in the CHAID model (70.83%). Thus, if a manager's goal is to increase the percent of correct prediction in the "yes" response group, the logistic regression model is still underperforming the CHAID model in this data set.

Although the AID/CHAID analysis looks deceptively simple, it belongs to a group of powerful multivariate techniques. Prerequisites for the most profitable uses of these techniques include:

- Understanding the characteristics of your data and removing or fixing any irregularities.

- Understanding the specific requirements of the program used to perform anAID/CHAID analysis.

- Finally, always validating the results of AID/CHAID analysis against a hold-out (validation) data set.

Principal Components Analysis

The objective of using Principal Components Analysis is to structure identification and variable reduction in a data set. The discussion here will focus on the use of variable reduction. Direct marketers are often faced with a large number of independent variables, many of which are highly correlated with each other. Although this problem was not discussed in the context of multiple regression, highly correlated independent variables create two types of problems in multiple regression. First, if the correlation is very high, it can create a computational problem resulting in very unstable estimates of regression coefficients and unreliable significance tests. Second, highly correlated independent variables create a problem in the interpretation of the coefficients of the correlated variables. This problem is referred to as multicollinearity in multiple regression.

Even without going into the statistical reasoning, intuitively it should be obvious that a very high correlation between two independent variables is unappealing because it implies a very high degree of redundancy of information contained in those two variables. Thus, instead of using both variables in the regression model, marketers may be better off using just one of them. Of course, it is not clear which one of the two variables should be retained in the model. The issue of variable selection becomes even more critical because multicollinearity creates huge instability in the forward, backward, or stepwise selection methods.

Principal components analysis offers a way to circumvent the problem of multicollinearity. It can be used to convert a set of "m" correlated variables into another set of "p" uncorrelated variables (where p is usually less than m) subject to certain conditions. First, the new variables, called the principal components, are linear combinations of the original variables. Second, the new variables (principal components) are constructed with the goal of retaining the maximum amount of information from the set of the original m variables. Usually, when p is less than m, there is some loss of information. However, many marketers believe that their data sets have so much error/redundancy/noise that reducing, say, 100 correlated variables to 20 uncorrelated principal components and, perhaps, retaining 80% of the original information is a small price to pay. Of course, if p equals m, all information from the original data set is retained in the principal components.

With respect to multicollinearity, once a data set has been subjected to principal components analysis, the principal components instead of the original variables can be used as independent variables in the multiple regression. Because these principal components are uncorrelated, their use will avoid the problems of multicollinearity. The downside of using principal components is that it may be very hard to get an intuitive understanding and explanation of the coefficients for each principal component used in building the regression model. However, if the direct marketer is simply using the regression model for predictive purposes, the lack of easy interpretability of the coefficients will not be a major deterrent.

Cluster Analysis

Segmentation, the cornerstone of marketing, is based on the principle of dividing a market into segments (groups) whose members have similar characteristics and/or needs; the members of different groups are dissimilar. Cluster analysis is the most commonly used tool for this purpose:Divide a data set of customers/prospects into nonoverlapping clusters (groups) in order to maximize the homogeneity of members within the clusters and maximize the heterogeneity between the clusters.

Because the goal of a cluster analysis is to group similar individuals together, some measure is needed in order to assess how similar or different the individuals are. For example, a direct marketer might have many pieces of information (demographic, psychographic, and behavioral) for each member in the house file. In order to figure out similarity of the individuals in his housefile, the direct marketer will have to construct an index of similarity between individuals based on the available pieces of information (variables). The most common approach is to measure similarity in terms of "distance" between individuals in the variable-space. Individuals with smaller distances between them are considered more similar to each other than those with larger distances between them. There are many ways to operationalize "distance" between individuals in the variable-space. The most common one is the "Euclidean Distance," which is the square root of the sum of the squared differences of variables for a pair of individuals.

Essentially, in cluster analysis, a data set containing n individuals and m variables is first converted into an n-by-n matrix of distances between each pair of individuals based on the m variables. Cluster analysis programs can then identify clusters of individuals by analyzing this matrix of distances. The technique assigns individuals to the same cluster when the "distances" between the individuals are small and assigns individuals to different clusters when the "distances" between the individuals are large.

Like other multivariate techniques, cluster analysis is a powerful and useful tool for assigning individuals to groups. In cluster analysis the groups are suggested by the data and are not defined a priori. The choice of the variables that go into the calculation of distances between individuals is, therefore, a critical issue in cluster analysis. We suggest that direct marketers use managerial judgment and past research in selection of such variables. Finally, unlike other multivariate techniques, there are no statistical significance tests for the number of clusters in a cluster analysis solution. Direct marketers are advised to use managerial judgment with respect to the number of clusters and validate their cluster analysis results on holdout data sets.

Interactive Workshop 6-1:

Using Excel for Cross-Tab Analysis

(For demonstration, go to the CD-Rom accompanying this book.)

We assume you have already installed "Analysis ToolPak" in EXCEL (instructions were given in Interactive Workshop 5-1). In this workshop, we will demonstrate how to use a spreadsheet package such as EXCEL® for doing cross-tabulation analysis.

Please open the data set labeled "workshop6.1.xls" in EXCEL. You will find three columns (A, B, and C) of data. The first column (A) contains subject ID (numbers ranging from 1 through 1000). The second column (B) contains values for the variable, GENDER (Male or Female). The third column (C) contains values for the variable, BALANCE (Yes or No). To run a cross-tab, please complete the following procedure:

- Open the data set using EXCEL
- Click on Data in the EXCEL menu
- Click on Pivot Table Report
- Select Microsoft Excel List in the pop-up; click Next
- Type "B1:C1001" in the Range box and click Next
- Click and drag the Gender button to area marked COLUMN
- Click and drag the Balance button to the area marked ROW
- Click and drag the Gender button to the area marked DATA
- Click Finish

If you followed the above procedure correctly, EXCEL should produce the cross-tab shown in Exhibit 6-14.

The data in the table are the counts and these numbers should match what is in the text. Unfortunately, EXCEL does not provide an easy interface for calculating Chi-square in the cross-tab. However, you can input these table numbers in the Interactive Workshop 10-3 to get the Chi-square values.

Count of Gender	Gender		
Balance	Female	Male	Grand Total
No	248	275	523
Yes	152	325	477
Grand Total	400	600	1000

Exhibit 6-14: Using Excel for Cross-Tab Analysis

Interactive Workshop 6-2:
Using EXCEL for Independent Sample T-Test for Means

(For demonstration, go to the CD-Rom accompanying this book.)

In this workshop you will replicate the independent sample t-test results for testing of means (average charge on credit card by males and females) as reported in the text using EXCEL®. Please open the data set labeled "workshop6.2.xls" in EXCEL. You will find two columns (A and B) of data. The first column contains a variable labeled "Charge_M." This variable represents the amount charged by males in the direct marketer's house file. The second column contains a variable labeled "Charge_F." This variable represents the amount charged by females in the direct marketer's house file. To run an independent sample t-test, please do the following:

- Open the data set using EXCEL

- Click on Tools in the EXCEL menu

- Click on Data Analysis

- Select "t-Test: Two sample assuming unequal variances" in the pop-up window and click OK

- Select column A for variable 1 range box

- Select column B for variable 2 range box

- Type "0" in the hypothesized mean difference box

- Make sure the Labels box is checked

- Check new worksheet ply and type "New1" in box; click OK

If you followed the above procedure correctly, EXCEL will run an independent sample t-test and will output a sheet labeled New1, as shown in Exhibit 6-15.

Note that the average amount charged by males and females match the numbers reported in the text. The two-sided p-value for testing whether the average amount charged by males and females in the population are equal or not is shown corresponding to "P(T<=t) two-tail." The two-sided p-value is 6.95×10^{-45}, i.e., 0.000 as reported in text.

Readers may note that EXCEL is also reporting one-sided p-value corresponding to "P(T<=t) one-tail." Note that the one-sided p-value is exactly one-half of the two-sided p-value. In other words, in calculating this one-sided p-value, EXCEL has automatically assumed that the

T-Test: Two-Sample Assuming Unequal Variances

	Charge_M	Charge_F
Mean	2629.471667	1796.89
Variance	630075.1912	812013.1859
Observations	600	400
Hypothesized Mean Difference	0	
df	780	
t Stat	15.00169482	
P (T <= t) one-tail	3.47804E-45	
t Critical one-tail	1.646808414	
P (T <= t) two-tail	6.95609E-45	
t Critial two-tail	1.96300798	

Exhibit 6-15: Using EXCEL for Independent Sample T-Test for Means

direction of the means in the data is consistent with the researcher's predictions in the alternative hypothesis. Since EXCEL's assumption may or may not be true, we strongly suggest that researchers use the two-sided p-value from the computer output and then use the conversion rule explained in this chapter.

Interactive Workshop 6-3:

Using EXCEL for Independent Sample T-Test for Response Rate

(For demonstration, go to the CD-Rom accompanying this book.)

In this workshop you will replicate the independent sample t-test results for testing of response rates from two lists as reported in the text using EXCEL®. Please open the data set labeled "workshop6.3.xls" into EXCEL. You will find two columns (A and B) of data. The first column contains a variable labeled "Response_List1." This variable represents responses from the first list (coded as 1 = yes, 0 = no). The second column contains a variable labeled "Response_List2." This variable represents responses from the second list (also coded as 1 = yes, 0 = no). To run an independent sample t-test, please do the following:

- Open the data set using EXCEL

- Click on Tools in the EXCEL menu

- Click on Data Analysis

- Select "t-Test: Two sample assuming unequal variances" in the pop-up window and click OK

- Select column A for variable 1 range box

- Select column B for variable 2 range box

- Type in 0 in the hypothesized mean difference box

- Make sure the Labels box is checked

- Check new worksheet ply and type "New1" in box; click OK

If you followed the above procedure correctly, EXCEL will run an independent sample t-test and output in a sheet labeled New1, as shown in Exhibit 6-16.

In the above table, the proportions of positive responses are 4.8% from the first list and 7.2% from the second list. The two-sided p-value is the number corresponding to "P(T<=t two-tail), or 0.0745. Note that these numbers match (within rounding errors) the numbers reported in the text.

t-Test: Two-Sample Assuming Unequal Variances

	Response_List1	Response_List2
Mean	0.048	0.072
Variance	0.045787575	0.066905207
Observations	500	750
Hypothesized Mean Difference	0	
df	1191	
t Stat	-1.78498075	
P (T <= t) one-tail	0.03725943	
t Critical one-tail	1.646135388	
P (T <= t) two-tail	0.074518859	
t Critial two-tail	1.961957423	

Exhibit 6-16: Using EXCEL for Independent Sample T-Test for Response Rate

Interactive Workshop 6-4:

Using EXCEL for Correlation Analysis

(For demonstration, go to the CD-Rom accompanying this book.)

In this workshop you will replicate the results of correlation analysis reported in the text using EXCEL®. Please open the data set labeled "workshop6.4.xls" in EXCEL. You will find three columns (A, B and C) of data. The first column (A) represents the subject ID in the house file (numbers ranging from 1 through 1000). The second column (B) contains a variable labeled "Charge." This variable represents the amount charged by each member in the house file. The third column (C) contains a variable labeled "AGE," which represents the age of each member. To run a correlation analysis, do the following:

- Open the data set using EXCEL
- Click on Tools in the EXCEL menu
- Click on Data Analysis
- Select "Correlation" in the pop-up window and click OK
- Type "B1:C1001" in the Input Range box
- Check Labels in First Row box
- Check New Worksheet Ply and type "New1" in box; click OK

If you followed the above procedure correctly, EXCEL will run a correlation analysis and will produce the output in a new sheet labeled New1, as shown in Exhibit 6-17.

Note that the correlation coefficient of 0.319 between "Charge" and "Age" match the number reported in the text. Unfortunately, there is no convenient interface in EXCEL to also produce the p-value for testing the significance of this correlation coefficient. However, as we explained in the text, the p-value from the simple regression can be used to test the significance of the correlation coefficient. How to use EXCEL for conducting simple regression is explained in Interactive Workshop 6-5.

Charge	1	
Age	0.319297	1

Exhibit 6-17: Using EXCEL for Correlation Analysis

Interactive Workshop 6-5:

Using EXCEL for Simple Regression Analysis

(For demonstration, go to the CD-Rom accompanying this book.)

In this workshop you will replicate the results of simple regression analysis reported in the text using EXCEL®. We will continue to use the data set labeled "workshop6.4.xls" for this workshop as well. You will find three columns (A, B and C) of data. The first column (A) represents the subject ID in the house file (numbers range from 1 through 1000). The second column (B) contains a variable labeled "Charge." This variable represents the amount charged by each member in the house file. The third column (C) contains a variable labeled "AGE," which represents the age of each member. To run a simple regression analysis, do the following:

- Open the data set using EXCEL
- Click on Tools in the EXCEL menu
- Click on Data Analysis
- Select "Regression" in the pop-up window and click OK
- Type "B1:B1001" in the Input Y Range box (this is the dependent variable)
- Type "C1:C1001" in the Input X Range box (this is the independent variable)
- Check Labels in First Row box
- Check New Worksheet Ply and type "New1" in box; click OK

SUMMARY OUTPUT

Regression Statistics

Multiple R	0.31929691
R Square	0.101950516
Adjusted R Square	0.101050667
Standard Error	883.6662925
Observations	1000

ANOVA

	df	SS	MS	F	Significance F
Regression	1	88470051.95	88470051.95	113.2973375	3.90085E-25
Residual	998	799304384.3	780866.1166		
Total	999	857774436.3			

	Coefficients	Standard Error	t Stat	P-value	Lower 95%	Upper 95%	Lower 95.0%	Upper 95.0%
Intercept	1436.689751	86.46938428	16.80940799	5.04789E-56	1268.969421	1604.41	1268.969	1604.41
Age	17.21702277	1.617514572	10.6441222	3.90085E-25	14.04290282	20.39114	14.0429	20.39114

Exhibit 6-18: Using EXCEL for Simple Regression Analysis

If you followed the above procedure correctly, EXCEL will run a simple regression and output a new sheet labeled New1, as shown in Exhibit 6-18.

Note that the values of multiple R, R square, and the coefficients for intercept and age match the numbers reported in the text. The p-value for testing the overall regression model is given in the ANOVA table under the column heading "Significance F." This p-value is equal to 3.9×10^{-25}, or 0.000 as reported in the text. Similarly, the p-value for testing whether the coefficient of age equals 0 is given under the column heading "P-Value." This p-value is equal to 3.9×10^{-25}, or 0.000 as reported in the text.

Interactive Workshop 6-6:

Using EXCEL for Multiple Regression Analysis

(For demonstration, go to the CD-Rom accompanying this book.)

In this workshop you will replicate the results of multiple regression analysis reported in the text using EXCEL®. Please open the data set labeled "workshop6.6.xls" for this workshop. You will find five columns (A - E) of data. The first column (A) represents the subject ID in the house file (numbers range from 1 through 1000). The second column (B) contains a variable labeled "Charge." This variable represents the amount charged by each member in the house file. The third column (C) contains a variable labeled "AGE," which represents the age of each member. The fourth column (D) contains a variable labeled "Homeval" (the value of each member's home). The fifth column (E) contains a variable labeled "Income" (each member's annual income). To run a multiple regression analysis, do the following:

- Open the data set using EXCEL
- Click on Tools in the EXCEL menu
- Click on Data Analysis
- Select "Regression" in the pop-up window and click OK
- Type B1:B1001 in the Input Y Range box (this is the dependent variable)
- Type C1:E1001 in the Input X Range box (this is the range of values for all three independent variables)
- Check Labels in First Row box
- Check New Worksheet Ply and type "New1" in box; click OK

SUMMARY OUTPUT

Regression Statistics

Multiple R	0.57893301
R Square	0.33516343
Adjusted R Square	0.33316091
Standard Error	761.081571
Observations	1000

ANOVA

	df	SS	MS	F	Significance F
Regression	3	290846258.7	96948753	167.37085	7.53191E-88
Residual	996	576928177.6	579245.16		
Total	999	867774436.3			

	Coefficients	Standard Error	t Stat	P-value	Lower 95%
Intercept	191.244953	99.50025573	1.9220549	0.0548839	-4.009224814
Age	12.6953179	1.414175136	8.9771893	1.357E-18	9.92021342
HOMEVAL	0.00142888	0.000191126	7.476093	1.675E-13	0.001053819
INCOME	0.01207235	0.000779002	15.497193	1.087E-48	0.010543676

Exhibit 6-19: Using EXCEL for Multiple Regression Analysis

If you followed the above procedure correctly, EXCEL will run a multiple regression and will output a new sheet labeled New1, as shown in Exhibit 6-19.

Note that the values of multiple R, R square, and the coefficients for intercept, age, homeval, and income match the numbers reported in the text (within rounding errors). The p-value for testing the overall regression model is given in the ANOVA table under the column heading "Significance F." This p-value is equal to 7.53×10^{-88}, or 0.000 as reported in the text. Similarly, the p-value for testing whether the coefficient of age equals 0 is given under the column heading "P-Value." This p-value is equal to 1.357×10^{-18} or 0.000 as reported in the text.

III
Database Marketing Strategies and Program Applications

Chapter 7

The Lifetime Value
of a Customer

Key Concepts
- Lifetime Value of a Customer
- Break-Even
- Recency/Frequency/Monetary Value

Applications
- Establishing Break-Even for a Single Sale
- Establishing the Continuity Value of a Customer over Time
- Establishing Enhanced Lifetime Value
- Forecasting Customer Value
- Using Recency/Frequency/Monetary Value

It has been mentioned several times throughout this book: You don't have a business until you have made a sale; you don't have a business for the long term without customers; and you don't have a customer until you have made a second sale to a newly acquired buyer. Add to these statements that not all buyers or customers are the same and you have the reasons why knowing LTV (lifetime value of a customer) is the financial lifeblood of virtually every successful organization.

Simply put, LTV is the future value of the amount of money that can be spent currently to acquire a new customer. It is the present value of profits to be realized over the life of a customer's relationship with an organization (whether for-profit or nonprofit). Of course, all buyers or customers are not the same. Some make only one purchase (and never really become customers), other make just a few, and still others buy on a regular basis for the life of the organization. And even among lifelong customers, there can be tremendous differences: Some buy only low-margin products that have limited profitability; others don't pay attention to price.

The ability to identify one's most profitable customers is intimately tied to segmentation (discussed in the following two chapters) and the key to marketing effectiveness and profitability. Thus, while traditional accounting and tax reporting practice requires treating all promotion expenditures as expenses, database marketers also view their customer list as an asset and a source of future revenue and, thus, treat promotion expenditures as an investment. The key issue is to determine what the lifetime value of one's customer is and how to increase it.

While the "percent of sales" method has long been used to budget advertising, the LTV-customer investment approach use by database marketers makes it possible to relate objective sales revenues to the need for and the cost of acquiring and retaining customers. Thus, promotion expenditures become a cause of sales rather than a result. This chapter will examine the important concepts related to lifetime value, including determination of break even and determining different levels of promotion.

Rate of Response: What Should It Be? How Is It Measured?

Response to a promotion varies with the product, the demand for it, price competition, brand preference, as well as the offer. The time frame for the prospect to make a decision varies as well. Is the promotion intended to garner an immediate response (e.g., as an impulse purchase) or is more likely to take place at some time in the future? Or is the purpose, as with brand or image promotion, a series of responses over a period of time in the future? Just how and when will results be measured?

Response varies, too, according to pre-qualification of the database or other promotion medium used. For example, customers typically will respond to an offer more readily than will cold prospects.

Realistically, the expectation question should be rephrased: "What advertising response is needed?" Even more apropos, "What is the lifetime value of a first-time customer?" Or, what lesser level of response would be required in order to break even over an extended period of time during which a first-time customer demonstrates value through repurchases or additional purchases?

Determination of Break-Even and the Lifetime Value of a Customer

One of the keys to maximizing profitability is the concept of break-even. Profit maximization, it is taught, occurs at the point where marginal revenue equals marginal cost. That is, revenue derived from the sale of one additional unit should not be less than the cost of producing and fulfilling (and selling!) that unit.

Production costs are generally a combination of fixed and variable costs. Fixed costs are those costs that remain fairly constant regardless of the volume of production; variable costs generally increase proportionate to the level of production.

Firms often view production costs as a combination of the costs-of-goods-sold plus general/administrative expenses (costs of fulfillment). Traditional cost accounting (and the Internal Revenue Service) views the costs of promotion as general/administrative expenses. But conceptually and in terms of building a profitable business, customer acquisition is an investment rather than an expense.

Database marketers change the traditionally accepted formula, *Revenue - Cost = Profit*, in the short run, to read:

> Revenue - Production Cost = Profit, including Promotion Cost Available for Customer Investment, in the long run.

Exhibit 7-1 presents two cost curves. One (TPC) considers only production costs while the other (TPPC) considers both production and promotion costs. Traditional production break-even occurs at point A, when total revenue (TR) is equal to total production costs (TPC). Total production costs, in turn, consist of the combination of fixed production costs (FPC) and variable production costs (VPC).

To the left of the TR line and under the TPC line is an area in which there is a total production loss (TPL). Beyond that point, TR divided by the quantity sold minus TPC divided by the quantity sold is equal to a unit profit (UP), which is break-even, at point A, without promotion costs, thus:

$$TR/Q - TPC/Q = UP$$

Unit profit is, in effect, the limit of the promotion budget based on a single sale to the newly acquired customer. Traditional break-even calculation includes promotion and production cost as overhead expenses. However, the smart marketer views these costs of customer acquisition as an investment rather than an expense.

For illustration, assume that a direct response promotion consists of an offer mailed to 250M prospects at a cost of $500/M pieces mailed, and a total promotion cost (TPRC) of $125,000. Super-imposing this $125,000

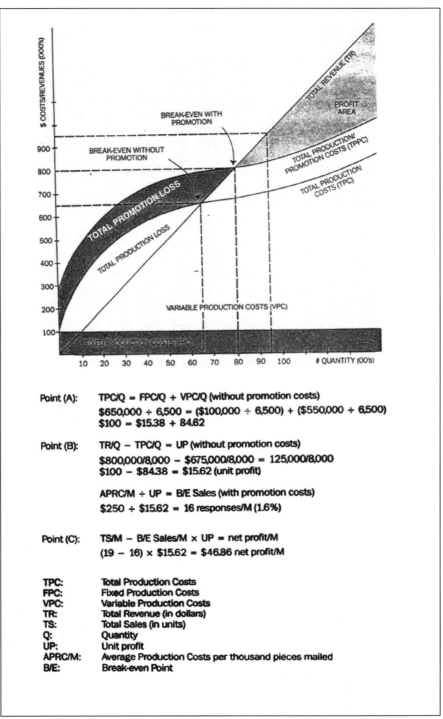

Point (A):   TPC/Q = FPC/Q + VPC/Q (without promotion costs)
$650,000 ÷ 6,500 = ($100,000 ÷ 6,500) + ($550,000 ÷ 6,500)
$100 = $15.38 + 84.62

Point (B):   TR/Q − TPC/Q = UP (without promotion costs)
$800,000/8,000 − $675,000/8,000 = 125,000/8,000
$100 − $84.38 = $15.62 (unit profit)

APRC/M ÷ UP = B/E Sales (with promotion costs)
$250 ÷ $15.62 = 16 responses/M (1.6%)

Point (C):   TS/M − B/E Sales/M × UP = net profit/M
(19 − 16) × $15.62 = $46.86 net profit/M

TPC: Total Production Costs
FPC: Fixed Production Costs
VPC: Variable Production Costs
TR: Total Revenue (in dollars)
TS: Total Sales (in units)
Q: Quantity
UP: Unit profit
APRC/M: Average Production Costs per thousand pieces mailed
B/E: Break-even Point

Exhibit 7-1: Break-even Determination With and Without Promotion

promotion cost (TPRC) on TPC, which varies with total production volume, it is apparent that sales must be increased by 1,500 units, from the production break-even of 6,500 units to the production plus promotion break-even of 8,000 units.

In this illustration, therefore, average promotion costs per thousand pieces mailed (APRC/M) divided by UP becomes break-even at point B with promotion, thus:

$$APRC/M \div UP = B/E$$

Note that total sales in units per thousand pieces mailed (TS/M) less break-even sales per thousand pieces mailed (B/E Sales/M) multiplied by the UP becomes equal to net profit per thousand pieces mailed, at point C, thus:

$$TS/M - B/E\ SALES/M \times UP = NET\ PROFIT/M$$

To break-even, the cost of making a sale and acquiring a customer cannot exceed unit profit for that sale. Let's look next at an example that assumes only one sale to a newly acquired customer. There is no opportunity for continuity sales.

Interactive Workshop 7-1:
Establishing the Break-Even Point for a Single Sale

(For demonstration, go to the CD-Rom accompanying this book.)

Establishing the break-even point for a single sale to a new customer is a first step. Here's the formula:

$$\frac{\text{Promotion Cost}}{\text{Unit Profit per Sale}} = \text{Break-even Number of Sales}$$

That is, if the marketer recovers promotion cost from the gross profit (beyond cost-of-goods sold and overhead) of the total number of units sold, he breaks even on those sales.

Exhibit 7-2 provides a profit worksheet for calculating the break-even point and profit at various levels of unit sales per thousand pieces of direct-mail promotion. A variation of this can be used for other print (newspaper, magazine), broadcast (television, radio), or electronic (telephone, Internet) promotion.

Product Offer: _Practical Mathematics_ @ $39.95, net 30 days

Assumptions:

# Promotions Mailed	9,508
Shipments Returned	8%
Sales Uncollectable	6%

Order Processing/Collection Costs:

Gross Orders	100 @ $1.80	=	$180.00
Less: Returns	8 @ 8% of 100		
Net Sales (A)	92 @ $0.50	=	$ 46.00
Total (B)			$226.00
Cost Per Net Sale (B/A) =			$2.46

Break-Even Calculation:

Line	Description		
1	Selling Price		$39.95
2	Cost-of-Goods Sold	$5.99	
3	G&A Allocation	$3.80	
4	Shipping/Delivery Costs	$2.20	
5	Processing/Collection Costs	$2.46	
6	Cost of Returns	$0.30	
7	Sales Uncollectable	$2.40	
8	Premium Gift Cost	$0.54	
9	Total Production Costs		$17.69
10	UNIT PROFIT (Line 1 - Line 9)		$22.26
11	Total Promotion Costs per M Pieces Mailed (includes database, print, mail, postage, overhead)		$345.83
12	Breakeven Nt Sales/M Pieces Mailed (Line11/Line10)		15.54

Cost of Returns:

Return Servicing	$1.30
Shipping/Delivery	$2.20
Total (C)	$3.50
Returns Projected (D)	8%
Cost Per Net Sale (C×D/1.00−D)	$0.30

Total Profit at Alternative Levels of Net Sales:

Line	Description							
13	Projected Net Sales per M Pieces Mailed	17	20	25	30	35	40	45
14	Less:Break-even Sales (Line 12)	15.54	15.54	15.54	15.54	15.54	15.54	15.54
15	Net Sales Earning Full Unit Profit (Line 13 – Line 14)	1.46	4.46	9.46	14.46	19.46	24.46	29.46
16	Unit Profit (Line 10)	$22.26	$22.26	$22.26	$22.26	$22.26	$22.26	$22.26
17	Net Profit per M Pieces Mailed (Line 15 × Line 16)	32.61	99.39	210.69	322.00	433.30	544.61	655.91
18	M Pieces Mailed	9,508	9,508	9,508	9,508	9,508	9,508	9,508
19	Total Net Profit (Line17 × Line 18/1000)	$310.01	$944.98	$2,003.26	$3,061.55	$4,119.83	$5,178.11	$6,236.40
20	NtPr'fit %NtSales: Line19/Line1 × Line13 × Line18/1000	4.80%	12.44%	21.10%	26.87%	30.99%	34.08%	36.49%

Exhibit 7-2: Direct Mail Marketing Profit Worksheet

Lines 2 through 8 of the break-even calculation in Exhibit 7-2 represent production costs, totaling $17.69 (line 9) per copy of Practical Mathematics. Order processing/collection costs (line 5) and costs of returns (line 6) are amortized and allocated to net sales, in the manner shown at the top of Exhibit 7-2.

Unit profit, calculated by subtracting $17.69 (line 9) from the selling price of $39.95 (line 1) is $22.26 (line 10). Unit profit divided into total promotion costs of $345.83 per thousand pieces mailed (line 11) provides break-even net sales (line 12). This is 15.54 units, or 1.55 percent. That is the answer to the initial question: "What rate of response is needed to break even?"

Having calculated a break-even response rate of 1.55 percent, lines 13-20 of Exhibit 7-2 present alternative profit amounts at assumed alternative levels of net sales.

Interactive Workshop 7-2:

LTV: The Continuity Value of a Customer Over Future Time

(For demonstration, go to the CD-Rom accompanying this Book.)

Relatively few marketers enjoy the luxury of breaking even on the first sale to a new customer, as just illustrated. Rather, it is more likely that this first sale will, in effect, be an investment in that customer, which will be returned through future sales.

LTV (Lifetime Value of a Customer) is continued value of that relationship over time and into the future. LTV can be calculated in this way:

1. Define a stream of total revenues over a period of future time. Take into account additional or repeat purchases by customers. Assume a particular frequency of reorder or renewal as well as a dollar value for reorders or renewals. Also, customers move, change interests, or die so provide for attrition; that is, for a lapse rate from one time period to the next.

2. From this total revenue stream, deduct for each time period the cost-of-goods-sold as well as general and administrative expenses. The residuals thus derived represent a series of contributions for defraying promotion costs associated with acquiring new customers and for producing a profit.

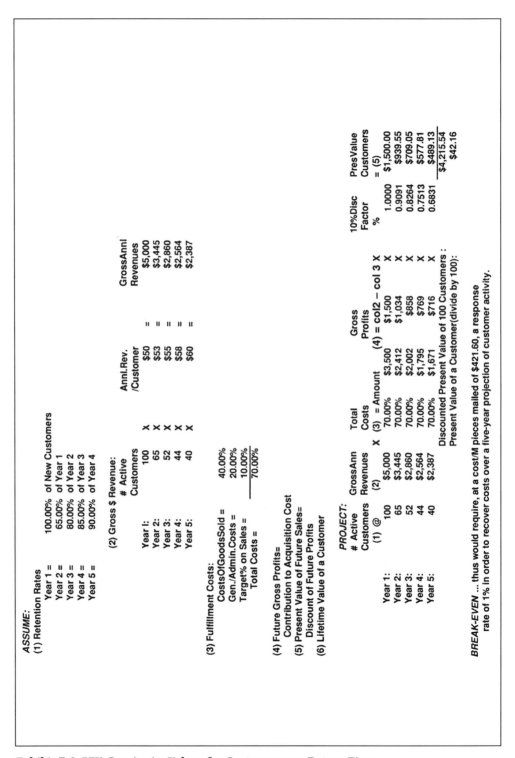

Exhibit 7-3: LTV, Continuity Value of a Customer over Future Time

3. The dollar value of this revenue stream is discounted to a present value at some rate appropriate to the risk of investing in new customers.

In insurance selling, for example, LTV measures the ongoing value of the initial sale of a single insurance policy as it is renewed, increased, and retained. It can also measure the value of magazine subscription renewals, record, or book club sales or future catalog purchases — all instances of continuity selling.

An example of calculating the continuity value of a customer is shown in Exhibit 7-3. Projected for a 5-year period, an initial base of 100 customers is assumed. Further assumed is a retention rate of 65 percent at the beginning of the second year; 80 percent of those remaining at the beginning of the third year; 85 percent entering the fourth year; 90 percent entering the fifth year. Revenue is assumed to increase year-to-year.

Costs-of-goods sold plus general/administrative costs and a target profit of 10 percent on sales, which is optional as an assumption, are estimated as percentages of revenues. These rates are assumed to be constant over the five-year projection, although in reality this is seldom the case.

With these assumptions, together with an assumed 10 percent discount factor, the present value of a customer is calculated to be $42.16 (6). This, then, is the maximum amount that can be spent to acquire a new customer. Breaking-even, at an assumed cost of $421.60 per thousand pieces mailed, requires an initial response rate of 1 percent in order to recover acquisition costs over a five-year projection of customer activity.

LTV calculation should be done by product line and, under some conditions, even by source of new business. The calculation should be done at least annually, updating the assumptions used.

Interactive Workshop 7-3:

Enhanced LTV: The Lifetime Value of a Customer with Cross-Selling

(For demonstration, go to the CD-Rom accompanying this book.)

LTV measures the value of continuity selling. Enhanced LTV measures the added value of cross-selling. When *Time* renews subscriptions of current customers, it is engaged in continuity selling. When it offers its present customers the opportunity to receive one or more of the other magazines it publishes, like *People* or *Sports Illustrated*, it engages in cross-selling. Each of these cross-selling opportunities opens the door to new continuity-selling efforts. Each successful additional sale adds to the value of a customer.

By anticipating these future sales and projecting the lifetime value of a current customer, Enhanced LTV might help an organization decide to spend more on promotion to acquire new customers than those customers appear to be worth initially.

Enhanced LTV is calculated as the ratio of promotion cost to LTV of the enhanced sale, i.e., the cross sale, thus:

$$\text{Enhanced LTV} = \frac{\text{Promotion Cost}}{\text{LTV of Cross-Sale}}$$

If the ratio is 1.00, the cross-sale is being acquired at exactly what it is worth over time and still yield an assumed rate of return on investment on the cross-sale.

If the ratio is less than 1.00 (0.85, for example), these cross-sales are being acquired at less than their future value.

If the ratio is greater than 1.00 (1.40, for example), more is being paid for the acquisition of the cross-sale than it is worth over its future life.

It follows from this rationale, then, that a cross-sale to an existing customer cannot be made profitably at a ratio greater than 1.00. The LTV ratio on initial sales made to newly acquired customers, on the other hand, may exceed 1.00. How much these may exceed 1.00 depends on the lower-than-1.00 ratios of cross-sales subsequently made to that customer.

Exhibit 7-4 illustrates a product and source mix forecast which views customer acquisition as an investment. Five products to be offered to present customers as well as qualified prospects, in order to acquire new customers, are identified by the letters A, B, C, D, and E. Anticipating that product offers to customers will generate a ratio less than 1.00, the

Pro-dct	Source	Promotion $ Cost	Inquiry Fulfill $ Cost	Order Fulfill $ Cost	Total $ Cost	Mail/Space Volume/ Circulation	#Inquirs & (/M)	#Orders & (/M)	$ Sales Revenue	Order LTV Value	Total LTV Value	LTV Ratio	Cumu lative LTV
A	Customers	$35,000		$40,000	$75,000	100,000		4,000 (40)	$200,000	24.38	$97,520	0.77	
	MailPrspts	$87,500		$25,000	$112,500	250,000		2,500(10)	$125,000	24.38	$60,950	1.85	
	SpcPrspts	$30,000	$20,000	$20,000	$70,000	500,000	5,000(10)	2,000(4)	$100,000	24.38	$48,600	1.44	
	Subtotal	$152,500	$20,000	$85,000	$257,500	850,000	5,000	8,500	$425,000	24.38	$207,070	1.24	1.24
B	Customers	$35,000		$18,000	$53,000	100,000		3,600(36)	$108,000	15.10	$54,360	0.97	
	MailPrspts	$90,000		$31,500	$121,500	300,000		6,300(21)	$189,000	15.10	$95,130	1.28	
	SpcPrspts	$2,700	$12,960	$8,100	$23,760	270,000	3240(12)	1,620(6)	$48,600	15.10	$24,462	0.97	
	Subtotal	$127,700	$12,960	$57,600	$198,260	670,000	3,240	11,520	$345,600	15.10	$173,952	1.14	1.20
C	Customers	$90,000		$16,000	$106,000	200,000		2,000(10)	$240,000	51.70	$103,400	1.03	1.16
D	Customers	$70,000		$16,800	$86,800	200,000		4,200(21)	$294,000	29.88	$125,496	0.69	1.06
E	Customers	$10,000	(Stuffer)	$2,400	$12,400	200,000		2,400(12)	$216,000	21.24	$50,976	0.24	1.00
	TOTAL	$450,200	$32,960	$177,800	$660,960	2,120,000	8,240	28,620	$1,520,600		$660,894		1.00

Exhibit 7-4: Enhanced LTV Calculated in a Product/Source Mix

need in this composite forecast is to determine how much solicitation of prospects, at a ratio greater than 1.00, can be accommodated.

The bottom-line objective, all products and all sources of orders combined, is a cumulative LTV ratio of 1.00—the point at which promotion costs, including inquiry follow-up and order fulfillment, but not cost-of-goods-sold or general administrative costs—exactly equal the value of the sales generated.

In Exhibit 7-4, costs related to acquisition of new sales (but not necessarily new customers) are shown left of the column titled "Mail/Space Volume/Circulation;" response results are shown to the right. Costs are related to the volume of promotion as well as the number of inquiries and orders to be processed.

The "# Inquiries" and "# Orders" are shown in column headings as are the response rates per thousand solicitations. Significant is the response rate from customers relative to that from prospects, which is 4:1 in the case of product A. Note, in the column headed "Order PAR (LTV) Value," that each product has a unique PAR, representing the continuity value of that sale, but not cross-sales, which are evaluated by Enhanced LTV ratios.

PAR (LTV) ratios for all orders from current customers—with the exception of product C—are below 1.00. Product C's ratio of 1.03 indicates that this effort should not be continued. The product should also be dropped from the line, since a product that cannot be sold profitably to a current customer likely has little appeal to prospective customers without a relationship.

Analyzing the PAR (LTV) ratios of products and sources of their sales can help enhance the profitability of promotions. In this example, PAR (LTV) ratios reveal that product B, marginally appealing to current customers, may not be worth offering. On the other hand, the low promotion cost for product E is as effective for creating profit as would be additional sales!

Interactive Workshop 7-4:

The Recency/Frequency/Monetary (R/F/M) Formula

(For demonstration, go to the CD-Rom accompanying this book.)

An essential tool for identifying an organization's best customers is the Recency/Frequency/Monetary (R/F/M) formula.

By carrying within each customer's record the date, volume and nature of purchases, over a period of time, it is possible to determine periodically the performance record of each customer. This enables the enterprise to estimate the future potential of that customer, and relate the cost of future promotion to the potential benefit to be derived from each customer in the database. This is the 80/20 principle in action!

The R/F/M formula is not new. It has been a standard for general merchandise catalogers for half-a-century. The exact R/F/M formulation for each directed marketer will vary according to the relative importance given to each of the three variables:

- the recency of purchase
- the frequency of purchase, and
- the monetary value of the purchase.

Under certain conditions, there might be need for weighting the calculations of particular promotions having more relevance, for example, to customers who had purchased most recently.

Exhibit 7-5 illustrates the use of the R/F/M formula in evaluating customers in an organization's database according to the combined R/F/M values of their transactions over a period of time. In this hypothetical example, three customers (identified as A, B and C) have a purchase history calculated over a 24-month period. Numerical points are assigned to each transaction, according to a historically derived R/F/M formula exclusive to this organization. Weighting is given to recency of purchase (times 5), frequency of purchase (times 3), and monetary value of purchase (times 2). Thus, on a scale of 10, recency is weighted at 50 percent, frequency at 30 percent, monetary at 10 percent.

The resultant cumulative scores—202 for A, 79 for B, and 280 for C—indicate a potential preference for customer C. Based on C's R/F/M history, a greater number of promotion dollars (such as mailing a seasonal catalog) could be justified. Sending a catalog could also be warranted for customer A. Customer B might be an unlikely risk and sending a catalog could be a misdirected marketing effort.

While recency of purchase has been given the greatest weight in this hypothetical example, each organization must determine through its own

ASSUMPTIONS:

Recency of Transaction: 20 Points if within Past 3 months
10 Points if within Past 6 months
5 Points if within Past 9 months
3 Points if within Past 12 months
1 Point if within Past 24 months

Frequency of Transaction: # Purchases within 24 Months X 4 Points each (Maximum = 20 Points)

Monetary Value of Transaction:$ Volume of Purchases within 24 Months X 10% (Maximum = 20 Points)

Weighting Assumption: Recency = 5
Frequency = 3
Monetary = 2

Custmr	#Purch	Rec'cy	Ass'nd Points	(x5) Weight Points	Frq'cy	Ass'nd Points	(x3) Weight Points	Mont'y	Ass'nd Points	(x2) Weight Point	Total Weight Points	Cumu-lative Points
A	#1	3Mths	20	100	1	4	12	$ 30	3	6	118	118
A	#2	9Mths	5	25	1	4	12	$100	10	20	57	175
A	#3	24Mths	1	5	1	4	12	$ 50	5	10	27	202
B	#1	12Mths	3	15	2	8	24	$500	20	40	79	79
C	#1	3Mths	20	100	1	4	12	$100	10	20	132	132
C	#2	6Mths	10	50	1	4	12	$ 60	6	12	74	206
C	#3	12Mths	3	5	2	8	24	$ 70	7	14	53	259
C	#4	24Mths	1	5	1	4	12	$ 20	2	4	21	280

Exhibit 7-5: Evaluation of Customer Database Records by Recency, Frequency and Monetary Values of Transactions (R/F/M)

analysis the factors that influence purchases. As a rule of thumb, however, the buyer who has purchased most recently is the one most likely to buy again.

Please be sure to read the instructions, in the Appendix, for accessing the CD-ROM accompanying this BOOK as well as working with the statistical tools and techniques that are contained thereon.

Planning, Forecasting, Budgeting, and Evaluating

Strategic planning is the essence of the database marketing process, from which evolves a system based on scientific decision-making. Planning looks at means versus ends, inputs versus outputs. Planning minimizes risks.

Profitable organizations engage in long-range planning for periods of two, three, five, and even 10 or more years. This kind of planning makes use of LTV and Enhanced LTV ratios to calculate the lifetime value of a newly acquired customer. To update plans and weather inevitable changes, these companies turn to short-range forecasting, budgeting and evaluating for periods of threemonths, six months, or a year.

Forecasts and budgets are mathematical models formulated in terms of statistical probabilities, calculated to be reasonably close to actual occurrences. There are two major categories of forecasting methodology. **Build-up techniques** derive estimates from components of the forecast, such as accumulation of promotion costs into a sales forecast. **Relationship techniques** derive estimates from correlation with market factors, such as demographics. (A Build-Up Forecast is shown in Exhibit 7-6.)

Among the variety of forecasting methodologies are some highly sophisticated computer models. Classified according to the techniques employed, these methods include the following:

- Judgment forecasts are "seat-of-the-pants forecasts" based mainly on prior experience and insight. They often include no data; they are possibly most widely used.

- Surveys of expectations use polling methods to ask knowledgeable people about future events. These become more suitable when there is a historic reference point.

- Time series or mechanical extrapolation forecasts attempt to identify movements or trends that existed over past time periods, presuming the future mirrors the past.

- Moving averages couple a series of averages that approximate a trend with exponential smoothing. This tends to cancel out the high and low values.

- Analytical forecasts predict on the basis of information obtained from economic variables rather than simply the past history of the variable being projected. It is a popular causal method, using correlation and regression.

Marketers often explain after the fact rather than predict. The process considers actual results relative to forecast results and budgeted costs, and looks at the factors responsible for these results in order to identify misdirected effort.

(1) Year	(2) Source/Lists	(3) Est.Size of Source/List	(4) Mailing Freq'cy	(5) Total Mailed (3)x(4)	(6) Mailing Cost/Pc	(7) Space $ Adv/Inq	(8) Promotion Cost Total (5)*(6)+(7)	(9) Response Rate of Col.5	(10) Ttl Mail Response (5)*(9)	(11) Ord/Inq Cost of Col.7
2000	Customer(Bounce-back)	3,184	1	3,184	0.15		$478	10.00%	318	
	Response-12ppMini	100,000	1	100,000	0.53		$53,000	1.47%	1470	
	Space Ads for Orders					$50,000	$50,000			$35.00
	Space Ads for Inquiries					$10,000	$10,000			$35.00
	TOTAL-2000			103,184			$113,478		1788	
2001	Customer-2000(90%)	2,866	5	14,329	0.85		$12,180	4.00%	573	
	Customer-2001(50%)	3,452	2	6,904	0.85		$5,868	4.00%	276	
	Response-12ppMini	150,000	1	150,000	0.43		$64,500	1.19%	1785	
	Response-36ppCatalog	150,000	1	150,000	0.85		$127,500	2.36%	3540	
	Space Ads for Orders					$50,000	$50,000			$38.00
	Space Ads for Inquiries					$10,000	$10,000			$38.00
	TOTAL-2001			321,233			$270,048		6174	
2002	Customer-2000(95%)	2,723	5	13,613	0.75		$10,210	4.00%	545	
	Customer-2001(90%)	6,214	5	31,068	0.75		$23,301	4.00%	1243	
	Customer-2002(50%)	6,143	2	12,287	0.75		$9,215	4.00%	491	
	Response-36ppCatalog	450,000	1	450,000	0.75		$337,500	2.08%	9360	
	Space Ads for Orders					$100,000	$100,000			$41.00
	Space Ads for Inquiries					$20,000	$20,000			$41.00
	TOTAL-2002			506,967			$500,226		11639	
2003	Customer-2000(95%)	2,586	5	12,932	0.70		$9,053	4.00%	517	
	Customer-2001(95%)	5,903	5	29,514	0.70		$20,660	4.00%	·1181	
	Customer-2002(90%)	11,058	5	55,291	0.70		$38,704	4.00%	2212	
	Customer-2003(50%)	13,974	2	27,947	0.70		$19,563	4.00%	1118	
	Response-36ppCatalog	1,300,000	1	1,300,000	0.70		$910,000	1.94%	25220	
	Space Ads for Orders					$100,000	$100,000			$44.00
	Space Ads for Inquiries					$20,000	$20,000			$44.00
	TOTAL-2003			1,425,685			$1,117,979		30247	
2004	Customer-2000(95%)	2,457	5	12,286	0.65		$7,986	4.00%	491	
	Customer-2001(95%)	5,608	5	28,039	0.65		$18,225	4.00%	1122	
	Customer-2002(95%)	10,505	5	52,526	0.65		$34,142	4.00%	2101	
	Customer-2003(90%)	25,153	5	125,763	0.65		$81,746	4.00%	5031	
	Customer-2004(50%)	25,259	2	50,518	0.65		$32,837	4.00%	2021	
	Response-36ppCatalog	2,650,000	1	2,650,000	0.65		$1,722,500	1.81%	47965	
	Space Ads for Orders					$100,000	$100,000			$47.00
	Space Ads for Inquiries					$20,000	$20,000			$47.00
	TOTAL-2004	|ActCstmrs|		2,919,131			$2,017,435		58730	
	GRAND TTL:2000-2004	94,241		5,276,201			$4,019,166		108579	

Exhibit 7-6: A Build-Up Forecast/Budget with LTV Enhancement

(12) TtlSpace Respons Orders (7)/(11)	(13) Total # Orders (10)+(12)	(14) Aver'g $Order	(15) Total $ Revenue (13)*(14)	(16) C.O.G.S. + G/A	(17) Fulfil't Costs (15)*(16)	(18) Total Costs (8)+(17)	(19) (Customer Investment) (15)-(18)	(20) LTV: New Customers	(21) LTV Recovery	(22) Net Inv +LTV -LTV Recovry (19)+(20)-(21)
	318	$12	$3,821	55.00%	$2,102	$2,579	$1,242		$1,242	
	1,470	$55	$80,850	55.00%	$44,468	$97,468	($16,618)	$51,450		
1,429	1,429	$55	$78,571	55.00%	$43,214	$93,214	($14,643)	$50,000		
286	286	$55	$15,714	55.00%	$8,643	$18,643	($2,929)	$10,000		
1,714	3,503		$178,957	55.00%	$98,426	$211,904	($32,947)	$111,450	$81,773	($3,270)
	573	$75	$42,988	55.00%	$23,643	$35,823	$7,165		$7,165	
	276	$70	$19,331	55.00%	$10,632	$16,500	$2,831		$2,831	
	1,785	$60	$107,100	55.00%	$58,905	$123,405	($16,305)	$67,830		
	3,540	$65	$230,100	55.00%	$126,555	$254,055	($23,955)	$134,520		
1,316	1,316	$55	$72,368	55.00%	$39,803	$89,803	($17,434)	$50,000		
263	263	$55	$14,474	55.00%	$7,961	$17,961	($3,487)	$10,000		
1,579	7,753		$486,361	55.00%	$267,499	$537,547	($51,186)	$262,350	$200,814	$10,350
	545	$85	$46,284	55.00%	$25,456	$35,666	$10,618		$10,618	
	1,243	$80	$99,417	55.00%	$54,679	$77,980	$21,437		$21,437	
	491	$75	$36,860	55.00%	$20,273	$29,488	$7,372		$7,372	
	9,360	$70	$655,200	55.00%	$360,360	$697,860	($42,660)	$383,760		
2,439	2,439	$60	$146,341	55.00%	$80,488	$180,488	($34,146)	$100,000		
488	488	$60	$29,268	55.00%	$16,098	$36,098	($6,829)	$20,000		
2,927	14,566		$1,013,371	55.00%	$557,354	$1,057,579	($44,209)	$503,760	$413,291	$46,260
	517	$90	$46,556	55.00%	$25,606	$34,658	$11,898		$11,898	
	1,181	$85	$100,349	55.00%	$55,192	$75,852	$24,497		$24,497	
	2,212	$80	$176,930	55.00%	$97,312	$136,015	$40,915		$40,915	
	1,118	$80	$89,431	55.00%	$49,187	$68,750	$20,681		$20,681	
	25,220	$75	$1,891,500	55.00%	$1,040,325	$1,950,325	($58,825)	$1,109,680		
2,273	2,273	$65	$147,727	55.00%	$81,250	$181,250	($33,523)	$100,000		
455	455	$65	$29,545	55.00%	$16,250	$36,250	($6,705)	$20,000		
2,727	32,975		$2,482,039	55.00%	$1,365,121	$2,483,101	($1,062)	$1,229,680	$1,028,938	$199,680
	491	$95	$46,685	55.00%	$25,677	$33,662	$13,023		$13,023	
	1,122	$90	$100,939	55.00%	$55,517	$73,742	$27,197		$27,197	
	2,101	$85	$178,589	55.00%	$98,224	$132,366	$46,223		$46,223	
	5,031	$85	$427,593	55.00%	$235,176	$316,922	$110,671		$110,671	
	2,021	$80	$161,658	55.00%	$88,912	$121,749	$39,909		$39,909	
	47,965	$80	$3,837,200	55.00%	$2,110,460	$3,832,960	$4,240	$2,254,355		
2,128	2,128	$70	$148,936	55.00%	$81,915	$181,915	($32,979)	$100,000		
426	426	$70	$29,787	55.00%	$16,383	$36,383	($6,596)	$20,000		
2,553	61,283		$4,931,388	55.00%	$2,712,264	$4,729,699	$201,689	$2,374,355	$2,044,189	$531,855
11,501	120,080		$9,092,116	55.00%	$5,000,664	$9,019,830	$72,286	$4,481,595	$3,769,006	$784,875

Interactive Workshop 7-5:

A Forecast Model That Views Customers as Investments

(For demonstration, go to the CD-Rom accompanying this book.)

Exhibit 7-6 shows a build-up forecast and budget with LTV enhancement. It demonstrates a five-year projection of lifetime customer value, its amortization and current market valuation.

This example, a start-up mail-order catalog, has no customer database at the outset. A "bounce-back" offer included with each shipment to a new customer is its first effort at cross-selling.

As detailed in column (2), it acquires new customers beginning in Year 2000 with the mailing of a 12-page mini-catalog to selected response lists. It also employs publication space ads to generate direct orders as well as to solicit inquiries for its catalog. This new-customer acquisition process is projected to continue for a five-year period, during which time the company builds its customer base—with each year's customer renewal rate shown in parentheses—and increases the size of its catalog.

Columns (3) through (8) detail the extent of each promotion effort—number and frequency of catalog mailings as well as space advertising expenditures—together with costs for each effort. Formulas are shown under each column heading.

Columns (9), (10), (12), (13), (14), and (15) detail predicted response and revenue, as well as the formulas for arriving at the numbers in these columns. Note that column (11) specifies an allowable order/inquiry cost (LTV), which increases year-to-year, and is applicable only to space advertising. This value has been calculated independently.

The constant 55 percent in column (16), applied to revenues in column (15), includes the combined costs-of-goods sold and general and administrative costs in column (17). These costs are next added to promotion costs in column (8) to determine total production and promotion costs in column (18). Then, subtraction of total costs in column (18) from total revenues in column (15) provides, in column (19), a picture of customer investment.

LTV (PAR), which is calculated independently for each product, is then multiplied times the number of new customers in column (13), as shown in column (20). PAR recovery, being the positive values in column (19), is shown in column (21). Finally, column (22) summarizes net cash investment, PAR and PAR recovery in order to reflect net customer value accumulation for each annual time period.

At the end of five years, as shown at the bottom of column (3), the firm projects that it will have 94,242 active customers. Their remaining lifetime value, shown at the bottom of column (22), is $784,875, an amount that can be considered to be the market valuation (goodwill) of the customer list. This amount is really understated, as customers acquired during the first year of operation are now fully amortized, although 2,457 of these are still active. Similarly, 5,608 customers remain from the second year with one year of amortization remaining. The resolution to this, which would reflect current market valuation more realistically, at a higher level, would be to extend the number of years for determination and amortization of LTV.

While relatively few organizations have adopted LTV as a formal accounting practice, treating their investment in the acquisition of customers as an asset, more and more are accepting the principle in marketing decision making.

Additional Exercises

- In Exhibit 7-2, Break-Even Calculator, raise or lower the selling price and see the impact on the number of sales needed to break-even. Recalibrate order processing/collection costs, costs of returns, and promotion costs and see what happens.

- In Exhibit 7-3, the Continuity Value of a Customer Over Future Time, increase the retention rates by ten percentage points for each sale following the first. What impact does such cultivation of existing customers have on the amount of money that can be spent to acquire a new customer? What impact does increasing the average revenue per sale by $25 have on the lifetime value of a customer? What is the bottom line impact of changing the discount factor?

- In Exhibit 7-4, Enhanced LTV Calculator, experiment with and define the factors that influence par ratios.

- In the Recency/Frequency/Monetary Calculator in Exhibit 7-5, change the inputs for each customer in the Recency, Frequency and Monetary Columns, and see what happens.

- In the Build-Up/Forecast shown in Exhibit 7-6, increase the number of 12-page minicatalogs mailed in the first year from 100,000 to 1,000,000. What effect does this have on the number of customers active and their value at the end of the fifth year? Next, increase the number of 36-page catalogs mailed in the fifth year from 2,650,000 to 3,650,000. What effect does this have on the number of customers active and their value at the end of the fifth year? How has each of these changes impacted revenues and cash flow?

■ Conduct other "what if?" experiments in Exhibit 7-6—extent of promotion, response rates, promotion costs, costs of goods sold, revenues—and note their impact on the bottom line.

■ See if you can fit your own numbers into the examples of spread-sheets provided in this chapter and on the CD-ROM.

Chapter 8

Consumer Market Segmentation

Key Concepts
- Market Segmentation and Penetration
- Geographic Segmentation
- Demographic Segmentation
- Psychographic Segmentation
- Product Differentiation and Positioning

Applications
- Identifying and Reaching a Consumer Market Segment

A market is defined as customers with needs and/or wants to satisfy, money to spend, and the willingness to spend it. A market segment is a homogenous subgroup of a heterogeneous aggregate market that is selected as a target market. A cluster is a grouping of smaller entities, such as ZIP Code areas or comparable individuals, into a market segment. Database marketing enables a marketer to target and focus on increasingly well-defined and profitable market segments. The process of segmentation (or market segmentation) begins with observing customers' actions and continues with learning about the demographic and psychographic (reflected in lifestyle) characteristics of these customers.

The Nature of Market Segmentation and Penetration

Market segmentation is a staple of direct marketing because it reflects a customer orientation. Market segmentation uses a rifle-shot approach that enables the marketer to target appeals to specific markets rather than a shotgun or scattershot approach that includes likely prospects but also includes many unlikely individuals.

The most basic form of market segmentation is the division between ultimate consumers and business-to-business markets. But this is only the beginning. Brand preferences, product characteristics, potential purchase volume, price/cost, and recency and frequency of purchase are just a few additional ways of segmenting markets.

How to Identify Consumer Market Segments

The consumer market contains an infinite number of subgroups. These clusters of buyers or prospective buyers share **geographic**, **demographic**, or **psychographic** (or lifestyle) features that can be used to identify and to organize (or cluster) them into logical groupings using a variety of techniques. Exhibit 8-1 lists a number of these features or characteristics.

Geographic Segmentation

Geographic segmentation seeks to identify whether a customer or prospect resides in an urban or rural area, then pinpoints the region, state, county or metropolitan area where he or she lives.

United States geographic groupings range from the country in its entirety down through 9 census regions and 12 Federal Reserve Districts. Beyond these are 50 states, 3,042 counties and 435 congressional districts. There are numerical codes, too, such as ZIP Codes, telephone area codes, and route numbers. Then there are endless arrays of state-defined areas of economic activity and trading areas. Overlapping these is an abundance of so-called media communications areas and retail trading zones associated with cities, towns, rural farm, and rural non-farm areas. Smaller geographic units include census tracts containing clusters of block groups and individual city blocks.

On a still more sophisticated level, the GPS (Global Positioning System) and the Census Bureau's TIGER (Topologically Integrated Geographic Encoding Referencing) systems have assigned latitude/longitude coordinates to millions of street addresses for site locations.

Geographic information can tell a lot about a market segment because people with like interests tend to cluster. Their buying decisions are often influenced by a desire to emulate friends, neighbors, and community innovators. The ZIP Code and other geographic indicators provide the means to identify the environments of such clusters of households.

DEMOGRAPHICS
Personal Information:
Age:
Gender:
Height:
Weight:
Eye Color:
Hair Color:
Race: —
Ethnicity
— Foreign Born:
— Country of Origin:
— Mother Tongue Spoken:
Religion:
Marital Status:
Family Size:
Education Level:
Occupation:
Industry:
Income:
Mobility:

Dwelling Information:
Type (single/multiple):
Size (square feet):
$ Value (if owner):
$ Rent (if not owner):
Structure Age:
Tenure of Residence:
Household Equipment —
— Dishwasher:
— Clothes Washer/Dryer:
— Refrigerator/Oven
— Computer:
— VCR/Camcorder:
— Freezer
— Television:
— Radio:
Structure Equipment —
— Heating:
— Cooling:
— Multi-Bath:
— Public Water:
— Public Sewer:
— Security System:
Kitchen:
Direct Access:
Telephone:
Autos Registered:

GEOGRAPHICS
Location Information:
Nationality —
— United States:
— Other American:
— European:
— Asian:
— Australian/New Zealand:
Other:
— Metropolitan Type —
— Urban:
— Suburban:
— Urban Fringe:
— Rural Farm:
— Rural Non-Farm:
Region:
Federal Reserve District:
Congressional District:
State:
County:
State Economic Trading Area:
Media Communication Area(s):
Retail Trading Area:
Metropolitan Statistical Area:
Census Tract:
Minor Civil Division:
Block Group:
Block:
Block Face:
ZIP Code Area:
Telephone Area Code:
Latitude/Longitude Coordinate:

PSYCHOGRAPHICS
Attitudes:
Interests:
Opinions:
Activities:
Biological Needs:
Psychological Motivations:
Environmental Influences:

ACTIONS TAKEN
What Purchases Lately:
What Lists On:
What Affinity Groups:
What Favorite Charities:
What Political Affiliation:
What Influencers:

**Exhibit 8-1: An Array of Characteristics Describing Consumers
within Market Segments**

ZIP Code Areas as Market Segments. For the most part, geographic areas available as market segments are imprecise indicators of customer identity as well as demographic and psychographic homogeneity. To achieve these, the physical boundaries of such units should define areas that are economically meaningful and also are environmentally measurable. ZIP Code areas, originally conceived by the United States Postal Service in the 1960s for the sorting and distribution of mail, have become a convenient as well as a logical method of market segmentation for direct marketers.

ZIP Codes provide similarity of identity in addresses and are homogeneous. Mail goes from people to people in the same manner in which trade is conducted and in the same manner in which cultural exchange takes place. This people-to-people relationship explains why ZIP Codes were established with regard to transportation patterns. It also explains why buyer behavior in ZIP Code areas can be measured by and predicted from environmental influences.

People with like interests tend to cluster and their buying decisions are often influenced by a desire to emulate friends, neighbors and community innovators. ZIP Code areas, part of everyone's address, provide the means to identify clusters of households that have a high degree of homogeneity. This homogeneity results from the manner in which ZIP Code areas were built. It is derived from accepted principles of reference group theory and the concept of environmental influences on behavior.

As generally accepted in marketing literature, behavior of buyers is interdependent. Purchase decisions are not so much caused by income *per se* as by the buyer's perception of his or her relative position, or that aspired to, in an environment that is measurable. Thorstein Veblen called it "conspicuous consumption." John Kenneth Galbraith referred to "the dependence effect." The less scholarly have simply called it "keeping up with the Joneses." The concept here is that who we think we are often exerts more influence on buying than who we actually are.

Demographic Segmentation

Demographic statistics include age, gender, marital status, occupation, or education. They are generally compiled for a geographic area, and are frequently related to some social or economic characteristic or to a comparison over time. The primary unit of observation in demography is the individual, with the family unit (related individuals living together) and/or the household (families plus individuals living alone plus non-related individuals living together) being secondary.

There are three main sources of demographic data:

1. By enumeration of a population as in a census.

2. By registration on the occurrence of an event such as birth, marriage, or death; by recording a purchase such as real estate or automobile or by application for licensing.

3. By sample surveys or tabulations of special groups.

Change in demography is important, too. If a single person marries or if a baby is born, these events have significance for certain marketers. So does population change or high mobility of the residents of a geographic area. Direct marketers capture such major events so as to offer differentiated products to geographic or demographic market segments.

Psychographic Segmentation

Much market segmentation is based on psychographic factors associated with lifestyles. Knowing an individual's personality, behaviors, values and "AIO's" (attitudes, interests, opinions) can help in understanding customers who share geographic and demographic characteristics, but have different buying behaviors.

Psychographic (lifestyle) information can be obtained from interaction of demographic variables and geographic locations. It can also be determined from actions taken, such as subscribing to a certain publication, or owning a certain product. Surveys are often used to determine attitudes, interests, and opinions.

One way to discover psychographic characteristics is to watch for multiple database identifications. For example, a registered owner of a particular automobile, residing in a 90-unit apartment building located in an affluent ZIP Code, might also appear as a subscriber to *The Wall Street Journal*, a customer of L.L.Bean, and a contributor to the Republican Party and Planned Parenthood. These multiple-list identifications can describe attitudes, interests, and opinions and provide names and addresses of prospects.

Segmentation Based on Actions Taken

Direct marketers have used market segmentation based on actions taken as the traditional way to select response mailing lists. The number of choices is nearly limitless, with consumer lists including buyers of all types of products, subscribers to specialized magazines, members of differentiated book and record clubs, donors to causes, collectors, and members.

Lists of respondents are enhanced when there is an affinity, a relationship, a membership, or some form of expressed loyalty or connection to the organization.

They are enhanced, too, when subgrouped by characteristics of recency, frequency, and monetary value. For example, recent buyers ("hotline" buyers) of books about the Civil War are a segment within a segment (i.e., recent buyers of Civil War books as a segment of buyers of Civil War books). So are those who have been buying the annual update of an encyclopedia for ten or more years. So are those who buy "the best."

The number of segments and subsegments is limited only by the amount of data and the ability of the database manager to manipulate it. So, those who send gifts to others, as distinct from buying for their own consumption, comprise a segment within a segment. So are those who purchase as members of a select "club." So is the very large segment of "conscientious wheelers and dealers"—the millions of people who enter contests and sweepstakes, solve puzzles, buy lottery tickets, and order "genuine synthetic diamonds!" At heart, every mailing list represents a market segment that has demonstrated interest in certain offers by responding to them.

Product Differentiation and Positioning

Market segmentation is used to divide the total heterogeneous market into smaller, more homogenous groupings. Unless a product or service is unique and can appeal equally to everyone (highly unlikely), it is vital to think in terms of market segments.

It also is desirable to differentiate specific products for specific market segments. Such differentiated products are positioned so that they will offer special benefits to the groups to which promotion is targeted.

Product differentiation, like market segmentation, is an alternative to price competition. The difference might be real and substantial or simply a matter of image or perception and can apply relative to a firm's other products as well as to its competitors.

A toothpaste containing fluoride is intrinsically different from another toothpaste without fluoride. On the other hand, Singapore Airlines, calling its Boeing 747 aircraft "Daily Megatop 747," may have planes physically identical to its competition, yet such a representation can make the company's aircraft *appear* significantly different even if they are not.

Positioning is the image projected by a product relative to a particular use of it or even its use by a market segment. Baking soda might be portrayed as a tooth cleaner or an odor-remover. In effect, positioning combines the principles of product differentiation with those of market segmentation.

"Everything You've Always Wanted in a Beer...and Less" is an example of positioning a differentiated product, "light" beer, so that its promotion is targeted to a calorie-conscious market segment. "7-Up, the Un-Cola" is a similar example, of a soft drink targeting its promotion to a caffeine-free segment.

Workshop 8-1:
Using a Database to Identify and Reach a Consumer Market Segment

Stoney Creek (SC) is a residential community located in central Virginia. It is a part of Mountain & Valley Resort (MVR), a highly regarded family resort that encompasses 11,000 acres of land centered in the Blue Ridge Mountains, adjacent to the George Washington National Forest, quite near Shenandoah National Park.

While the mountain resort today attracts vacation skiers and golfers from as far away as Washington, D.C., and Charlotte, North Carolina, a major part of its use is by the owners of condominium and single-family residences there. These property owners in effect own the resort through an entity called MVR Partners, Inc.

The market for MVR residence units has been well defined and segmented geographically, demographically, and psychographically. The more than 2,000 mountain condominiums at present sold as quickly as they were planned and built. Most of the 500 homes on the mountain have been custom-built by owners.

In the 2,000-acre valley development known as Stoney Creek, more than 250 single-family units, virtually all custom-built and nearly all primary residences, are occupied year-around. The geographic, demographic, and psychographic mix of these MVR Partners is, however, diverse! While some view it as a retirement community, most do not. Many have full-time occupations.

MOUNTAIN & VALLEY PROPERTY OWNERS (RESIDENTS) DATA

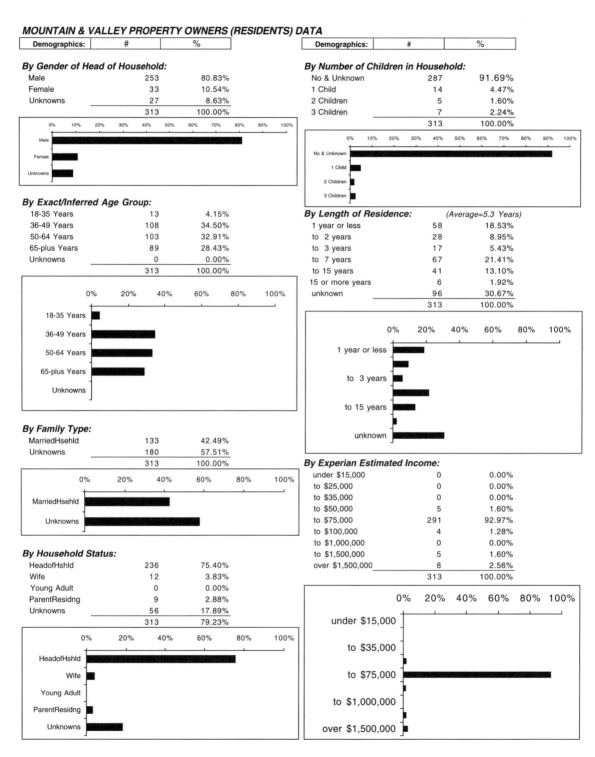

Exhibit 8-2: Mountain & Valley Resort Resident Property Owners Data

MOUNTAIN & VALLEY PROPERTY OWNERS (NONRESIDENTS) DATA

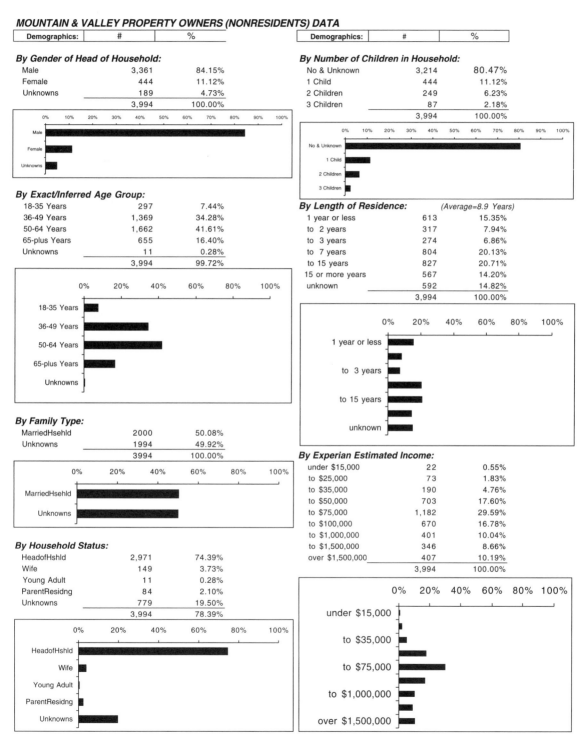

Exhibit 8-3: Mountain & Valley Non-Resident Property Owners Data

Stoney Creek has succeeded up to now in attracting both retired and working individuals, many of the permanent residents having upgraded from part-time condominium status. Could there, however, be a potential market segmentation conflict here?

One market study conducted years earlier for a condominium retirement community near Chicago revealed some misconceptions and prejudices toward these. Respondents to this survey viewed a particular community as an "old people's home," clearly identified with the retirement, perhaps even the nursing home, market. Most respondents, regardless of their ages, just did not think they were "old enough" to move there yet.

In the study, many associated the community's activities and facilities with regimentation and even institutionalism. Some saw it as "not quite respectable" and suggested that the residents were probably shiftless and hedonistic. They used words like "playground," "leisure-living," "fun," and "pleasure," respondents apparently drawing these words entirely from the community's own advertising. The majority of the respondents identified the community as an expensive, high income, high cost place to live. They used these words in an unfavorable sense: "exclusive," "luxurious," and "country-club atmosphere."

Developers learned that buying a home and moving were emotion-laden activities and, further, different segments of the total market had substantially different motives for changing residences. Unfortunately, it also appeared that the motives of various segments were often at cross-purposes, so advertising appeals to one segment may well alienate other segments.

While the MVR development has been eminently successful, the Stoney Creek residential community may have to identify and select those market segments that are most compatible. As a step in this direction, it will be useful to look at the demographics of those who own property within the MVR complex, many of whom initially experienced the environment as a guest of the Resort.

The Mountain & Valley Property Owners Association (MVPOA) maintains a database containing 4,547 owner records, including individual records for multiple owners of a single property. This database distinguishes those properties located in the mountain area from those in the valley area. It is not yet able to distinguish those properties that are developed from those that are undeveloped lots.

As will be done with both the Ski and Guest databases in Chapters 13 and 14, the MVPOA records were matched to the Experian database for enhancement with demographic, although not lifestyle, data. Matches were obtained for 85% of the records.

Frequency distributions of demographic variables associated with permanent residents appear in Exhibit 8-2. Variables associated with non-residents appear in Exhibit 8-3. Not all data variables could be identified for all records, so distribution totals vary. Note, too, that these distributions are not a measure of market penetration but are an allocation of records.

Exercise: It could be helpful to compare the Property Owners profiles with each other (resident vs. nonresident) as well as with MVR's Ski and Guest databases in Chapters 13 and 14, so as to target resort guests who might be prospects for properties. Recall that many of these first experienced the environment as a Resort guest.

Chapter 9

Business-to-Business Market Segmentation

Key Concepts
- SIC and NAICS Coding
- TIGER System
- Extended Data
- Business Ecosystems
- Input-Output Analysis
- Impact Analysis
- Econometric Footprints
- Cluster Analysis
- Location Analysis

Applications
- Segmenting Business-to-Business Markets
- Analyzing B2B Customer Penetration
- Developing Customer Profiles

Customer knowledge has always been vital to success in the business-to-business (B2B) arena and the practices of the old-style "industrial" rep who knew everything about his customers' business needs in many ways have provided the model for contemporary database attitudes and applications. Fifty years ago, that kind of information might have been written on the back of an envelope or on a 3x5 index card. Today, that information is most likely in a database, probably a relational database that includes important information about their customers' customers as well as their customers. In other words, they have online access to a complete picture of a customer's needs, objectives, and operating environment before ever making a call. Like consumer marketers, they perform statistical analyses to identify their own best customers and then seek prospects that look just like them.

Tremendous changes in today's global economy are forcing business-to-business marketers to adapt to many challenges. To be successful, these marketers must be able to account for each nuance of change in their customers' organizations, their own organizations, and in the overall economy. In addition to facing these market changes, business-to-business marketers must find new ways to cultivate their current customers, locate qualified prospects, and reduce marketing costs.

Some of the challenges facing business marketers include:

- Marketing costs are increasing while the audience reached is decreasing. It costs more to generate awareness than ever before.

- Face-to-face selling, down in efficiency, is up in cost. Travel expense is up, and the cost of a sales call is a larger part of revenue than ever before.

- Communication clutter results in individuals receiving up to 10,000 messages per day, and many have tuned out all marketing messages as irrelevant, whether they in fact irrelevant or not. In other words, it's increasingly difficult to cut through the clutter even when one's message is unquestionably relevant to the target prospect.

- Customer relationship managers often do not use an integrated analytical approach to combining operations with marketing programs and campaigns. The availability of analytics that assess customer data is limited. (It helps to think of operational customer relations as the body of the system and analytics as the brain.)

- In the current business environment Standard Industry Classification (SIC) is not as predictive as it used to be. The current method of SIC segmentation assumes similar businesses within the same industry type; however, a business in a rural area with a similar SIC as one located in an inner-city area can be a very different entity. Both manage the same type business, but the picture of the environment where they are located could be dramatically different.

How to Identify Business-to-Business Market Segments

Of the statistical tools available, cluster analysis seems most capable of producing useful B2B marketing information. Such analysis is used to segment customers that share similar characteristics across a wide range

Consumer	Business-to-Business
Name/Address	Name/Address
Source code	Source code
Age	Year started
Gender	Gender of decision-maker
Income	Revenue
Wealth	Net worth
Family size	Number of employees
Children	Parent firm or subsidiary
Occupation	Line of business (SIC)
Credit evaluation	Credit evaluation
Education	Education of decision-maker
Urban/rural resident	Headquarters/branch
Own or rent home	Private or public ownership
Ethnic group	Minority ownership
Gender	Gender of decision makers
Interests	Interests of decision makers
Life-style of ZIP area	Socio-economics of location
Mail respondent	Mail respondent
Transactions & R/F/M	Transactions & R/F/M

Exhibit 9-1: Similarities Between Consumer and Business-to-Business Markets

of demographic and behavioral variables and has long been used in the consumer marketplace. Recently, such analysis has proven to be valuable for B2B marketers as well.

In the United States, there are at least ten times as many purchasing households (i.e., consumer purchasing entities or units) as there are business-to-business organizations, and about twenty-five times as many individual consumers. But when the customer characteristics of consumer and business-to-business markets are compared, as in Exhibit 9-1, striking similarities emerge.

First, information about an individual purchaser is similar whether the person is acting on his or her own behalf or that of an organization, but it is obtained through a different set of segmenting tools.

Second, in business-to-business distribution, producers and middlemen call on industrial users *at the buyer's location*, whereas users of consumer goods call on the producers and middlemen for their needs *at the seller's location*.

Third, because the typical business-to-business buying decision is more complex than the typical consumer buying decision, direct marketing has long played an important role in business-to-business marketing.

For example, lead generation and qualification are used extensively in business-to-business direct marketing to enhance the effectiveness of personal selling. Direct contact in the form of sales calls to B2B buyers takes more time and is more costly than "calls" on consumers, which generally means that the consumer goes to the seller's place of business. Business-to-business purchases typically involve much larger dollar amounts, and B2B buyers are usually much better informed, have more specialized interests, and are involved in a process of joint decision making with others in their organizations. Repeat purchases, too, are more frequent in industrial situations.

These factors have combined to explain the need for, as well as the growing use of, market segmentation techniques described below in business-to-business direct marketing.

Standard Industrial Classification (SIC) Coding System

A common means of industrial market segmentation is the Standard Industrial Classification (SIC) coding system developed and maintained by the federal government. This system is used to designate industry groups by function and product and, in a way, parallels the demographic characteristics used for segmenting markets and analyzing demand of consumer markets. The first two digits of the four-digit code indicate major classifications of industry, of which there are ten:

01 - 09	Agriculture, Forestry and Fisheries
15 - 17	Construction
20 - 39	Manufacturing
40 - 49	Transportation, Communications, Public Utilities
50 - 51	Wholesale Trade
52 - 59	Retail Trade
60 - 67	Finance, Insurance, Real Estate
70 - 89	Services
91 - 97	Public Administration
99	Non-classifiable Establishments

The final two digits of the four-digit SIC code classify individual organizations by subgroup and further detail within industry. For example, SIC #2300 identifies manufacturers of wearing apparel. Within this classification, SIC #2311 identifies men's suit and coat manufacturers.

North American Industrial Classification System (NAICS)

SIC codes did a good job detailing the manufacturing industry in the post-World War II era, but many feel it fails to recognize today's information technology age. With rapid growth of the service industry, high technology, and international trade, a new system has arisen, largely in response to the North American Free Trade Agreement (NAFTA) of 1994. It has been felt that a new system was needed to compare U.S. statistical information with that of Canada and Mexico. Desirable, too, would be future compatibility with an International Standard Industrial Classification System being developed by the United Nations.

All three groups have agreed on a system now called the North American Industrial Classification System (NAICS). This system has formulated a six-digit code, with the first five digits denoting the NAICS levels used by all three countries to produce compatible data. NAICS is an entirely different classification system focused on production activities rather than on the industries served, which is what SIC codes do.

Different agencies within governments are now converting to NAICS coding, but business has done little if anything to adopt the new coding system in marketing applications.

The Census Bureau's TIGER System

The Global Positioning System (GPS) and the Census Bureau's TIGER (Topologically Integrated Geographic Encoding Referencing) system associate latitude and longitude coordinates with street addresses. Used to pinpoint geographic locations, they can establish business sites, locate competition, measure distance, and generate data about the demographics of a business location.

With mapping capabilities and information in its database, a business-to-business direct marketer can visualize reach and penetration of the geographic territories of its resellers.

Other Industrial Market Segmentation Methods

Business-to-business organizations can be categorized by financial strength or size, number of employees, and/or sales volume. Geographic selectivity, including city size and location, is often used, too. Other criteria include headquarters or branch office, a parent or a subsidiary, form of ownership, and extent of telephone directory Yellow Pages advertising (a proven predictor for many business-to-business direct marketers).

It was already mentioned that the typical B2B sale differs from the typical consumer sale. This difference is most clearly reflected in the number of decision levels that characterize most business-to-business purchase decisions. Direct marketers must appeal not only to organizations but also to relevant individuals within these organizations. Purchasing agents alone do not generate demand within business organizations. More likely, engineers, chemists, architects, production managers, and a host of other specialists make joint decisions. Personalities and demographics of these decision-makers and influencers are now also becoming a basis for market segmentation. With data available on contacts within a prospect organization, a direct marketer can further segment on the basis of job titles and utility of particular job functions in order to enhance response rates.

This process applies equally to public-sector and other nonprofit organizations, which can include governments, medical services, legal services, schools, libraries, social services, churches, cultural, and arts organizations.

Despite the preceding discussion, the most important basis for business-to-business market segmentation is the organization's own database—i.e., its house list. Its own customer list, including prior brand and product purchase behavior, actions taken, credit evaluation, recency/frequency/monetary scoring, and each customer's own enhanced demographic profile, offers the most accurate means of targeting relevant B2B market segments.

Extended Data—New Business Enhancement Variables

In recent years, data describing more than the traditional standard industry classifications and usual business demographics has been developed. This information enables direct marketers to identify business operational characteristics and environments within which they are physically located, providing fuel for modeling and predicting business customer behavior. Discussion of these new techniques and sources of information follows.

Input-Output Matrices: Business Ecosystems and Lifestyles

Businesses, like individual consumers, have lifestyles. A small business may retain characteristics of its CEOs personal lifestyle; a large business culture often develops its own unique characteristics of consumption and behavior. Like an ecosystem in the physical world, the business world is made up of different parts that function and interact in tandem to and in reaction to each other. The patterns and the interactions of the various components of this culture are called the business *ecosystem*.

There is, of course, a correlation between the production and the demand of an economy. Changes in either component in the regional economy will likely lead to changes in the other. Viewing the economic system in this way, as a broad-based system of interdependence, will provide insights into the functioning of businesses at the site level.

Input-output matrices, derived basically from U.S. Department of Commerce data, trace the distribution of goods from their origin to their destination. In such a matrix, an industry (SIC) appears as both seller and buyer in row and column headings. At the point where the row and column of any two industries intersect, the matrix records the transaction between those two SIC classifications.

Input-output analysis, in its broader form, thus determines the impact that specific industries have on the total economy in terms of what they sell and what they buy. A decrease in sales of new automobiles, for example, would result in reduced purchases from the tire industry. This, in turn, would result in reduced sales by the tire industry and would ultimately reduce the tire industry's purchases from the rubber industry. In a sense the business ecosystem can be traced and defined from region to region, from business site to site, to give a robust view of business activity beyond standard compiled demographics.

Much of input-output analysis is a component of regional science that attempts to discover the overlapping interests in economics, geography, city and regional planning with a practical application of using statistical tools to take incomplete data sets and arrive at accurate estimations for planning situations.

There is, of course, a correlation between the production and the demand of an economy. Changes in either component in the regional economy will likely lead to changes in the other. Viewing the economic system in this way, as a broad-based system of interdependence, will provide insights into the functioning of businesses at the site level.

Impact Analysis

Tools used by city planners estimate the impact of program expenditures on surrounding economic components, such as employment, earnings, and output of goods. Such science is an outgrowth of input-output analysis and is used to measure direct dollar impacts from a first round, to a second round, to a third round and so on.

The following is a simple example. A dollar spent at a local store may produce an impact of $.80 on the local economy, $.30 on the surrounding economy and $.15 on the regional economy. Thus, the total impact of one dollar spent is $1.25.

Econometric Footprints

Econometric footprints considerably enhance business-to-business direct marketing by using an extensive array of data variables that take traditional B2B market segmentation beyond the traditional demographic variables (e.g., SIC codes, number of employees, revenues, etc.). Using econometric footprints enables direct marketers to address factors often overlooked in business-to-business segmentation—local economic and social conditions of a business' location—that can impact that business' buying behavior. Augmenting traditional business demographics with data elements that capture these local influences, a new and powerful analytical dimension becomes available.

Econometric footprints can be created through statistical processes, primarily principal components and multidimensional scaling. These techniques reduce large sets of descriptive economic, industry, and consumer variables into newly created numeric or composite variables. These variables (called factors) present the pattern of the original data set in terms of a single number that enables the use of a huge amount of available raw data without having to include each raw data element individually. Hundreds of econometric footprints can be utilized to help explain the variances in industrial buying behavior. An example of an econometric footprint for Available Labor is represented in the map shown in Exhibit 9-2.

Variables embraced in econometric footprints include:

- Census data trends
- Economic input/output data

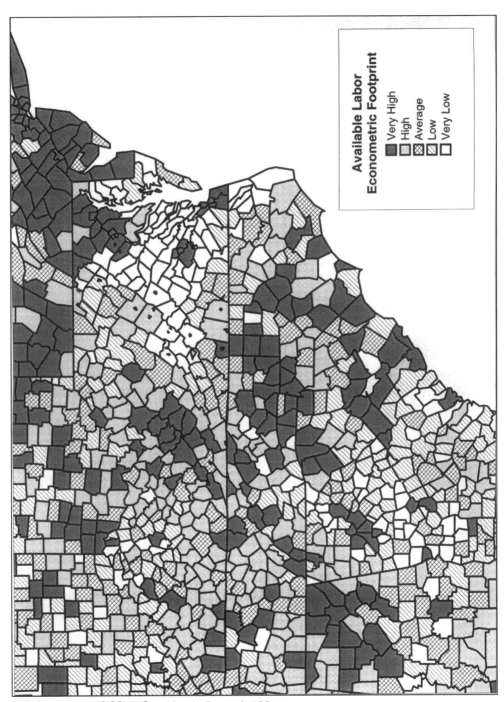

Exhibit 9.2: Available Labor Metric Footprint Map

- Compiled business demographics
- Compiled consumer demographics
- Credit data
- Automotive data
- Crime data
- Labor data
- Agricultural data
- Retail data
- Earnings data

This list, which might seem exhaustive, barely scratches the surface of the possibilities available.

Business Clusters

As in consumer markets, business-to-business markets can be clustered. Data for individual firms by SIC classifications can be associated with other data for such areas. Ruf Strategic Solutions of Olathe, Kansas, has identified such areas in terms of economic activity (number of businesses, commerce input-output, bank savings, retail sales, etc.) as well as in terms of consumer demographics and lifestyles (number of households, home value, income, autos owned, etc.) Such clusters reveal the impact that economic and social variables prevailing in a business environment have on the buying behavior of businesses (and their buyers) located there.

Cluster Analysis: Targeting Business Customers

Most marketing professionals know that each customer in a database is not equal in value. In fact, it is quite simple to distinguish between the repeat customer and the customer who has made a single, inexpensive purchase some time ago. The difficulty, until now, has been to isolate the best customers that appear to fall in the middle of the spectrum.

It is obvious that socioeconomic and demographic factors impact business activity, but the key is finding out which factors are important and how they interact within the overall business environment. Traditional customer segmentation methods have used Standard Industrial Classification (SIC) codes and such variables as annual revenues and number of employees.

Cluster analysis is more descriptive than traditional segmentation methods because it can reveal hidden relationships. For example, cluster analysis may reveal that past purchasing patterns, economic growth, and interdependency factors are far better predictors of future purchases than the size of the firm, its revenues or industry classification.

Customers can be segmented into clusters, which, when combined, become the overall customer profile. Companies can then target each group effectively through individualized marketing messages.

Customer profiles are the key to effective prospecting; businesses should target prospects that look like their best customers. By using hundreds of underlying variables, clusters can essentially differentiate between two similar businesses in the same approximate location by comparing differences to an average of the universe of all businesses.

For example, a company that sells computer software designed specifically for small businesses could reduce its prospecting costs by eliminating large businesses and those small businesses that do not use computers. Traditional market segmentation techniques, relying on address, SIC Codes, number of employees, annual revenues and other conventional demographic factors, would have been able to eliminate the companies that were considered too large, but would not have been able to eliminate the small businesses unlikely to use computers. However, cluster analysis would be able to show those unlikely to use computers by revealing the purchasing habits, preferences, and other related traits of those companies.

By analyzing data from many firms across the spectrum of industries, a marketer can derive business "lifestyles." Using input/output tables, the marketer can use statistical models to describe the *consumption and digestion* of products and services a company uses to produce its final products and services. Once indexes are attached to a business file, hidden relationships of the business environment are revealed. Clusters thus provide detailed understanding of businesses by summarizing their lifestyles.

Understanding the Consumer Component

Business cluster analysis can also incorporate consumer factors to provide an additional dimension to the picture. A correlation exists between the location of a business and the consumer behavior in the same location. Businesses locate in areas where they can find good employees, low costs, and customers to purchase their goods. Consumers locate in areas where they can find good jobs, good schools for their children, and needed products and services. The final demand of consumers can define the commerce area's footprint.

By incorporating the consumer component, business clusters can reveal the hidden relationships of the surrounding economy. Additional matches allow business owners and their employees who purchase to be linked to their home addresses. This results in a descriptive profile giving expanded information on consumption, media usage, and credit behavior.

Business clusters provide meaning to the thousands of variables and hidden relationships in the business ecosystem. They allow the zeroing-in of target markets necessary to survive and thrive. Business-to-business marketers can identify their best customers, increase market penetration, and boost advertising effectiveness. They can optimize location of markets, target new customers more precisely, and more clearly visualize their markets for better strategic decision-making.

Unleashing the Power of Database Marketing: Location Analysis

Advances in technology, data collection, and outsourcing have given marketers powerful new projective marketing tools that were unheard of only a few years ago. These tools enable marketers to correlate who customers are, what they do, and where they reside with their future purchase behavior and why they purchase. Data warehouses provide compiled information that, along with a customer database, can build intelligence for targeting segments that exhibit the most desired behavior.

These tools and methods can be used for evaluating and segmenting a firm's best customers, acquiring new prospects, cross-selling services or products, positioning advertising in proper media areas, locating new sales offices or retail sites.

In the past, choosing a new site for a retail location was as easy as determining the corner with the highest traffic count or visiting as many physical sites as possible to get a gut feel of the environment. One simple method was to divide the number of potential customers by the population of a trade area.

Another technique, the gravity model, evaluates store size and distance friction to conclude that, in most cases, people who live or work near the store are most likely to shop there. Each of these methods has been used to define site location with limited success, mainly because of limited data.

Collecting the Data

Several data sources can be helpful in determining who a firm's customers are. Syndicated data collected by compilers can provide information on income, education, and housing as well as lifestyle. Primary data from surveys can give understanding of different components and variables that make up the lifestyles of customers or prospects. Customer transaction data, however, is possibly the most important component of information, providing answers to such questions as these: "Who are my customers?" "When do they purchase?" "What do they purchase?" "Where do they purchase?" "What did they spend?"

Even retailers who do not maintain a customer database have access to credit card transaction data. Working with a bank card processor and a service bureau, reverse matching of credit card data can build a name and address file that will provide powerful information about customers. This information can provide purchase activity patterns that can be evaluated by time of day in order to determine whether a customer is shopping from home or from work.

Another innovative database-building technique includes collecting license tag information and reverse matching to address. These methods allow proactive targeting to businesses or employees who do not even live in the trade area but, because of their work location, shop there.

When collecting the data sample, it is important to remove bias. All sites—high, medium and low performing locations—should be collected. Factors that impact a site in an urban area may be different from factors that impact a rural site.

Once data is collected, analysis can provide understanding of the distance a customer or prospect will travel to utilize a specific service. Latitude/longitude coordinates of residence address, determined from the Census Bureau's TIGER file, can be attached to customer records, along with data that predicts driving time to and from the site location. Such modeling can show the decay that occurs as distance increases from the individual customer's residence. Geographic (GPS) mapping, too, can provide evidence of barriers to customer convenience, such as highway crossings, bridges, traffic or lack of access.

Utilizing business databases that include SIC codes of the competition and sales volume within the trade area, it is possible to subtract the relative impact on prospective sites. Matching license tag information of a competitor's parking lot can provide additional competitive insight.

Market Analysis

Statistical tools—regression and correlation analysis or cluster analysis—applied to a customer database can provide detailed profiles of the demographics and lifestyles of those customers. Penetration within market segments and future potential of the best segments can be determined. Clusters can then be studied further to understand why some segments perform better than others. Correlating key influencing variables with market penetration can answer the question of why people buy, thus determining market areas with similar characteristics.

Once the analysis is completed, scoring of optimum trade areas, current customers, prospect lists, and prospective sites will narrow down those that deliver the best opportunities for new customer growth within the known competitive environment.

Utilizing business econometric modeling techniques, analysis can be done from the site outward to evaluate the potential success of any business to locate there. Factors that include economic input/output and commerce area analysis can predict success of a particular business and aid economic development. An illustration of a site trade area gravity model is shown in Exhibit 9-3.

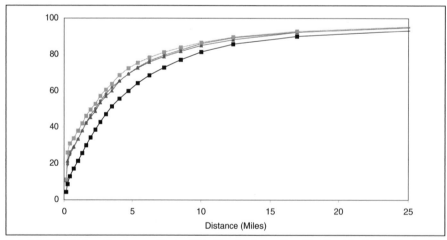

Exhibit 9-3: Using Customer Data, Site Trade Area Gravity Can Be Evaluated with a Distance Decay Graph

Interactive Workshop 9-1:

Business-to-Business Market Segmentation

Company X, a business-to-business marketer, seeks to:

1. Establish an overall picture of customers;
2. Segment these customers by market penetration;
3. Determine characteristic traits of its top customers.

Utilizing business-clustering technology developed by Ruf Strategic Solutions, 52,275 customers are analyzed. Of these, 41,959 (80.3%) are determined to be active (defined as those customers who purchased from the company within the last 12 months); the remaining 10,316 (19.7%) are considered inactive. The Ruf model appends a cluster code to each record on the business customer database based on each customer's demographic and purchase behavior. The records are grouped together and summarized by cluster code.

The model then compares the percentage of customers to the percentage of market-area businesses within each cluster, in order to develop an index, i.e., [(% of revenue) / (% of businesses) * 100)]. Finally, each cluster is ranked from the highest to the lowest based on this index.

A market penetration report, shown in Exhibit 9-4, details the four top-performing business clusters.

These top four clusters represent 22.26% of the company's customer file but only 13.87% of the market area. The lift for these top four clusters is 110.91% (210.91-100). The indices show that targeting these top four clusters would generate results 2.1 times better than targeting the entire file.

The top quintile of business clusters captures 35% of the total customers. This quintile has an overall/cumulative index of 179, signifying nearly 1.8 times the likelihood to become a customer than the average market area business. In contrast, the bottom quintile only contains 11.9% of the customers in 24.5% of the prospect base. This may warrant eliminating these segments from future marketing promotions or repositioning how this market is approached based on the demographic makeup.

Rank Order	Cluster ID	% of Revenue	% of Businesses	Index
1	7023	1.13	0.04	2,825
2	7020	6.39	0.27	2,367
3	7018	1.67	0.07	2,386
4	7034	5.54	0.27	2,051

Exhibit 9-4: Top-Performing Business Clusters

Rank Order	SIC Code	Description	% of Revenue	% of Businesses	Index
1	38	Instruments and Related	1.86	0.13	1,431
2	37	Transportation Equipment	1.56	0.13	1,200
3	36	Electronic Equipment	2.49	0.21	1,186
4	33	Primary Metal Industries	0.89	0.09	989

Exhibit 9-5: Top Performing Standard Industrial Classifications

The four top-performing Standard Industrial Classification (SIC) codes (Revenue/Businesses*100) are shown in Exhibit 9-5.

The Ruf business-to-business customer segmentation analysis shows Company X's market penetration by industry classification, employee size, annual sales volume, years on file and census division. These demographic data are charted in Exhibit 9-6.

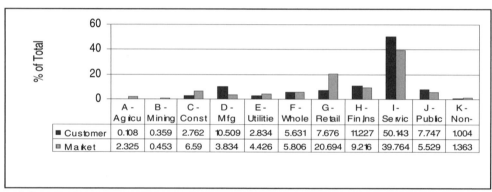

	A - Agricu	B - Mining	C - Const	D - Mfg	E - Utilitie	F - Whole	G - Retail	H - Fin Ins	I - Servic	J - Public	K - Non-
Customer	0.108	0.359	2.762	10.509	2.834	5.631	7.676	11.227	50.143	7.747	1.004
Market	2.325	0.453	6.59	3.834	4.426	5.806	20.694	9.216	39.764	5.529	1.363

Exhibit 9-6.1: Market Penetration by Industrial Classifications

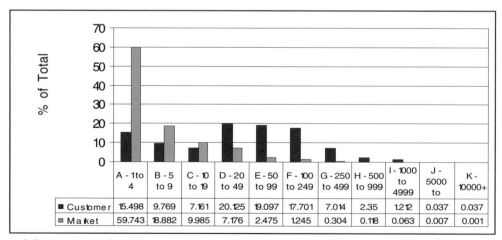

	A - 1 to 4	B - 5 to 9	C - 10 to 19	D - 20 to 49	E - 50 to 99	F - 100 to 249	G - 250 to 499	H - 500 to 999	I - 1000 to 4999	J - 5000 to	K - 10000+
Customer	15.498	9.769	7.161	20.125	19.097	17.701	7.014	2.35	1.212	0.037	0.037
Market	59.743	18.882	9.985	7.176	2.475	1.245	0.304	0.118	0.063	0.007	0.001

Exhibit 9-6.2: Market Penetration by Employee Size

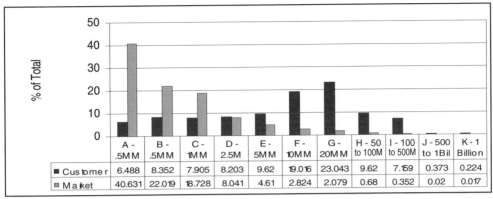

	A -.5MM	B -.5MM	C -1MM	D -2.5M	E -5MM	F -10MM	G -20MM	H - 50 to 100M	I - 100 to 500M	J - 500 to 1Bil	K - 1 Billion
■ Customer	6.488	8.352	7.905	8.203	9.62	19.016	23.043	9.62	7.159	0.373	0.224
▣ Market	40.631	22.019	18.728	8.041	4.61	2.824	2.079	0.68	0.352	0.02	0.017

Exhibit 9-6.3: Market Penetration by Annual Sales Volume

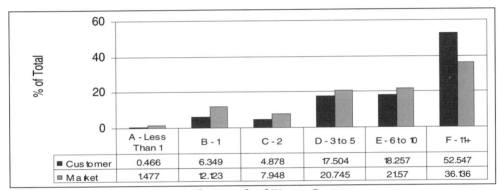

	A - Less Than 1	B - 1	C - 2	D - 3 to 5	E - 6 to 10	F - 11+
■ Customer	0.466	6.349	4.878	17.504	18.257	52.547
▣ Market	1.477	12.123	7.948	20.745	21.57	36.136

Exhibit 9-6.4: Market Penetration by Length-of-Time a Customer

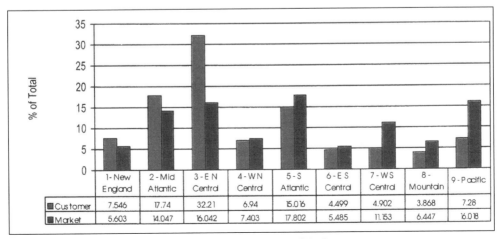

	1- New England	2 - Mid Atlantic	3 - E N Central	4 - W N Central	5 - S Atlantic	6 - E S Central	7 - W S Central	8 - Mountain	9 - Pacific
■ Customer	7.546	17.74	32.21	6.94	15.016	4.499	4.902	3.868	7.28
■ Market	5.603	14.047	16.042	7.403	17.802	5.485	11.153	6.447	16.018

Exhibit 9-6.5: Market Penetration by Census Geographic Area

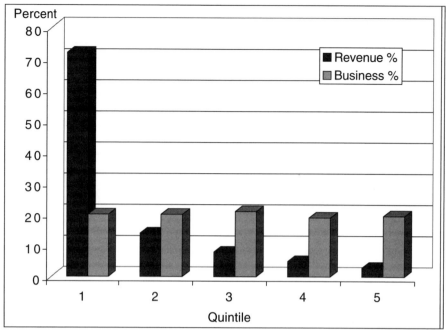

Exhibit 9-7: Distribution of Company X Customer Revenue within All Businesses

Business Cluster Penetration Analysis of Customers

An initial step in the profiling of the business-to-business customer database of Company X is determination of market penetration within the business clusters described in this chapter. Once these clusters are derived and associated with individual customers of Company X, revenues within clusters are indexed to the frequency distribution of all businesses within the clusters. Business Cluster Penetration Analysis then records the degree of cumulative marketing effectiveness in quintiles (20% groupings) of clusters. When rank-ordered differences are observed—as is distinctly apparent in this analysis—it remains to determine the reasons for such differences in terms of the economic, industry and social make-up of the clusters as well as the characteristics applicable to individual customers.

The purpose of such determination is to direct future customer acquisition and development of promotional efforts to those segments that have a high propensity for response or else to avoid expenditures to those segments that have a low probability for success. Such profiles can also help to position specific products and create advertising messages targeted to them.

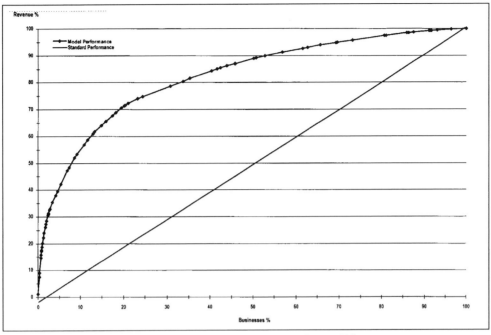

Exhibit 9-8: Lift in Market Penetration Resulting from the Model

Market penetration itself is arithmetically measured by dividing revenues (or customers) within a cluster by the total number of businesses in each such cluster or, similarly, dividing direct mail responses by the number of solicitation pieces mailed. Certain key statistics are thus derived, such as a Revenue/Businesses or Response/Mailings index (whose base is an overall mean of penetration) on which the clusters are then rank ordered, with subtotals at quintiles of all businesses.

A portrayal of business-to-business segmentation, indexing distribution of Company X revenue derived from the businesses in a cluster, grouped by quintiles of all businesses, is shown in Exhibit 9-7. A chart portraying the lift in penetration from the model is shown in Exhibit 9-8.

The detailed Company X Business Cluster Penetration Analysis, rank ordered by an index to average and grouped by quintiles of all businesses, is shown in Exhibit 9-9.

The ultimate need is to determine, through correlation of cluster penetration with the economic, industry, and social variables associated with these clusters, why penetration of the clusters at the top of the ranking are better than average so that we might find prospective customers most like these. To enable this, as example, detailed composition of the top three penetrated clusters (7023, 7020, 7018) is shown in Exhibit 9-10.

Quintile	Rank	Cluster	Revenue	Revenue %	Revenue Tot. %	Businesses	Businesses %	Businesses Tot. %	Revenue/ Business	Index	Index Total
1	1	7023	577,076	1.131	1.131	3,819	0.040	0.040	151.10657	2,829.08	2,829.08
	2	7020	3,259,459	6.386	7.516	25,791	0.270	0.310	126.37971	2,366.26	2,425.96
	3	7018	850,877	1.667	9.183	6,788	0.071	0.381	125.35018	2,347.09	2,411.25
	4	7034	2,826.14	5.537	14.72	26,105	0.273	0.654	108.26052	2,027.06	2,250.79
	5	7038	625,729	1.226	15.946	6,441	0.067	0.721	97.14780	1,819.11	2,210.46
	6	7026	603,270	1.182	17.128	6,683	0.070	0.791	90.26934	1,690.12	2,164.48
	7	7016	230,448	0.452	17.579	2,730	0.029	0.820	84.41319	1,580.88	2,144.15
	8	7032	618,725	1.212	18.791	9,83	0.103	0.923	62.94252	1,178.51	2,036.51
	9	7033	694,900	1.361	20.153	12,143	0.127	1.050	57.22639	1,071.55	1,19.720
	10	7028	1,041,039	2.039	22.192	18,537	0.194	1.244	56.16006	1,051.51	1,784.32
	11	7025	895,051	1.754	23.945	17,366	0.182	1.425	51.54042	965.05	1,679.89
	12	7027	1,089,695	2.135	26.08	22,535	0.236	1.661	48.35567	905.38	1,569.96
	13	7029	587,499	1.151	27.231	12,361	0.129	1.791	47.52844	889.90	1,520.83
	14	7031	568,928	1.115	28.346	14,908	0.156	1.947	38.16260	714.53	1,456.22
	15	7040	1,159,830	2.272	30.618	33,031	0.346	2.292	35.11338	657.45	1,335.78
	16	7015	164,757	0.323	30.941	5,380	0.056	2.348	30.62398	573.46	1,371.51
	17	7017	153,997	0.302	31.243	5,199	0.054	2.403	29.62050	554.60	1300.24
	18	7036	625,364	1.225	32,468	21,226	0.222	2.625	29.46217	551.62	1,236.90
	19	7024	231,015	0.453	32.92	8,897	0.093	2.718	25.96549	486.20	1,211.90
	20	7042	1,253,879	2.457	35.377	58,851	0.616	3.334	21.30599	398.93	1,061.16
	21	7041	1,326,645	2.599	37,976	72,599	0.760	4.093	18.27360	342.14	927.73
	22	7048	753,300	1.476	39,452	41,393	0.433	4.527	18.19873	340.75	871.57
	23	7047	1,360,250	2.665	42.116	76,763	0.803	5.330	17.72013	331.78	790.22
	24	7057	2,580,090	5.055	47.171	151,339	1.583	6.913	17.04841	319.21	682.33
	25	7054	631,179	1.236	48,407	40,157	0.420	7.333	15.71778	294.29	660.10
	26	7053	1,862,992	3.650	52.057	119,377	1.249	8.582		292.20	
	27	7045	657,579	1.288	53.346	56,824	0.595	9.177		216.68	
	28	7064	1,757,432	3.443	56,789	157,908	1.652	10.829		208.39	
	29	7056	923,715	1.810	58.598	84,035	0.879	11.708		205.81	
	30	7066	1,29,013	2.388	60.986	116,675	1.221	12.929		195.63	
	31	7051	325,123	0.637	61.623	37,498	0.392	13.322		162.33	

Exhibit 9-9.1: Business Cluster Penetration Analysis

Quintile	Rank	Cluster	Revenue	Revenue %	Revenue Tot. %	Businesses	Businesses %	Businesses Tot. %	Revenue/ Business	Index	Index Total
	32	7055	1,191,187	2.334	63.957	146,254	1.530	14.852		152.50	
	33	7061	837,138	1.640	65.597	103,086	1.079	15.931		152.05	
	34	7065	1,090,745	2.137	67.734	146,818	1.536	17.467		139.10	
	35	7044	545,931	1.069	68.803	73,759	0.772	18.238		138.58	
	36	7058	867,732	1.700	70.503	119,790	1.253	19.492		135.63	
	37	7052	419,736	0.822	71.325	62.781	0.657	20.149		125.07	
Quintile Totals: Observations: 37			36,407,106	71.325		1,925,677	21.149				
2	38	7037	166,474	0.326	71.651	25,073	0.262	20.411	6.63957	124.3	351.04
	39	7049	316,759	0.620	72.271	62,205	0.651	21.062	5.08929	95.29	343.14
	40	7063	894,273	1.752	74.023	211,104	2.209	23.271	4.23617	79.32	318.10
	41	7069	386,460	0.757	74.780	108,538	1.136	24.406	3.56050	66.67	306.40
	42	7076	2,001,854	3.922	78.702	597,382	6.251	30.657	3.35105	62.74	256.72
	43	7070	935,818	1.833	80.535	283,863	2.970	33.627	3.29672	61.72	239.50
	44	7068	516,556	1.012	81.547	159,200	1.666	35.293	3.24470	60.75	231.06
	45	5402	1,452,967	2.846	84.394	477,758	4.999	40.292	3.04122	56.94	209.46
Qunitle 2 Totals: Observations: 8			6,670,981	13.069		1,925,123	20.143		Mean: 3.46522		
3	46	7050	340,410	0.667	85.061	119,583	1.251	41.543	2.84664	53.3	204.75
	47	7060	219,903	0.431	85.492	85,563	0.895	42.438	2.57007	48.12	201.45
	48	5393	355,487	0.696	86.188	138,666	1.451	43.889	2.56362	48.00	196.38
	49	7062	433,467	0.849	87.037	170,687	1.786	45.675	2.53954	47.55	190.56
	50	7035	30,227	0.059	87.096	12,460	0.13	45.805	2.42592	45.41	190.14
	51	5404	925,517	1.1813	88.91	415,556	4.348	50.153	2.22718	177.28	
	52	7059	118,052	0.231	89.141	58,760	0.615	50.768	2.00905	175.58	
	53	7067	370,514	0.726	89.867	195,825	2.049	52.817	1.89207	170.15	
	54	6178	680,220	1.333	91.199	384,454	4.023	56.84	1.76931	160.45	
	55	7071	773,090	1.515	92.714	444,411	4.65	61.49	1.73958	150.78	
Quintile 3 Totals:Observations: 10			4,246,887	8.32		2,025,965	21.198		Mean: 2.09623		

Exhibit 9-9.1: Business Cluster Penetration Analysis (continued)

Quintile	Rank	Cluster	Revenue	Revenue %	Revenue Tot. %	Businesses	Businesses %	Businesses Tot. %	Revenue/ Business	Index	Index Total
4	56	5394	187,894	0.368	93.082	115,489	1.208	62.698	1.62758	30.48	148.46
	57	6174	434,302	0.851	93.933	280,856	2.939	65.637	1.54635	28.95	143.11
	58	7072	472,383	0.925	94.859	335,961	3.515	68.152	1.40606	26.33	137.17
	59	6162	53,568	0.105	94.963	40,723	0.426	69.578	1.31542	24.62	136.48
	60	7075	414,040	0.811	95.775	330,537	3.458	73.037	1.25263	23.45	131.13
	61	6180	885,405	1.735	97.509	718,406	7.517	80.553	1.23246	23.08	121.05
Quintile 4 Totals:Observations:	6		2,447,682	4.795		1,821,982	19.064		Mean:1.34342		
5	62	7039	34,608	0.068	97.577	37,850	0.396	80.949	0.91435	17.12	120.54
	63	7073	427,712	0.838	98.414	475,258	4.973	85.922	0.89996	16.85	114.54
	64	6147	39,551	0.077	98.492	44,552	0.466	86.388	0.88775	16.63	114.01
	65	6170	91,064	0.178	98.671	108,005	1.130	87.518	0.84315	15.79	112.74
	66	7074	270,733	0.530	99.201	336,845	3.524	91.043	0.80373	15.05	108.96
	67	5382	21,076	0.041	99.242	26,412	0.276	91.319	0.79797	14.94	108.68
	68	5388	19,951	0.039	99.281	26,405	0.276	91.595	0.75558	14.15	108.39
	69	6166	99,908	0.196	99.477	137,476	1.438	93.034	0.72673	13.61	106.93
	70	6181	157,864	0.309	99.787	318,921	3.337	96.371	0.49499	9.27	103.54
	71	6173	109,057	0.214	100	346,846	3.629	100.000	0.31442	5,89	100.00
Quintile 5 Totals:Observations:	10		1,271,524	2.491		1,858,570	19.447		Mean: 0.68414		
			51,044,180	100.000		9,557,317	100.000		Mean: 5.34085		

Exhibit 9-9.1: Business Cluster Penetration Analysis (continued)

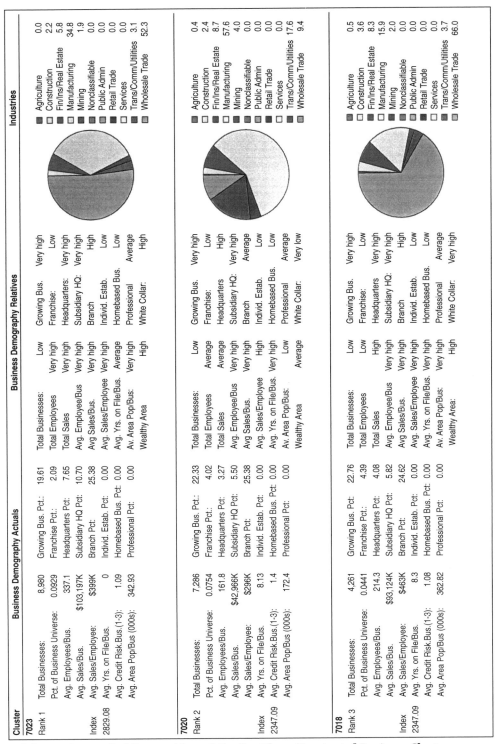

Cluster 7023 — Rank 1

Business Demography Actuals

Measure	Value	Measure	Value
Total Businesses:	8,980	Growing Bus. Pct.:	19.61
Pct. of Business Universe:	0.0929	Franchise Pct.:	0.0929
Avg. Employees/Bus.:	337.1	Headquarters Pct:	7.65
Avg. Sales/Bus.:	$103,197K	Subsidiary HQ Pct:	10.70
Avg. Sales/Employee:	$399K	Branch Pct:	25.38
Index 2829.08		Individ. Estab. Pct:	0.00
Avg. Yrs. on File/Bus.:	0	Homebased Bus. Pct:	0.00
Avg. Credit Risk.Bus.(1-3):	1.09	Professional Pct:	0.00
Avg. Area Pop/Bus (000s):	342.93		

Business Demography Relatives

Measure	Value	Measure	Value
Total Businesses:	Low	Growing Bus.:	Very high
Total Employees	Very high	Franchise:	Low
Total Sales	Very high	Headquarters:	Very high
Avg. Employee/Bus	Very high	Subsidiary HQ:	Very high
Avg Sales/Bus.	Very high	Branch	Very high
Avg. Sales/Employee	Very high	Individ. Estab.	Low
Avg. Yrs. on File/Bus.	Average	Homebased Bus.	Low
Av. Area Pop/Bus.:	Very high	Professional	Average
Wealthy Area	High	White Collar:	High

Industries

Industry	Pct
Agriculture	0.0
Construction	2.2
Fin/Ins/Real Estate	5.8
Manufacturing	34.8
Mining	1.9
Nonclassifiable	0.0
Public Admin	0.0
Retail Trade	0.0
Services	0.0
Trans/Comm/Utilities	3.1
Wholesale Trade	52.3

Cluster 7020 — Rank 2

Business Demography Actuals

Measure	Value	Measure	Value
Total Businesses:	7,286	Growing Bus. Pct.:	22.33
Pct. of Business Universe:	0.0754	Franchise Pct.:	0.0754
Avg. Employees/Bus.:	161.8	Headquarters Pct:	3.27
Avg. Sales/Bus.:	$42,966K	Subsidiary HQ Pct:	5.50
Avg. Sales/Employee:	$296K	Branch Pct:	25.38
Index 2347.09		Individ. Estab. Pct:	0.00
Avg. Yrs. on File/Bus.:	8.13	Homebased Bus. Pct:	0.00
Avg. Credit Risk.Bus.(1-3):	1.4	Professional Pct:	0.00
Avg. Area Pop/Bus (000s):	172.4		

Business Demography Relatives

Measure	Value	Measure	Value
Total Businesses:	Low	Growing Bus.:	Very high
Total Employees	Average	Franchise:	Low
Total Sales	Average	Headquarters	High
Avg. Employee/Bus	Very high	Subsidiary HQ:	Very high
Avg Sales/Bus.	Very high	Branch	Average
Avg. Sales/Employee	High	Individ. Estab.	Low
Avg. Yrs. on File/Bus.	Very high	Homebased Bus.	Low
Av. Area Pop/Bus.:	Low	Professional	Average
Wealthy Area	Average	White Collar:	Very low

Industries

Industry	Pct
Agriculture	0.4
Construction	2.4
Fin/Ins/Real Estate	8.7
Manufacturing	57.6
Mining	4.0
Nonclassifiable	0.0
Public Admin	0.0
Retail Trade	0.0
Services	0.0
Trans/Comm/Utilities	17.6
Wholesale Trade	9.4

Cluster 7018 — Rank 3

Business Demography Actuals

Measure	Value	Measure	Value
Total Businesses:	4,261	Growing Bus. Pct:	22.76
Pct. of Business Universe:	0.0441	Franchise Pct.:	0.0441
Avg. Employees/Bus.:	214.3	Headquarters Pct:	4.08
Avg. Sales/Bus.:	$93,124K	Subsidiary HQ Pct:	5.82
Avg. Sales/Employee:	$463K	Branch Pct:	24.62
Index 2347.09		Individ. Estab. Pct:	0.00
Avg. Yrs. on File/Bus.:	8.3	Homebased Bus. Pct:	0.00
Avg. Credit Risk.Bus.(1-3):	1.08	Professional Pct:	0.00
Avg. Area Pop/Bus (000s):	362.82		

Business Demography Relatives

Measure	Value	Measure	Value
Total Businesses:	Low	Growing Bus.:	Very high
Total Employees	Low	Franchise:	Low
Total Sales	High	Headquarters	Very high
Avg. Employee/Bus	Very high	Subsidiary HQ:	Very high
Avg Sales/Bus.	Very high	Branch	Low
Avg. Sales/Employee	High	Individ. Estab.	Low
Avg. Yrs. on File/Bus.	Very high	Homebased Bus.	Low
Av. Area Pop/Bus.:	Very high	Professional	Average
Wealthy Area:	High	White Collar:	Very high

Industries

Industry	Pct
Agriculture	0.5
Construction	3.6
Fin/Ins/Real Estate	8.3
Manufacturing	15.9
Mining	2.0
Nonclassifiable	0.0
Public Admin	0.0
Retail Trade	0.0
Services	0.0
Trans/Comm/Utilities	3.7
Wholesale Trade	66.0

Exhibit 9-10: Detailed Composition of the Top Three Penetrated Business Clusters

Item Name	Item Description	Description	Customer		National		Index
			Total	Percent	Total	Percent	
Credit rating	The credit risk score of the company. Indicates risk of delinquency	Very good	5,969	15.515	560,057	6.478	239.5
		Good	11,518	29.938	1,858,936	21.503	139.2
		Satisfactory	8,376	21.771	3,506,046	40.555	53.7
		Unknown	2,835	7.369	2,275,454	26.321	28
		Professional	817	2.124	444,602	5.143	41.3
		Institutional/Government	8,958	23.284	1,145,864	13.254	175.7
		Non-Matches		0.000		0.000	
Population code	The size of the city in which the business resides	1-24,999	17,486	45.450	4,282,167	44.559	102
		25,000-49,999	4,901	12.739	1,213,074	12.390	102.8
		50,000-99,999	4,378	11.379	1,031,555	10.536	108
		100,000-249,999	4,320	11.229	1,032,006	10.540	106.5
		250,000-499,999	2,188	5.687	776,940	7.935	71.7
		500,000+	5,200	13.516	1,455,217	14.863	90.9
		Unknown/Non-Matches		0.000		0.000	
Wealth code	The company's Wealth Area status	Wealthy	25,903	67.328	6,859,857	70.063	96.1
		Non-wealthy/Non-Matches	12,570	32.672	2,931,102	29.937	109.1
White collar	Indicates a company with greater than 50% white collar employees	White collar	9,426	24.500	3,431,296	35.046	69.9
		Non-white collar/Non-Matches	29,047	75.500	6,359,663	64.954	116.2
Growing company	Indicates a company with > 10% increase in employment for companies with 3+ employees	Growing companies	35,672	92.720	9,478,426	96.808	95.8
		Non-Growing/Non-Matches	2,801	7.280	312,533	3.192	228.1
Work at Home code	Indicates a home business	Home business	37,181	96.642	8,882,903	90.726	106.5
		Non-home business/Non-Matches	1,292	3.358	908,056	9.274	36.2

Exhibit 9-11: Business Customer Profile Examples with Characteristics Indexed to U.S. Average

The business customers of Company X can also be profiled on a variety of other dimensions: employee size, sales volume, years on file, headquarters/branch, individual/firm, public/private, franchise, standard industrial classification, census division, street type, credit rating, state where located, population of location, wealth code, white collar/non-white collar, growing company, work at home enterprises, extent of telephone book advertising. Examples of such profiling are shown in Exhibit 9-11.

Interactive Workshop 9-2:

Building a Business-to-Business Customer Profile

(For demonstration, go to the CD-ROM accompanying this book.)

- Explain the rationale of business clusters and suggest why these offer greater opportunities for B2B market segmentation than do the traditional techniques.

- How does business-to-business buying differ from consumer purchase and why might the consumer lifestyles of B2B buyers impact on their business-to-business purchase?

- Why do businesses selling to other businesses need to know the demographics and lifestyles, as well as the site locations, of the ultimate customers of the intermediaries?

- With reference to Exhibit 9-6, what can you say about the business customers of Company X relative to their standard industrial classifications, sales volumes and census areas?

- From the CD-ROM, extract the descriptions of those business clusters comprising the top quintile of market penetration. From this, how would you define Company X's top market segments? How will this information aid you in prospecting for new customers?

- Do the same thing for the business clusters comprising the bottom quintile of market penetrations. What implication does this have for prospecting?

Chapter 10

Structuring and Evaluating an Experiment

Key Concepts
- Experimental Designs
- Sample Types:
    Simple Random
    Systematic Random
    Stratified Random
    Cluster
    Replicated
    Sequential
- Sampling Error
- Sample Size
- Measuring Difference

Applications
- Developing A Priori Assumptions and Computing Sample Size
- Structuring and Performing Tests
- Developing A Posteriori Analysis and Testing Validity
- Identifying Optimum Decisions

The purpose of an experiment, or test, is to manipulate (change) an independent variable (over which the marketer has control) to see the effect of the change on a dependent variable (over which the marketer has no direct control but has a strong interest in). Examples of independent variables (also called factors) include a product's features, a product's price, copy, layout, and nature of an offer, etc. Examples of dependent variables include the rate of response to an offer, the cumulative penetration of a market segment, reactions to a product, the overall rating of a brand preference, etc.

Theoretically, anything can be tested in a direct marketing context, but only important variables—products, offers, media, formats, and timing—should be tested. Mail-order marketers of an earlier time tested many relatively insignificant factors, such as the color of ink used for a letter's signature or the type of covering used on a window envelope. Testing should be limited to factors that affect the bottom line.

In order to have a claim to validity and reliability, an experiment must adhere to established standards of *control, randomization,* and *sampling.* Valid experiments are characterized by:

1. The presence of a *control* group, along with one or more test groups on which an experiment is not conducted but which is otherwise identical to the test groups.

2. *Random* assignment of subjects to groups so that differences in composition between the control and test groups occur by chance alone.

3. A *sample* that is of an adequate size and drawn from a population so that the results of the test, when known, will be statistically valid at a confidence level and an error limit that are acceptable to the researcher.

The mathematician Blaisé Pascal demonstrated the importance of control in 1648 when he hypothesized that atmospheric pressure declined with increasing altitude. Pascal took two barometric readings: the first in his village; the second, a short time later, from the top of a 3,000-foot peak. The second observation did indeed show significantly lower atmospheric pressure. What Pascal did not know, however, was whether the atmospheric pressure had become lower at the bottom as well as the top of the mountain during the time that it took to climb.

Pascal changed his experimental design to eliminate this alternative interpretation. He calibrated two barometers before he began his trek up the mountain. At the precise time he read the barometer at the top of the mountain, another villager read the control barometer at the bottom. His comparison, now with a control, showed that although both barometers had lower readings at the end of the time it took him to climb the mountain; the barometer he carried to the top had a significantly lower reading.

An experiment without control is frequently invalid. A beer distributor hypothesized that an increasing level of advertising spending (the independent variable) would result in increased sales (the dependent variable). Over a 13-week period, the distributor increased the amount of advertising each week. Sure enough, sales increased each week. Overlooked, however, was the simultaneous increase in heat and humidity during the three summer months of the experiment. The distributor's control should have been a measurement of the sales trend without an increase in advertising during the same 13-week span in a comparable market with similar climate.

The effect of a marketing experiment is often expressed as the difference between the observation of the dependent variable of the test group—for example, response rate—after the subjects received an experimental treatment (an offer with a price change) and the observation of the dependent variable of the control group, which did not receive the experimental treatment (an offer with no price change). The control group generally is hard to beat because it usually represents the cumulative "best" that an organization knows how to do at any point in time. That is why, as the search for something better continues, 8 out of 10 trials will likely not beat the control.

In a well-designed experiment, one has complete control over what is tested and the manner in which the experiment is conducted. But neither the marketplace nor human behavior can be controlled completely. Seasonality may affect sales; human behavior may be inconsistent. And the actual level of response to an experiment, even when meticulously controlled, may not always be projectable into an unknown future environment. For example, the environment in which the experiment is conducted may not precisely compare with the environment of the continuation effort. Economic conditions or consumer optimism may change. Competition may heat up due to new models and innovations. Such uncontrollable factors may affect the test so that, while the relative relationship between a test and its control may be the same, the absolute levels of response for both may be higher or lower.

Experimental Designs

A series of notations has evolved to describe the design of statistically designed experiments. D.T. Campbell and J.C. Stanley originally presented those designs shown in Exhibit 10-1. Listed are the basic experimental designs, together with a key to the notations they used to describe them.

Campbell and Stanley assigned the term *pre-experiment* to designs in which there was no randomly assigned control group, and measurement did not go beyond that observed after the experiment or that derived from pre-measurement as well as post-measurement, but without a valid comparison. The first three designs in Exhibit 10-1—One-Shot Study Case, Pre-Measurement and Post-Measurement, and Static Group Comparison—are designated as pre-experiments because they have neither

X = an experimental manipulation of an independent variable
O = an observation of a dependent variable
b = observation before manipulation
a = observation after manipulation
R = random assignment to group
P = pairings
S = matched pairings
———— = groups equated randomly
- - - - - = groups not equated randomly

Name of Design	Form of Design				Comment	
One-Shot Study Case	X	O_a			No control	
Pre-Measurement and Post-Measurement	O_b	X	O_a		No control	
Static Group Comparison	X	O_a			No control; groups not	
		O_a			randomly equated	
Simple Randomization	R	X	O_a		Experimental group	
	R	—	O_a		Control group	
Random Matched Subjects	O_b	P	X	O_a	Experimental group	
(Determined after O)	O_b	P	-	O_a	Control group	
Single Group Control	S	X_1	O_a		Same individual —	
(Successive trials)	S	X_2	O_a		usually impossible	
Single Group Control	R I S_1	X_1	—	$O1_a$	Experimental group #1	
(Simultaneous trials)	I S_1	—	X_2	$O2_a$	Experimental group #2	
	R I S_2	X_2	—	$O3_a$	Experimental group #3	
	I S_2	—	X_1	$O4_a$	Control group	
Randomized Pre-Test	R	O_b	X	O_a	Experimental group	
and Post-Test	R	O_b	—	O_a	Control group	
Solomon Four-Group	R	$O1_b$	X	$O1_a$	Experimental group	
	R	$O2_b$	—	$O2_a$	Control group #1	
	R	—	X	$O3_a$	Control group #2	
	R	—	—	$O4_a$	Control group #3	

Exhibit 10-1: Experimental Designs for Structuring Tests

control nor randomization enabling comparative measurement. The Static Group Comparison injects a control but is not equated randomly.

Direct marketers most frequently use the Simple Randomization design shown in Exhibit 10-1, to structure and evaluate tests. The design injects control as well as randomization into the test. However, as demonstrated in the following section on designing a random sample, test and control groups are more likely to be systematic random samples rather than simple random samples. After drawing such a sample from a database, the control and test groups typically are "every other" or "every nth" name, when two or more test groups are paired with a single control.

The effect of the experiment is the difference between the observation of the dependent variable (for example, response rate) after the experimental treatment and the observation of the dependent variable of the control group, which did not receive the experimental treatment.

At this juncture, it is important to reemphasize that even a well-designed and statistically sound experiment randomized with control does not guarantee that the composition of the two groups is identical. Differences arising by chance alone may be substantial.

One method of obtaining groups that are better matched involves selecting subjects in pairs in a pretest after observation. This is the Randomized Matched Subjects design in Exhibit 10-1. This experimental design helps minimize potential differences between the chosen groups.

Even the pairing of randomized matched subjects, however, does not guarantee that the two resultant groups will be identical. If each subject served as its own control during successive treatments, as shown in the Single Group Control (successive treatments) design, that would be ideal. Of course, this is usually impossible because the first treatment results in a residual influence on the subsequent treatment.

An improvement is the Single Group Control (simultaneous treatments) design, which involves simultaneous, rather than successive, treatments on randomized matched pairs. However, even single group control with simultaneous treatments is virtually impossible.

The advantage of matched pairs without actual matching is shown in the Randomized Pre-Test and Post-Test design in Exhibit 10-1. Here, there is observation of the randomized groups before and after the experiment. Researchers who like to doublecheck their test results favor this design.

The final experimental design, Solomon Four-Group, combines elements of the two designs most relevant for marketing tests: Simple (or Systematic) Randomization and Randomized Pre-Test and Post-Test, with the injection of more than one control group.

Note that in all of the designs considered so far, the focus is on changing one independent variable (factor) and observing its effect on a dependent variable. Direct marketers most commonly use these designs, referred to as single factor designs—perhaps because these are easy to administer and allow the marketer to unambiguously ascertain the effect of one change in the mailing piece or offer on the desired dependent variable. Direct marketers often have several things to test (such as the copy, the price, etc.) and employ a sequential testing approach changing one factor at a time. However, sometimes there are good reasons to consider more advanced designs (such as factorial designs), where multiple independent variables can be changed simultaneously and their effects on a dependent variable can be assessed. An example of a factorial design is illustrated in Interactive Workshop 10-4.

Designing a Random Sample

Sampling is a method of choosing a subset of members from a population such that the results from the sample can be projected with a certain degree of statistical confidence to all the members of the population. Without proper sampling, the resultant prediction will be invalid. Thus, marketers must know the major means of selecting samples of potential respondents from a population, a database, or a list. At a minimum, the marketer should be able to draw adequate samples from a population and to compute sample sizes, variances, and confidence levels. It is also helpful to be familiar with the key terms shown in Exhibit 10-2, as well as topics discussed in Chapter 5.

Ideally, marketers want to ensure that test and control groups are as nearly alike in makeup as possible such that any differences between the two should be attributable to a chance factor alone. These are the major ways to obtain such samples:

- **Simple Random Sample:** Using preprinted tables or computer-generated random numbers assures the equality of probability of sample selection. Each consecutive selection is made randomly from a population from which the preceding selection is removed. Statisticians call this "drawing without replacement."

- **Systematic Random Sample:** Starting with a random number, every nth name is selected in the proportion that the desired sample represents of the total population. This is technically not a pure random sample but, because of its convenience, is the sampling method most often used.

- **Stratified Random Sample:** The names in this selection are drawn in proportion to a particular parameter of a population; i.e., a distribution of the sample by age is proportioned to the known distribution of the population.

- **Cluster Sample:** Area clusters are picked at random and the entire cluster is selected; i.e., the entire ZIP Code is an nth selection of all

Accuracy - The difference between the sample statistic and the actual population parameter.

Bias - Methodical error occurring in the selection of respondents or measurement; a difference between expected value of a statistic and the population parameter.

Population or Universe or Sampling Frame - The total domain or group of items being considered.

Random Event - An occurrence that has several possible values and occurs with some definable frequency if many repetitions are undertaken.

Reliability - Standard error of a statistic; its precision.

Sampling Error - The difference between sample result and the population parameter (which most often is unknown). Sampling error declines as the sample size increases, assuming an unbiased sampling procedure.

Sampling Method - Means of drawing sample from population.

Simple Random Sample - Every possible sample of equal size has an even probability of selection.

Valid - A statistic without bias.

Exhibit 10-2: Sampling Terminology

ZIP Codes. This technique is convenient when responses are to be followed up in person to minimize travel time.

■ **Replicated Sample:** Several independent random samples are drawn, such as first choosing a stratum from among all 50 of the United States; then choosing a stratum of census tracts within counties of those states. A variation would be selections over periods of time.

■ **Sequential Sample:** Projection is evolved from progressive data; i.e., selection is based on prior predictions. This is the manner in which television news teams project outcomes of political elections.

It is possible that the arrangement of a list from which a sample is to be drawn could itself bias the selection. Sequencing of a list alphabetically by surname, for example, could result in ethnic concentrations within certain initial letters. A similar problem could occur when a list is arranged geographically (such as urban/rural) so that location differences are concentrated. Lists arranged in ZIP Code sequence allow nth name selection without undue bias.

Sampling error can occur when not everyone in the population of interest is available for selection. Names drawn from a telephone directory compilation that includes neither households without telephones nor unlisted numbers are not representative of a total population. Sampling error might also occur if a sample includes nonprospects; for example, obtaining a sample from a database that includes apartment dwellers to test a lawn furniture offer. Nonresponse error occurs when an individual is included in the sample but, for one reason or another, is not reached or else refuses to respond.

How to Determine the Size of the Sample

Sample size is influenced by two major considerations:

1. The cost involved in reaching the sample

2. The need for enough responses to be able to predict response within a comfortable limit of uncertainty.

The size of a sample can be determined by a judgment call, but the scientific basis for sample-size determination is found in probability theory. Using the Law of Large Numbers described in Chapter 5, it is possible to calculate the desired sample size based on the researcher's preference for confidence level, limit of error, and expected response rate.

The formulas for calculating sample size and error limit are in Interactive Workshop 10-2. These can be useful when determining a proper sample size or error limit for response rates beyond the limits of the table or for confidence levels other than 95 percent and 99 percent.

Fortunately, it is not necessary to perform cumbersome calculations to determine optimum sample size. The tables shown in Interactive Workshop 10-2 provide, with 95 percent and 99 percent levels of confidence, the sample-size requirements at various levels of response, within acceptable limits of error.

Interactive Workshop 10-1:

Setting Up an Experiment

(For demonstration, go to the CD-Rom accompanying this book.)

Assume that an organization wants to test a new promotion versus its present promotion, which will be offered to the control group in the experiment. Experience indicates that a 2 percent response rate can be expected from the present promotion.

Here is the framework for implementation of the experiment:

1. State the hypothesis

2. Develop *a priori* assumptions; compute sample size

3. Structure and perform the test experiment

4. Develop a posteriori statistics; judge test validity

5. Make the decision

State the Hypothesis

In testing a hypothesis, the researcher is deciding whether an assumption, stated in advance of an experiment, is valid. The logic of hypothesis testing and the related terms were covered in much greater details in Chapter 5. A review of those concepts will be helpful to appreciate the following discussion. In testing response to the new direct-mail promotion offer (test promotion) compared to the promotion currently employed (control promotion), the null (H_0) and the alternative (H_a) hypotheses can be stated as:

- H_0: Direct-mail response from the test promotion is equal to or less than direct-mail response from the control promotion.
- H_a: Direct-mail response from the test promotion is more than direct-mail response from the control promotion.

Develop *A Priori* Assumptions and Compute Sample Size

A response rate of 2 percent from the control group is the first of three assumptions made prior to the experiment.

The second assumption is about significance or the α-level for testing the null-hypothesis as discussed in Chapter 5. This α-level has to be decided prior to testing the hypothesis. If $\alpha = 0.05$ is chosen, it means that the marketer is asking for 95 percent confidence in test results. In

Expected (Assumed) Response Rate: 2%, 20/M pieces mailed.

Significance Level (α): 0.05

Confidence Level $(1.0 - \alpha) * 100\%$: 95%

Limits of Error:

Percent	Response/M Pieces Mailed
+15%	20/M + 3/M = 23/M (2.3%)
−15%	20/M − 3/M = 17/M (1.7%)

Sample Size: 8,365 Pieces to be mailed

Exhibit 10-3: A Priori Assumptions and Sample Size Determination

other words, the test result must diverge far enough from the control result, so that such a result could occur with a probability of 0.05 or less if the hypothesis were true. Or 95 times out of 100 the test result could be expected to be better, within limits, than the control results. As you would expect, smaller values (or higher confidence) will increase the sample size requirement, i.e., increase the cost of the test.

The third assumption relates to the limit of error or the acceptable variance around the mean, i.e., the predicted response rate. Acceptable variance is here assumed to be 15 percent. This is a number that has to be chosen by the marketer based on his preference. The trade-off is that a lower error limit will require a larger sample size, i.e., increase the cost of testing.

Having established these three assumptions, one can either access the 95 percent confidence table or use the formula given in Interactive Workshop 10-2 to calculate the required sample size. Assumptions and resulting sample size determination are summarized in Exhibit 10-3. This shows that if a randomly drawn group of 8,365 were mailed an offer expected to generate 2 percent response, then 95 times out of 100 the response rate would fall in the range of 2% ± 15% of 2%. A response rate below 2.3 percent or above 1.7 percent would be considered the "same as" 2 percent.

Structure and Perform the Test

Having determined a sample size of 8,365 pieces to be mailed for the test promotion and a comparable group for the control promotion, the next step is to draw the two groups from a database that contains 170,000 prospects. Since 8,365 times two equals about 17,000, 10% of the total list of 170,000 is drawn. A random number between 1 and 10 (say 8) is chosen. Starting with the 8th name in the list, every 10th name is selected: 8, 18, 28, 38, and so on. As names are drawn, they are alternately assigned to the test and to the control groups.

When the promotion is ready, both the test group and the control group are mailed simultaneously. Use a promotion scheduling form to assure proper database selection and mailing and to evaluate test results. Instructions should include:

- A general description of the test and its purpose

- Special production and fulfillment instructions

- Database and/or segment(s) mailed

- Print, broadcast, or electronic media components

- Product and offer

- Distribution date

- Sample sizes and how drawn

- Control and test costs

- Responses expected or required for break-even

- Prior tests (if any)

- Key coding

- Considerations pertinent to evaluation of the analysis

Develop *A Posteriori* Analysis and Test Validity

When results of the experiment are final, or at some statistically projectable point, the response rates from both the test and control groups are evaluated. One evaluation procedure for determining if an observed difference is or is not *statistically significant* is an independent sample t-test (covered in detail in Chapter 5). It is computed from the observed results and computer programs typically produce a two-sided p-value for the t-test as explained in the earlier chapter. For this example, the two-sided p-value has to be converted (using the conversion rule) to one-sided p-value because the alternative hypothesis is one-sided.

A posteriori analysis is essential in that it faces the rigors of statistics and the tests of significance. But results cannot adequately be analyzed unless there is a record of these results for all segments of the experiment.

Tracking is facilitated by the use of a *key code* on each response device. Response received by mail can be tracked through a code on the order form. The source of telephone orders can be identified if trained communicators ask for the source identification key code printed on the label of a catalog or other mailed promotion. Broadcast promotion responses can be coded to a unique 800-telephone number, possibly even cross-referenced to a ZIP code for geographic location. Or telephone respondents can ask to speak to a department or an individual.

Make the Decision

Finally, one makes a decision to accept or to reject the test promotion. While there can be subjective considerations-relative costs, repetitiveness of an offer, suitability—the decision must be an objective one, not influenced by personal preferences, author of the copy, or even a higher authority.

Statistically, the decision is taken to reject the null hypothesis if the p-value is less than the pre-specified α-level. Of course, rejecting the null hypothesis means accepting that the test promotion produced a better result than the control. It is a good practice to do a back test if a test beats the control (i.e., null hypothesis is rejected). That is, because the control represents the cumulative knowledge of the organization, before throwing it out based on only one experiment, marketers often to do a follow-up experiment with the same test and control offers using a different sample. If the results from the second experiment corroborate the result from the first experiment, the marketer has more justification in accepting the test offer as the new control offer.

Interactive Workshop 10-2:
Calculating Sample Size and Limit of Error

(For demonstration, go to the CD-ROM accompanying this book.)

The size of a sample drawn from a population (database)—e.g., the number of observations in an experiment or test—needs to be carefully calculated in order to assure the validity of the results. Sample sizes can be established by referring to the charts or by following the formula in this workshop.

Let's first define the four terms—confidence level (z-value), limit of error, expected (or actual) response rate, and sample size—that enter into the calculation:

- **Confidence Level (z-value):** This is the value from a normal distribution that corresponds to the chosen confidence level. For example, the 90%, 95%, 99% confidence levels correspond to z-values of 1.65, 1.96, 2.58 respectively.

■ **Limit of Error:** The number of percentage points by which the researcher is allowed to miscalculate the actual response rate. A 20 percent limit of error, assuming a 1 percent response rate, for example, could result in a range of actual response as low as 0.8 percent to as high as 1.2 percent; or $1\% \pm 20\%$ of 1%.

■ **Expected (Actual) Response Rate:** The number of times, in percentage, that a response has or is expected to occur.

■ **Sample Size:** The number of observations in the experiment, or test. This is, for example, the number of pieces mailed in a test from which the response is to be determined.

The formula for determining sample size is:

$$N = \frac{(R)\,(1-R)\,(Z)^2}{E^2} \qquad \text{where:}$$

R is the frequency of response, the response rate, a percentage expressed as a decimal

$1-R$ is the frequency of nonresponse, also a percentage expressed as a decimal

Z is the number from a standard normal distribution that corresponds to the confidence level chosen by the researcher

E is the limit of error expressed as a decimal; and

N is the sample size, the number of pieces to be mailed

To illustrate the use of the above formula, one can determine the sample size required to be mailed as a test when the expected response rate is 1%; the desired limit of error is $\pm 0.2\%$; at a confidence level of 95%. Thus:

$$
\begin{aligned}
R &= 1\% \dots 0.01, \text{ expressed as a decimal} \\
1-R &= 99\% \dots 0.99, \text{ expressed as a decimal} \\
Z &= 1.96, \text{ corresponding to a 95\% confidence level} \\
E &= 0.2\% \dots 0.002, \text{ expressed as a decimal} \\
N &= \text{to be determined}
\end{aligned}
$$

Substituting the above values into the formula for the determination of sample size, provides this solution:

$$N = \frac{(0.01)\,(0.99)\,(1.96)^2}{(0.002)^2}$$

R   LIMITS OF ERROR (EXPRESSED AS PERCENTAGE POINTS)

(Response)	.02	.04	.06	.08	.10	.12	.14	.16	.18	.20	.30	.40	.50	.60	.70
.1	95,929	23,982	10,659	5,995	3,837	2,665	1,957	1,499	1,184	959	426	240	153	106	78
.2	191,666	47,916	21,296	11,979	7,667	5,324	3,911	2,994	2,366	1,917	852	479	307	213	156
.3	287,211	71,803	31,912	17,951	11,488	7,978	5,861	4,487	3,546	2,872	1,276	718	459	319	234
.4	382,564	95,641	42,507	23,910	15,303	10,627	7,807	5,977	4,723	3,826	1,700	956	612	425	312
.5	477,724	119,431	53,080	29,858	19,109	13,270	9,749	7,464	5,987	4,777	2,123	1,194	764	530	390
.6	572,693	143,173	63,632	35,793	22,908	15,908	11,687	8,948	7,070	5,727	2,545	1,432	916	636	467
.7	667,470	166,867	74,163	41,717	26,699	18,541	13,622	10,429	8,240	6,675	2,966	1,669	1,068	741	545
.8	762,054	190,514	84,673	47,628	30,482	21,168	15,552	11,907	9,408	7,621	3,387	1,905	1,219	847	622
.9	856,447	214,112	95,160	53,528	34,258	23,790	17,478	13,382	10,573	8,564	3,806	2,141	1,370	951	699
1.0	950,648	237,662	105,628	59,415	38,026	26,407	19,401	14,854	11,736	9,506	4,225	2,376	1,521	1,056	776
1.1	1,044,656	261,164	116,072	65,291	41,786	29,018	21,319	16,322	12,897	10,446	4,643	2,611	1,671	1,160	853
1.2	1,138,472	284,618	126,496	71,155	45,539	31,624	23,234	17,788	14,055	11,385	5,060	2,846	1,821	1,265	929
1.3	1,232,097	308,024	136,899	77,006	49,284	34,225	25,145	19,251	15,211	12,321	5,476	3,080	1,971	1,369	1,006
1.4	1,325,529	331,382	147,280	82,845	53,021	36,820	27,051	20,711	16,364	13,255	5,891	3,314	2,121	1,473	1,082
1.5	1,418,769	354,692	157,640	88,673	56,751	39,410	28,954	22,168	17,515	14,188	6,305	3,547	2,270	1,576	1,158
1.6	1,511,818	377,954	167,980	94,489	60,473	41,995	30,853	23,622	18,664	15,118	6,719	3,780	2,419	1,680	1,234
1.7	1,604,674	401,168	178,297	100,292	64,187	44,574	32,748	25,073	19,811	16,047	7,132	4,012	2,567	1,783	1,310
1.8	1,697,338	424,334	188,592	106,083	67,894	47,148	34,639	26,521	20,955	16,973	7,543	4,243	2,716	1,886	1,385
1.9	1,789,810	447,452	198,868	111,863	71,592	49,717	36,526	27,966	22,096	17,898	7,955	4,474	2,863	1,988	1,461
2.0	1,882,090	470,523	209,121	117,631	75,284	52,280	38,410	29,407	23,235	18,821	8,365	4,705	3,011	2,091	1,536
2.1	1,974,178	493,544	219,352	123,386	78,967	54,838	40,289	30,846	24,372	19,742	8,774	4,935	3,158	2,193	1,611
2.2	2,066,074	516,518	229,564	129,129	82,643	57,391	42,165	32,282	25,507	20,661	9,182	5,165	3,306	2,295	1,686
2.3	2,157,778	539,444	239,753	134,861	86,311	59,938	44,036	33,715	26,638	21,578	9,590	5,394	3,452	2,397	1,761
2.4	2,249,290	562,322	249,920	140,581	89,972	62,480	45,903	35,145	27,769	22,493	9,997	5,623	3,599	2,499	1,836
2.5	2,340,609	585,152	260,068	146,288	93,624	65,017	47,767	36,572	28,896	23,406	10,403	5,851	3,745	2,600	1,911
2.6	2,431,737	607,934	270,192	151,983	97,269	67,547	49,627	37,996	30,021	24,317	10,807	6,079	3,891	2,702	1,985
2.7	2,522,673	630,668	280,296	157,667	100,907	70,074	51,483	39,416	31,144	25,227	11,211	6,307	4,036	2,803	2,059
2.8	2,613,416	653,354	290,380	163,339	104,537	72,595	53,335	40,834	32,264	26,134	11,615	6,534	4,181	2,904	2,133
2.9	2,703,968	675,992	300,440	168,998	108,159	75,110	55,183	42,249	33,382	27,039	12,017	6,760	4,326	3,004	2,207
3.0	2,794,328	698,582	310,480	174,645	111,773	77,620	57,026	43,661	34,497	27,943	12,419	6,986	4,471	3,105	2,281
3.1	2,884,495	721,124	320,499	180,281	115,380	80,125	58,867	45,070	35,611	28,845	12,820	7,211	4,615	3,205	2,355
3.2	2,974,470	743,618	330,496	185,904	118,979	82,623	60,702	46,476	36,721	29,745	13,220	7,436	4,759	3,305	2,428
3.3	3,064,254	766,063	340,471	191,516	122,570	85,118	62,535	47,878	37,830	30,642	13,619	7,660	4,903	3,404	2,501
3.4	3,153,845	788,461	350,427	197,115	126,154	87,607	64,364	49,278	38,936	31,538	14,017	7,884	5,046	3,504	2,574
3.5	3,243,244	810,811	360,360	202,703	129,730	90,089	66,188	50,675	40,040	32,432	14,414	8,108	5,189	3,603	2,647
3.6	3,332,452	833,113	370,271	208,278	133,298	92,568	68,009	52,069	41,141	33,325	14,811	8,331	5,332	3,702	2,720
3.7	3,421,467	855,367	380,163	213,842	136,859	95,041	69,825	53,460	42,240	34,214	15,207	8,554	5,474	3,801	2,793
3.8	3,510,290	877,572	390,031	219,398	140,412	97,507	71,638	54,848	43,336	35,103	15,601	8,776	5,616	3,900	2,865
3.9	3,598,921	899,730	399,878	224,932	143,957	99,969	73,446	56,233	44,430	35,989	15,995	8,997	5,758	3,998	2,938
4.0	3,687,360	921,840	409,706	230,460	147,494	102,426	75,252	57,615	45,522	36,874	16,388	9,218	5,900	4,097	3,010

Exhibit 10-4: Sample Sizes for Response Rates Between 0.1% and 4.0%.
        Confidence Level of 95%

LIMITS OF ERROR (EXPRESSED AS PERCENTAGE POINTS)

R (Response)	.02	.04	.06	.08	.10	.12	.14	.16	.18	.20	.30	.40	.50	.60	.70
.1	165,709	41,427	18,412	10,357	6,628	4,603	3,381	2,589	2,046	1,657	736	414	265	184	135
.2	331,087	82,772	36,787	20,693	13,243	9,197	6,756	5,173	4,087	3,311	1,471	827	529	368	270
.3	496,132	124,033	55,126	31,008	19,845	13,781	10,125	7,752	6,125	4,961	2,205	1,240	794	551	405
.4	660,846	165,212	73,427	41,303	26,434	18,356	13,486	10,325	8,158	6,608	2,937	1,652	1,057	734	539
.5	825,228	206,307	91,692	51,577	33,009	22,923	16,841	12,894	10,187	8,252	3,667	2,063	1,320	916	673
.6	989,279	247,320	109,919	61,380	39,571	27,480	20,189	15,457	12,213	9,893	4,396	2,473	1,582	1,099	807
.7	1,152,997	288,249	128,111	72,062	46,120	32,027	23,530	18,015	14,234	11,530	5,124	2,882	1,845	1,281	941
.8	1,316,384	329,096	146,265	82,274	52,655	36,565	26,864	20,569	16,251	13,164	5,850	3,291	2,106	1,462	1,074
.9	1,479,439	369,859	164,381	92,465	59,178	41,095	30,192	23,116	18,264	14,794	6,575	3,698	2,367	1,643	1,208
1.0	1,642,163	410,541	182,463	102,635	65,687	45,616	33,513	25,658	20,273	16,422	7,299	4,105	2,627	1,825	1,340
1.1	1,804,554	451,138	200,505	112,784	72,182	50,126	36,827	28,195	22,278	18,045	8,020	4,511	2,887	2,004	1,473
1.2	1,966,614	491,654	218,512	122,913	78,845	54,628	40,134	30,728	24,279	19,666	8,740	4,917	3,146	2,185	1,605
1.3	2,128,342	532,085	236,482	133,021	85,134	59,121	43,435	33,255	26,275	21,283	9,459	5,321	3,405	2,365	1,737
1.4	2,289,739	572,435	254,414	143,108	91,590	63,603	46,729	35,777	28,268	22,897	10,176	5,724	3,663	2,544	1,869
1.5	2,450,803	612,700	272,310	153,175	98,032	68,077	50,016	38,293	30,256	24,508	10,892	6,127	3,921	2,723	2,000
1.6	2,611,536	652,884	290,170	163,221	104,461	72,542	53,296	40,805	32,241	26,115	11,607	6,529	4,178	2,901	2,132
1.7	2,771,937	692,984	307,992	173,246	110,877	76,997	56,569	43,311	34,221	27,719	12,319	6,930	4,435	3,079	2,263
1.8	2,932,007	733,002	325,777	183,250	117,280	81,444	59,836	45,812	36,197	29,320	13,030	7,330	4,691	3,257	2,393
1.9	3,091,744	772,936	343,527	193,234	123,670	85,881	63,096	48,308	38,169	30,917	13,741	7,729	4,946	3,435	2,523
2.0	3,251,150	812,788	361,238	203,197	130,046	90,309	66,350	50,799	40,137	32,512	14,449	8,128	5,202	3,612	2,654
2.1	3,410,224	852,556	378,912	213,139	136,409	94,728	69,596	53,284	42,100	34,102	15,156	8,525	5,456	3,789	2,783
2.2	3,568,967	892,242	396,551	223,060	142,759	99,138	72,836	55,765	44,061	35,690	15,862	8,922	5,710	3,965	2,913
2.3	3,727,377	931,844	414,152	232,961	149,095	103,537	76,068	58,239	46,016	37,273	16,566	9,318	5,964	4,141	3,042
2.4	3,885,456	971,364	431,716	242,841	155,418	107,929	79,294	60,710	47,968	38,855	17,268	9,714	6,216	4,317	3,172
2.5	4,043,203	1,010,800	449,245	252,700	161,728	112,311	82,513	63,174	49,915	40,432	17,970	10,108	6,469	4,492	3,300
2.6	4,200,619	1,050,155	466,734	262,538	168,025	116,682	85,726	65,634	51,859	42,006	18,669	10,501	6,721	4,667	3,429
2.7	4,357,702	1,089,425	484,187	272,356	174,308	121,046	88,932	68,088	53,798	43,577	19,367	10,894	6,972	4,842	3,557
2.8	4,514,454	1,128,614	501,606	282,153	180,578	125,402	92,131	70,538	55,734	45,145	20,064	11,286	7,223	5,016	3,685
2.9	4,670,874	1,167,718	518,984	291,929	186,835	129,745	95,324	72,982	57,664	46,708	20,759	11,677	7,473	5,189	3,812
3.0	4,826,963	1,206,741	536,327	301,685	193,079	134,081	98,508	75,421	59,591	48,270	21,453	12,067	7,723	5,363	3,940
3.1	4,982,719	1,245,679	553,635	311,420	199,309	138,409	101,687	77,854	61,514	49,827	22,145	12,457	7,972	5,536	4,067
3.2	5,138,144	1,284,536	570,903	321,134	205,526	142,725	104,858	80,284	63,433	51,381	22,836	12,845	8,221	5,709	4,194
3.3	5,293,237	1,323,309	588,135	330,827	211,729	147,034	108,024	82,706	65,348	52,932	23,525	13,233	8,469	5,881	4,321
3.4	5,447,999	1,362,000	605,333	340,500	217,920	151,333	111,183	85,124	67,258	54,480	24,213	13,620	8,716	6,053	4,447
3.5	5,602,428	1,400,607	622,490	350,152	224,097	155,621	114,334	87,537	69,165	56,024	24,899	14,006	8,964	6,224	4,573
3.6	5,756,526	1,439,132	639,611	359,783	230,261	159,903	117,479	89,945	71,067	57,565	25,584	14,391	9,210	6,395	4,699
3.7	5,910,292	1,477,573	656,699	369,393	236,412	164,174	120,616	92,347	72,966	59,103	26,268	14,775	9,456	6,567	4,842
3.8	6,063,727	1,515,932	673,746	378,983	242,549	168,435	123,749	94,745	74,860	60,637	26,949	15,159	9,702	6,737	4,949
3.9	6,216,829	1,554,207	690,756	388,552	248,673	172,688	126,872	97,137	76,750	62,168	27,629	15,542	9,947	6,907	5,074
4.0	6,369,600	1,592,400	707,733	398,100	254,784	176,933	129,991	99,525	78,636	63,696	28,309	15,924	10,191	7,077	5,199

Exhibit 10-5: Sample Sizes for Response Rates Between 0.1% and 4.0%. Confidence Level of 99%

$$= \frac{(0.01\,(0.99)\,(3.8416)}{(0.000004)}$$

$$= \frac{0.03803184}{0.000004}$$

$$= 9{,}508 \text{ pieces to be mailed}$$

Suppose that, having proceeded with the experiment and having mailed 9,508 pieces as a test (with another 9,508 pieces as a control), the actual response from the test segment turned out to be 1.5% rather than the anticipated 1%? Still at a 95% confidence level, what would be the limit of error for continuation mailings projected from this experiment? Here is the formula for determining that:

$$E = \sqrt{(R)(1-R)/N} * Z$$

Substituting into this formula the actual response rate of 1.5%, with the same notation as before, here is the calculation for limit of error:

$$E = \sqrt{(0.015)(0.985)/9580} * 1.96$$

$$E = \sqrt{0.000001554} * 1.96$$

$$E = 000124 * 1.96$$

$$E = 0.00243 \ldots \text{ or, } 0.243\% \text{ limit of error}$$

These two examples illustrate the statistical importance of setting up direct-mail tests in a manner to assure a sample size adequate for meaningful projection of response rates within acceptable tolerances, i.e., limits of error.

Additionally, they demonstrate the need for accurate determination of the limit of error, the variance that could occur by chance alone, not as a result of significant differences in particular direct marketing efforts.

When predicting the response rate from a market segment, after testing, one must recognize "error by chance." In the calculation above, in which actual test response was 1.5% and error limit was calculated to be ±0.243%, any response rate from continuation mailings to this market segment within the range of 1.257% and 1.743% would be statistically "same as" the 1.5% prediction. Such variation could have occurred by chance alone.

Note, too, that a ±0.243 variance is 16% of a response rate of 1.5% whereas a ±0.2 variance is 20% of a lower response rate of 1%. This demonstrates that the relative amount of variance decreases as the response rate increases. Variance also decreases as sample size increases.

Decreasing error limits or increasing confidence levels both increase the sample-size requirement. Thus, there is a trade-off between the cost of additional mailing pieces and the value of the precision of information derived from a test.

Fortunately, it is not usually necessary to perform cumbersome calculations like these. Tables for 95 percent and 99 percent confidence levels, for response rates up to 4 percent and limits of error up to 70 percent, are provided in this workshop in Exhibits 10-4 and 10-5. Also, a Sample Size Calculator and Limit of Error Calculator are provided in CD-ROM format accompanying this text.

Interactive Workshop 10-3:

Measuring Difference

(For demonstration, go to the CD-ROM accompanying this book.)

There needs to be an understanding of the methods used for *validating difference* between the response rates of a test and of a control. Only through such understanding can one decide whether to change from one promotional strategy to another or to enter a new market segment or to adopt a new product.

Typically, the response rate to a targeted promotion is the average number of responses for each offer sent. Response is attributed to the test in comparison to the control. The variable tested could be the database segment used, a price variance, a product difference, or a difference in advertising.

In such a comparison, the researcher must determine if the response rate difference is real (in a statistical sense) or if the difference might have occurred through chance alone. In effect, one tests the hypothesis that there is no difference between the response rates from the test and the control.

Assume that a sample of an adequate size has been properly selected. Assume the experiment has been implemented in a valid manner. It remains for the marketer to be able to recognize the difference in response rates from a test and a control, with a degree of confidence and within an acceptable limit of error.

When evaluating the results of an experiment, one needs to know if a difference is *statistically significant.* The independent sample t-test may be used for validating such a difference. The null hypothesis offered is that there is no difference between the responses from the test and the control. The alternative hypothesis is that there is a difference between the

Group Statistics

	Group	N	Mean	Std. Deviation
RESPONSE	Control	500	8.000E-02	.2716
	Test	500	.1320	.3388

Exhibit 10-6: Response Rates from Test and Control Groups

responses from the test and the control. Note that the alternative hypothesis is two-sided. That is, in this case, the researcher has no a prioi expectation whether the test group is going to perform better than the control group. A t-statistic is computed from the observed results and this is compared with a table of probabilities for a theoretical sampling distribution to calculate the p-value.

Suppose the following results have been obtained:

	Test	Control	Totals
Response	66	40	106
Nonresponse	434	460	894
Total mailed	500	500	1000

The response rate in the test group is 13.2% and the response rate in the control group is 8%. Before concluding that the test group performed better than the control, the researcher needs to conduct an independent sample t-test. Suppose the researcher specifies a significance level of 5%. Running an independent sample t-test on the above data results, utilizing SPSS, a statistics software program, provides the output shown in Exhibit 10-6.

Independent Samples Test

		Levene's Test for Equality of Variances		t-test for Equality of Means			
		F	Sig.	t	df	Sig. (2-tailed)	Mean Difference
Response	Equal variances assumed	29.398	.000	-2.678	998	.008	-5.200E-02
	Equal variances not assumed			-2.678	952.820	.008	-5.200E-02

Exhibit 10-7: Independent Sample T-Test Measurement of Significance of Difference Between Test and Control Responses

The values for mean response in Exhibit 10-6 are response rates. The t-statistic based on this data and the 2-sided p-value are given in Exhibit 10-7.

The p-value for testing the hypothesis is 0.008 {in the last row under the column labeled Sig. (2-tailed)}. Because the p-value is lower than the 5% significance level, the conclusion is to reject the null hypothesis. In other words, the marketer concludes that the observed response rates are not due to chance alone and that test response is better than the control response rate. As said before, the marketer is likely to conduct a "back test" before switching to the test offer for future promotions.

Interactive Workshop 10-4:

Factorial Designs

(For demonstration, go to the CD-ROM accompanying this book.)

In a factorial design, two or more independent variables (factors) are manipulated (changed) simultaneously. The values that the factors take are called the levels of the factors. A treatment in a factorial design is the combination of levels of the factors. Subjects are assigned at random to these treatments. A factorial design is often denoted as mXn, where m is the number of levels of the first factor and n is the number of levels of the second factor. If executed and analyzed properly, factorial designs allow marketers to test the main (individual) effect of each factor as well as the interaction (joint) effect of all factors.

Suppose that a direct marketer sets out to test two things – a new copy and a new incentive in the offer. If he does not know about factorial designs, he has to conduct two sequential experiments. In the first experiment the new copy is tested against the control copy (the one that the marketer has been using). He sends 500 offers with the test copy and 500 offers with the control copy and observes a response rate of 12.6% and 8.0% respectively. He conducts an independent sample t-test at a 5% level and gets a p-value of 0.04. He therefore concludes that the test copy is better than the control copy.

Then, he conducts the second experiment, where he tests the new incentive against the control incentive (the incentive that the marketer has been using in the past). He sends 500 offers each using the test and the control incentive and gets response rates of 13.2% and 8% respectively. He conducts an independent sample t-test at 5% level, and gets a p-value of 0.008. He, therefore, concludes that the test incentive is better than the control incentive. Based on the results of these two sequential experiments, he concludes that the combination of "test copy and test incentive" represents the best possible future offer. The danger of doing sequential experiments, as described above, is the possibility that the marketer's final decision will be a less-than-desirable combination of copy and incentive!

If the direct marketer knows about factorial design, he will realize that he is testing two factors (copy and incentive) each with two levels (test and control). The correct way to test is to use a 2×2 factorial design with 4 treatments (test copy/test incentive, test copy/control incentive, control copy/test incentive, and control copy/control incentive).

Suppose the direct marketer has 1,000 names in his database and he assigns each name at random to receive one of the 4 treatments. Then, he sends an offer to each prospect based on which treatment the prospect was randomly assigned to receive and records responses. He observes the following response rates for each treatment:

	Incentive		
Offer	Test	Control	
Test	11.2%	14%	12.6%
Control	15.2%	2%	8.6%
	13.2%	8%	10.6%

The numbers in the Test and Control columns of the table show response rates for each combination of copy and incentive. The numbers in the last column of the table are the average response rates for the two factors, considered one at a time. Note that these average response rates match those used in the sequential testing example.

To analyze data from factorial experiments, researchers subject the data to an analysis of variance (ANOVA). The ANOVA produces a test and p-value for each factor considered by itself (main effect) and the joint (interaction) effects of both factors. The ANOVA output for this data derived from the statistical software program, SPSS, is shown in Exhibit 10-8. The column labeled "Sig." contains the p-values.

In the table in Exhibit 10-8, the p-value for the test of main effect for copy is 0.038, the p-value for the test main effect for incentive is 0.007, and the p-value for the test of interaction effect of copy and incentive together is 0.000. Assuming a 5% significance level for testing, both main effects and the interaction effect are statistically significant. These significant effects can be interpreted in the following manner.

The significant main effect of copy indicates that the average response rates for test (12.6%) versus control (8.6%) is different. In other

Tests of Between-Subjects Effects[b]

Source	Type III Sum of Squares	df	Mean Square	F	Sig.
COPY	.400	1	.400	4.326	.038
INCENTIV	.676	1	.676	7.311	.007
COPY * INCENTIV	1.600	1	1.600	17.305	.000
Error	92.088	996	9.246E-02		
Total	94.764	999			

Exhibit 10-8: ANOVA Test of 2×2 Factorial Experiment

words, considered by itself, the test copy performs better than the control copy. The significant main effect of incentive indicates that the average response rates for test (13.2%) versus control incentive (8%) is different. In other words, considered by itself, the test incentive performs better than the control incentive. Note that these main-effects tests are only considering the average response rates in the margin of the table. That is, conclusions based on the main effects alone will be similar to conclusions reached via sequential experiments of two factors one at a time.

The significant interaction effect suggests that there is a joint effect of copy and incentive. Stated differently, it implies that the marketer needs to consider the average response rate for all combinations of the two factors in order to identify the "best" combination. In this case, control copy and test incentive together is clearly the optimal combination (15.2%) as shown in the numbers reported inside the table.

We have constructed this data set deliberately to show how misleading the conclusions can be if marketers run sequential versus factorial experiments. In this data set, if the marketer conducted only sequential experiments (one factor at a time), he would have concluded that the optimal combination is "test copy with test incentive" (11.2% response rate) which is clearly not the case as illustrated by the ANOVA results. Only when there is no significant interaction in ANOVA, it may be possible to identify the best combination by running sequential experiments. Thus, we recommend that direct marketers carefully consider the factors they want to test and, if testing more than one factor, consider using factorial designs in order to determine if there is any possibility of interaction between the factors.

Interactive Workshop 10-5:

Using EXCEL for Independent Sample t-Test for Testing Response Rates between Test and Control Groups

(For demonstration, go to the CD-ROM accompanying this book.)

In this workshop you will replicate the independent sample t-test results for testing response rates from the test versus the control group as reported in the text using EXCEL®. Please open the data set labeled "workshop10.5.xls" in EXCEL. You will find two columns (A and B) of data. Column (A) contains a variable labeled "Response_Cont." This variable represents responses from the control group (coded as 1 = yes, 0 = no). Column (B) contains a variable labeled "Response_Test." This variable represents responses from the test group (also coded as 1 = yes, 0 = no). To run an independent sample t-test, do this:

- Open the data set using EXCEL

- Click on Tools in the EXCEL menu

- Click on Data Analysis

- Select "t-Test: Two sample assuming unequal variances" in the pop-up window and click OK

- Select column A for variable 1 range box

- Select column B for variable 2 range box

- Type "0" in the hypothesized mean difference box

- Make sure the Labels box is checked

- Check new worksheet ply and type "New1" in box; click OK

If you followed the above procedure correctly, EXCEL will run an independent sample t-test and will output a new sheet labeled New1, as shown in Exhibit 10-9.

Note that the response rates from the control and test groups are 8% and 13.2% respectively and these match the numbers reported in the text. The two-sided p-value is the number corresponding to "P(T<=t) two-tail." This p-value equals 0.0075, which matches the p-value reported in the text (with appropriate rounding to 3 places of decimal).

t-Test: Two-Sample Assuming Unequal Variances

	Response Cont	Response Test
Mean	0.08	0.132
Variance	0.073747495	0.114805611
Observations	500	500
Hypothesized Mean Difference	0	
df	953	
t Stat	-2.677759077	
P (T <= t) one-tail	0.00376956	
t Critical one-tail	1.646453711	
P (T <= t) two-tail	0.00753912	
t Critial two-tail	1.962457645	

Exhibit 10-9: Utilizing EXCEL for Independent Sample T-Test for Testing Response Rates between Test and Control Groups

Interactive Workshop 10-6:

Using EXCEL for Analysis of Variance

(For demonstration, go to the CD-ROM accompanying this book.)

In this workshop you will replicate the results of ANOVA reported in the text using EXCEL®. Please open the data set labeled "workshop10.6.xls" for this workshop. You will find three columns (A - C) of data. Column (A) represents the "copy" variable (takes two values: control or test). Column (B) contains a variable labeled "Incent_control." The numbers in this column represent the responses (coded as 1 = yes, 0 = no) to the offer with the control incentive. Column (C) contains a variable labeled "Incent_test." The numbers in this column represent the responses (coded as 1 = yes, 0 = no) to the offer with the test incentive. Note that the Excel data set is set-up with table rows representing "copy," and columns representing "incentive." Numbers in the table represent the responses to an offer as described by combinations of copy and incentive.

To run an ANOVA, do the following:

- Open the data set using EXCEL

- Click on Tools in the EXCEL menu

- Click on Data Analysis

- Select "ANOVA: Two Factor with Replication" in the pop-up window and click OK

- Type "A1:C501" in the Input Range box

Anova: Two-Factor With Replication

SUMMARY

	Incentiv_Control	Incentiv_Test	Total
Control			
Count	250	250	500
Sum	5	38	43
Average	0.02	0.152	0.086
Variance	0.019678715	0.1294137	0.0787615
Test			
Count	250	250	500
Sum	35	28	63
Average	0.14	0.112	0.126
Variance	0.120883534	0.0998554	0.1103447
Total			
Count	500	500	
Sum	40	66	
Average	0.08	0.132	
Variance	0.073747495	0.1148056	

ANOVA

Source of Variation	SS	df	MS	F	P-Value	F-Crit
Sample	0.4	1	0.4	4.3263	0.03778	3.85081
Columns	0.676	1	0.676	7.31144	0.00697	3.85081
Interaction	1.6	1	1.6	17.3052	3.5E-05	3.85081
Within	92.088	996	0.0924578			
Total	94.764	999				

Exhibit 10-10: Utilization of EXCEL for Analysis of Variance

- Type "250" in the Rows per Sample box

- Check New Worksheet Ply and type "New1" in box; click OK

Following this procedure, EXCEL will run an ANOVA and will output a new sheet labeled New1, as shown in Exhibit 10-10.

The top panel of the table shows that the average response rate for "control copy and control incentive" is 0.02 (or 2%) and for "control copy and test incentive" is 0.152 (or 15.2%). The next panel shows that the average response rate for "test copy and control incentive" is 0.14 (or 14%) and for "test copy and test incentive" is 0.112 (or 11.2%).

In the panel labeled ANOVA in the table above, sample refers to the copy factor and columns refer to the incentive factor. Thus, the p-values for testing the main effects of copy and incentive are 0.0377 and 0.0069 respectively. The p-value for testing the interaction effect of copy and incentive is 3.5×10^{-5}. All of these numbers match the corresponding numbers reported in the text (within rounding errors).

Exercises in Structuring and Conducting an Experiment

■ Design a statistically-valid experiment to measure response to a direct mail promotional offer to be sent to the "cautious" skiers segment of the Mountain & Valley Resort Ski Rental database described in Chapter 13. How would you structure and control such an experiment? Why would you conduct such a test?

■ Anticipating a 2% response to the offer and assuming a 95% confidence level and a maximum acceptable variance of 15%, calculate the required sample size. How would you calculate the limit of error when the actual response rate is 3%?

■ With a response rate of 5% from a test copy approach and a response rate of 2% from the control copy approach, how would you determine whether, in fact, there is a statistically valid difference between the two response rates?

■ How would you design an experiment to determine s difference in response to the offer between midweek and weekend skiers? How would you measure the difference statistically?

Chapter 11

Decision Making

Key Concepts
- Decision-Making Process
- Predictive Modeling

Application
- Using Mulitvariate Analysis to Make Decisions

Business and marketing management are about making decisions. This chapter is about the process of making those decisions.

Four steps are involved in using research and testing to make a decision or to solve a problem.

1. **Determine objectives.** Is the objective increased sales volume, increased response to advertising, greater return on investment, or accelerated cash flow?

2. **Array alternatives.** What are the possible courses of action? How can these best be evaluated, including (but not limited to) such statistical techniques as decision trees, payoff matrices, and mathematical models?

3. **Deal with uncertainty.** How can one assign probabilities, based on judgments, simulations, and statistics, in order to arrive at a proper choice?

4. **Perform evaluation.** How does one determine the alternative that best suits the objective under conditions of uncertainty? Then, how does one implement it, monitor it, and provide for feedback?

The Case of the Raincoat Vendor

A middleman purchases raincoats from an overseas manufacturer for $10 each and resells them to his customers at $35 each through a general clothing catalog mailed seasonally. Since the raincoats are distinctively styled, it is assumed that, if they are not sold, they have no further value. For each individual seasonal catalog promotion, he needs to decide how many raincoats should be purchased in order to maximize profit. The condition of uncertainty in the equation is the weather: *Will it be a rainy selling season?*

Following the four steps of the decision-making process, the raincoat vendor arrays the following:

- **Objective:** Maximize profits through determination of how many raincoats to buy for resale in a seasonal catalog

- **Alternatives:** (1) Buy 100 raincoats at $10 each; sell them all at $35 each; gross profit is $2500. (2) Buy 200 at $10 each; sell them all at $35 each; gross profit is $5000. (3) Buy none, leave the item out of the catalog and avoid the uncertainty (risk) entirely.

- **Uncertainty:** It might not be a rainy season. If the mail-order merchant sells only 50, gross profit would be just $750 on the purchase of 100. There would be a loss of $250 on the purchase of 200! (Example assumes no later salvage value.) The probability that it will not be a rainy season is calculated to be 40 percent.

- **Evaluation:** The three alternatives assumed, along with the associated probabilities of rain, are arrayed in the Decision Tree and Pay-Off Matrix in Exhibit 11-1.

There could be an infinite number of purchase alternatives and a great many other uncertainties, such as timely delivery of the catalog, economic conditions and competition. Of course, promotion cost of the catalog also needs to be considered.

In the Decision Tree shown in Exhibit 11-1, the purchase possibilities are arrayed—i.e., buy 100, buy 200 or buy none along with the sale and profit/loss potential of each, as well as the risk and uncertainty associated with the probability of a rainy selling season.

In the Pay-Off Matrix shown in Exhibit 11-1, amounts that are contained in the column headed "Expected Value" are derived by multiplying the percentages shown in the "Probability" column by the corresponding amounts shown in the "Profit" column. From this calculation is derived the expected profit under each condition of uncertainty for each alternative given. In one instance, the column headed "Risk" displays a $250 loss in the event that 200 raincoats are purchased and there is no rain.

The "Attitude" column displays how an individual's intuition might influence what action would be taken. Such models as these do not recommend an action, but they do provide a basis on which to make a decision that fits comfortably with one's risk tolerance.

DECISION TREE:

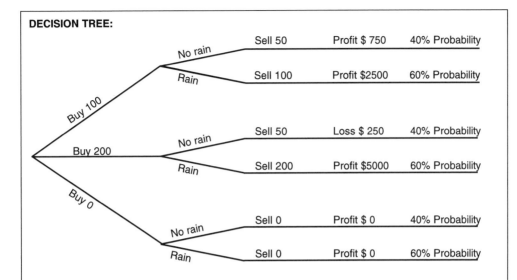

PAY-OFF MATRIX:

Alternative	Probability	Expected Profit	Value	Risk	Attitude
Buy 100:	40%-No Rain	$750	$300	$0	Play it safe; earn
	60%-Rain	$2500	$1500		a modest profit
			$1800		
Buy 200:	40%-No Rain	($250)	($100)	$250	Take a risk; earn
	60%-Rain	$5000	$3000		a higher profit
			$2900		
Buy 0:	40%-No Rain	$0	$0	$0	Do nothing;
	60%-Rain	$0	$0		lose/gain nothing

Exhibit 11-1: A Simplified Example of Decision-Making: The Raincoat Vendor

Predictive Modeling

Models like that of the Entrepreneurial Raincoat Vendor can be used to explain, predict, or solve problems. Models that explain can provide descriptions, frameworks, and aids to systematic thinking and discussion or hypothesis testing. Models that predict can help explain the impact that the inclusion of variables might have on results. And, models that solve problems can help facilitate the decision process involved in, say, determining how many telephone communicators and 800-service telephone lines are required to handle high-traffic periods of response to seasonal mail-order catalogs.

Models take many forms and display many characteristics:

- **Iconic models:** are basically images such as road maps, photographs or architectural mock-ups.

- **Analog Models:** are representations in the form of, as examples, flow charts or graphs that represent differences of sales resulting from different flights of a direct mail test.

- **Symbolic models:** are concerned with mathematical and/or logical symbols and include definitional equations such as "Profit = Revenue – Cost." Or the equation might be a more complex technical one such as "Commission = $1,000 + 0.05 × Sales."

- **Behavioral models:** look at events over time, such as time series or trend analysis. Or, they establish functional relationships such as "D = f(P)," read as "Demand is a function of Price."

Modeling techniques can correlate market penetration with census demographics, lifestyle research, transaction data, and buyer behavior. These models can very accurately predict response from selected market segments of prospects. Decision-support models can build profiles of those most likely to respond to an offer. Models, whether used for explanation, prediction or problem solving, rely heavily on causation.

Sometimes a model can be constructed to predict response, from particular segments of a database or from particular promotional strategies, as examples, which we are unable to explain. In other words, we generally know what happens but not why it happens. These are referred to as "black box" models.

Exhibit 11-2 illustrates differences in response among demographic segments of a database. The response rate from those persons on the list that are identified as "older age" is somewhat higher than that from those identified as "younger age." The response rate seems to increase even more among "older age" persons who are also "widowed." It thus appears

Age/Marital Status	Single	Married	Widowed	Divorced
Under Age 30	.53%	.64%	87%	.56%
Ages 30-39	.75%	1.40%	1.50%	.85%
Ages 40-49	1.03%	1.75%	1.95%	1.09%
Ages 50-59	1.10%	1.80%	2.05%	1.15%
Ages 60-69	1.30%	1.92%	2.23%	1.32%
Ages 70-79	1.36%	2.03%	2.38%	1.40%
Over Age 79	1.42%	2.56%	2.72%	1.50%

Exhibit 11-2: Response Rates Illustrative of Differences in Age and Marital Status within a Broad-based Compiled Mailing List

that "older age" and/or "widowed" marital status are the cause of higher response. The higher response could also be the effect of mailing only to older-aged persons who are also widowed.

Such a model, representing response percentages from 28 cells of a total solicitation, is represented as a 4x7 matrix. The four columns represent a marital status; the seven rows represent age bands. A response percentage is given where each column intersects with each row. The intersect is called a cell.

This model is relatively simple to construct. Each segment of a prospect list was key-coded on the response device so that all responses could be apportioned among 28 cells representing all possible combinations of age and marital status.

Workshop 11-1:
Using Multivariate Analysis to Make Decisions

A travel company that offers package tours through mail order to older persons desires to increase its marketing effectiveness. It seeks to do this through segmentation of its marketplace within the state of Florida using demographic independent variables in addition to age. It constructs a predictive model utilizing three multivariate statistical techniques: regression and correlation analysis, cluster analysis, and factor analysis.

The firm has developed, from census and proprietary data sources, a total of 103 demographic variables describing each of 35,000 geographic ZIP Code areas. These variables are expressed as either averages or frequency distributions. The 103 variables, describing 27 characteristics of each ZIP Code area, are shown in Exhibit 11-3.

Characteristic	Variable Description	Characteristic	Variable Description
Type of Area	% Urban % Rural Non-Farm % Rural Farm	**Industry of Work Force**	% Construction % Manufacturing % Transportation % Communication % Wholesale/Retail % Finance % Professional % Educational % PublicAdministration % Other
Race	% White % Black % Indian % Japanese % Chinese % Filipino % Spanish American % Other		
		Family Size	Average Family Size
Nativity	% Native/NativeParents % Native/Fore'nParents % Foreign Born	**Poverty**	% Indiv Below Poverty % Famil Below Poverty
		Mobility	% Moved Past 2 Years
Origin of Foreign Born	% United Kingdom % Ireland % Sweden % Germany % Poland % Czechoslovakia % Austria % Hungary % Russia % Italy % Canada % Mexico % Cuba % Other	**Home Ownership**	% Owner-Occupied
		Home/Rent Value	Median Value of Owned Median Rent Paid
		Age of Structure	Median Structure Age
		Tenure Residence	Median Tenure of Resid
		Income	Median Indiv Income Median Family Income
		Conspicuous Consumption	Mean Current AutoValue
Mother Tongue	% English % German % Polish % Yiddish % Italian % Spanish % All Others % Not Reported	**Dwelling Size**	Median Owner-Occupied Median Renter-Occupied
		Dwelling Type	% SingleFamilyDwellngs % 2-Unit Structures % 3/4-Unit Structures % 5/49-Unit Structures % 50+-Unit Structures % Mobile Homes/Trailers
Marital Status	% Married % Widowed % Divorced % Separated % Never Married	**Household Equipment**	% With Washer % With Dryer % With Dishwasher % With Freezer % With Television % With UHF-TV % With Battery Radio
Age	Median Age		
Education	Median Education Level	**Structure Equipment**	% With AirConditioning % With Multi-Bath % With Central Heat % With Public Water % With Public Sewer
Occupation of Work Force	% Professionl/Technicl % Farm Manager % Managerial % Clerical % Sales % Craftsmen % Operatives % Service % Farm Laborer % Other Laborer % Armed Services % Unemployed		
		Kitchen	% Lacking Kitchen
		Direct Access	% Lacking DirectAccess
		Telephone	% Having Telephone
		Autos Registered	% With One Auto % With Two Autos % With Three+ Autos

Exhibit 11-3: A Listing of 27 Characteristics and 103 Variables Describing 35,000 ZIP Code Areas

FACTOR 1:	**AFFLUENCE**	
	Education:	16+ years of school completed
		13-15 years of school completed
	Occupation:	manager, official, proprietor
		professional, technical, sales
	Industry:	finance
	Value/Owner-occup'd:	$100,000+
	Rent Paid/Renter:	$600+
	Structure Equipment:	Multibath
	Household Equipment:	Dishwasher
	Average Auto Value:	High
	Family Income:	$50,000+
	Individual Income:	$30,000+
FACTOR 2:	**SETTLED SINGLES**	
	Household Relation:	primary individual or non-relative
		of the head of the household
	Marital Status:	divorced
	Housing Occupancy:	renter
	Dwelling Type:	multiple family unit
	Dwelling Size:	1/2-room owner-occupied
		1/2-room renter-occupied
	Auto Registration:	one auto
FACTOR 3:	**POVERTY**	
	Education:	1-8 years school completed
	Kitchen:	lacking kitchen
	Telephone	lacking telephone
	Value/Owner-occup'd:	under $10,000
	Rent Paid/Renter:	under $100
	Poverty:	individuals below poverty level
		families below poverty level
	Family Income:	under $14,000
	Individual Income:	under $5,000
FACTOR 4:	**SENIOR CITIZEN**	
	Nativity:	native born of foreign parents
	Country of Origin:	eastern Europe
	Age:	65+
		50-64
	Marital Status:	widowed
	Structure Age:	50+ years
	Tenure of Residence:	35+ years
FACTOR 5:	**RURAL RESIDER**	
	Type of Area:	rural farm
	Occupation:	farmer, farm manager, farm laborer
	Industry:	other

Exhibit 11-4: Lifestyle Factors with Associated Variables

Several of these variables have been normalized; that is, they have been indexed to some larger area such as a Sectional Center (the first three digits of a five-digit code) or a state (such as Mississippi vs. New York) in order to achieve environmental, as opposed to absolute, measurement. This means that the *relative* income level in a rural Mississippi area is compared with the *relative* income level of an urban area in New York rather than in *absolute* dollars. A "high" dollar income level in rural Mississippi could be "low" in urban New York.

Variables have also been subjected to *factor analysis* to discover the typical lifestyle factors and the associated independent variables. These are shown in Exhibit 11-4. The *dependent* variable is market penetration, defined in this instance as the *response rate* (total responses divided by the total number of pieces mailed) to the travel company's direct mail offer of tours to the older residents of Florida.

To maximize the number of observations and to assure statistical validity of measurement and prediction, the response rate is calculated within *clusters* of ZIP Code areas that have common characteristics produced using *cluster analysis*. Ultimately, these clusters will be described as market segments in which penetration levels can be correlated with their characteristics. At this stage, both *environmental* (indexed) measurement and *interaction* among the variables defining clusters are important considerations.

Calculation of penetration is simple. Within each cluster of ZIP Code areas, the response rate is calculated as shown in the table below:

ZIP Code Area Clusters	Total No. of Pieces Mailed	Total No. of Responses	% Responses/ Mailed
A	5,793	60	1.04
B	2,735	33	1.21
C	6,731	136	2.02
D	4,341	119	2.74

From this table, it is readily apparent that there is an increasing rate of response from A to B, from B to C, and from C to D. These differences can be explained by evaluating the independent variables associated and deemed significant through regression and correlation analysis as shown in Exhibit 11-5, which enables the transfer of the findings from a sample to the total population without having mailed to that total population.

The derived linear regression equation ($Y = a + bX$) becomes a formula for predicting estimated response rates from ZIP Code area clusters having similar characteristics to those sampled. Correlation analysis identifies the relationship between cluster response rates and 103 selected demographics.

```
STEP #  1
   VARIABLE ENTERING        X- 5
R =0.583959     R SQ. =0.341008
   F LEVEL =      23.8036
   STANDARD ERROR OF Y =       0.06341
   CONSTANT TERM =      0.27470726

   VARIABLE NO.          COEFFICIENT              STD ERR OF COEFF
      X- 5               -0.28683022E-01                  0.00594


STEP #  2
   VARIABLE ENTERING        X- 2
R =0.717396     R SQ. =0.514658
   F LEVEL =      16.1004
   STANDARD ERROR OF Y =       0.05504
   CONSTANT TERM =      0.25037676

   VARIABLE NO.          COEFFICIENT              STD ERR OF COEFF
      X- 2                0.11710477                       0.02951
      X- 5               -0.25006641E-01.                  0.00524


STEP #  3
   VARIABLE ENTERING        X- 16
R =0.814453     R SQ. =0.663334
   F LEVEL =      19.4310
   STANDARD ERROR OF Y =       0.04637
   CONSTANT TERM =      0.17120540

   VARIABLE NO.          COEFFICIENT              STD ERR OF COEFF
      X- 2                0.12946498                       0.02503
      X- 5               -0.21160301E-01                   0.00450
      X- 16               0.10500204E-01                   0.00241


STEP #  4
   VARIABLE ENTERING        X- 14
R =0.831825     R SQ. =0.691934
   F LEVEL =       3.9919
   STANDARD ERROR OF Y =       0.04488
   CONSTANT TERM =       0.11676645

   VARIABLE NO.          COEFFICIENT              STD ERR OF COEFF
      X- 2                0.12659431                       0.02427
      X- 5               -0.18140811E-01                   0.00462
      X- 14               0.27103789E-01                   0.01373
      X- 16               0.99606328E-02                   0.00235
```

```
STEP # 10
   VARIABLE ENTERING        X- 22
R =0.896520     R SQ. =0.803748
   F LEVEL =       2.8542
   STANDARD ERROR OF Y =       0.03766
   CONSTANT TERM =      0.39812356

   VARIABLE NO.          COEFFICIENT              STD ERR OF COEFF
      X- 2                0.13928533                       0.02095
      X- 9               -0.20301903E-02                   0.00064
      X- 10              -0.87198131E-02                   0.00257
      X- 14               0.69082797E-01                   0.01875
      X- 15               0.13623666E-01                   0.00421
      X- 16               0.22368859E-01                   0.00380
      X- 22              -0.15226589E-02                   0.00091
      X- 23              -0.21373443E-02                   0.00081
```

Exhibit 11-5: Stepwise Multivariate Regression Analysis

Exhibit 11-5 reproduces a condensed printout of the stepwise multi-variate regression and correlation analysis. From an availability of 27 independent variables, 8 variables remain at the conclusion of Step 10. The reference numbers of these eight variables, together with their simple correlation coefficients, are shown at the bottom of Exhibit 10-5. The R^2 value of 0.803748 (the multiple coefficient of determination) indicates that 80% of the variance in response is explained by presence or absence of these eight variables.

The derived regression equation enables a rank ordering of predicted response rate attributable to each five-digit ZIP Code area within each cluster. This is visualized in Exhibit 10-6, which shows highest to lowest, as well as cumulative, predicted penetration percentages (response rates). It also shows both individual and cumulative base mailing list counts for each ZIP Code area within each cluster. Note the variance of the actual response rate, shown for each ZIP Code area in the third column, attributable to the small number mailed in each area.

Exhibit 10-6 reveals that, from a total mailing of 1,277,262 pieces, an overall response rate is predicted to be 1.95 percent. The response rate from the top cluster (#39) is predicted at 4.49 percent; that from the bottom cluster (#30) is predicted at 0.76 percent. The ratio, top versus bottom, is nearly 1:6. Note that the response rate from the top cluster is 2.3 times the overall average of 1.95 percent; that from the bottom is 39 percent.

To attain an average response of 2.55 percent (which is 31 percent better than the overall average), the company should stop after cluster #10, with a marginal response of 2.06 percent from mailing only 511,276 pieces.

Limiting the mailing to 242,935 pieces, about 20 percent of the list availability, the response rate would be 2.87 percent, an improvement of 47 percent over the 1.95 percent overall average.

From this analysis, the company decides how big a market segment is needed, then predicts what overall response rate will be. Or it sets its minimum response rate requirement (average or marginal), and then determines how many pieces it can mail.

At this point, of primary importance to the travel company is a description of the profiles that exist in Florida. Just what influence might each of these exert on the response rate to a travel tour offer directed to older persons? Factor analysis produces these three explanatory lifestyle profiles that are present in clusters with high response rates:

- **Rural Residers** — Variables positively associated with this factor include rural farm and rural non-farm areas; farm manager and farm laborer occupations; housing is often in mobile homes and

Rank Ordering of Zip Code Area Clusters
According to Predicted Penetration

CLUSTER #	ZIP #	PENETRATION ACTUAL	PERCENTAGES PRED	CUM PRED	*****BASE COUNTS**** ZIP ONLY	CUMULATIVE
39	32009	.00	.0449	.0449	89	89
	32265	.00	.0449	.0449	4	93
	32560	.1070	.0449	.0449	93	186
	32563	.00	.0449	.0449	6	192
	32710	.00	.0449	.0449	37	229
	32732	.00	.0449	.0449	200	429
	32740	.00	.0449	.0449	42	471
	32766	.1500	.0449	.0449	200	671
	33070	.0460	.0449	.0449	651	1322
	33470	.00	.0449	.0449	132	1454
	33527	.00	.0449	.0449	716	2170
	33554	.0590	.0449	.0449	505	2675
	33550	.00	.0449	.0449	194	2869
	33556	.0750	.0449	.0449	528	3397
	33569	.0480	.0449	.0449	1637	5034
	33584	.0390	.0449	.0449	1001	6035
	33586	.00	.0449	.0449	62	6097
	33592	.0770	.0449	.0449	518	6615
	33600	-.0750	.0449	.0449	398	7013
	33943	.00	.0449	.0449	139	7152
	32600	420	342	0363	2885	36007
II	32301	.0560	.0327	.0360	3533	39540
	32304	.0230	.0327	.0358	2532	42072
	32500	.0360	.0327	.0355	4873	46945
	32570	.0120	.0327	.0354	2312	49257
	32601	.0330	.0327	.0350	7826	57083
	33030	.0120	.0327	.0348	5564	62647
13	32211	.0240	.0246	.0291	6134	222185
	32303	.0160	.0246	.0290	4243	226428
	32561	.0330	.0246	.0289	1203	227631
	32701	.0140	.0246	.0289	2038	229669
	32751	.0140	.0246	.0288	3379	233048
	32786	.00	.0246	.0288	229	233277
	32789	.0170	.0246	.0287	7543	240820
	33511	.0370	.0246	.0287	2115	242935
10	33900	0210	0206	0255	53503	511276
	33062	0170	0111	0198	6834	1234153
	33140	00	0111	0198	56	1234209
	33134	0060	.0111	0198	3120	1237329
	33160	0130	0111	.0197	16354	1253683
	33306	0100	0111	.0197	986	1254669
30	33064	0210	.0076	.0196	8201	1262870
	33516	.00	.0076	.0195	11202	1274072
	33570	0090	.0076	.0195	3190	1277262

Exhibit 11-6: Rank Ordering of ZIP Code Area clusters According to Response Rate Predicted by Regression Analysis

trailers; housing is equipped with food freezers but often lacks formal kitchens; ancestry is East European. Negatively associated variables are access to public water and public sewers; finance industry; and multi-family dwelling units.

- **Social Class** — "Lower half" variables positively associated with this factor include occupation as laborers, operatives, service workers, unemployed; poverty levels; divorced, separated, and widowed marital status; older housing; and longer tenure of residence. "Upper half" variables, negatively associated, are high housing value; housing equipped with amenities such as air conditioning and dishwashers; two or more autos; high income; high education levels; occupations in management, sales, professional, technical; and finance industry.

- **Ancestry/Heritage** — Variables with positive association are native-born with English as a mother tongue; foreign-born with countries of origin including the United Kingdom, Canada, Ireland, Austria, and Germany; and housing in owner-occupied single-family units. Negatively associated variables include foreign born; emigrated from Cuba; Spanish is mother tongue; multiple family rental housing.

Because the overall response to this offer is double the break-even requirement for the acquisition of new customers, the travel company decides to validate its research. Six months after the first offer, the entire list is remailed, and rank-ordered in quintiles of response as predicted from regression analysis.

As expected, the overall response drops to about half of the first effort. What is important, however, is that the relationship (response rate indices) of the quintiles are virtually the same for both efforts, as detailed in this table:

Rank Ordered Quintile	Number of Pieces Mailed	First Effort Response %	First Effort Index	Second Effort Response %	Second Effort Index
1	242,935	2.87	147%	1.36	143%
2	268,341	2.26	116%	1.08	111%
3	230,592	1.94	99%	0.96	99%
4	290,001	1.54	79%	0.81	84%
5	245,393	1.19	61%	0.67	67%

Chapter 12

Using Database Information to Create More Effective Promotions

Key Concepts
- Physiological and Psychological Buying Influences
- Nature of Demand
- Learning Theory
- Environmental Buying Influences
- Offers, Features, and Benefits

Application
- Developing Targeted Promotions

The process for developing direct marketing promotions, whether individual pieces or entire programs and campaigns, begins with research that leads to idea generation and finally to actual execution (copywriting, creation of artwork, etc.). Regardless of the media form, every successful promotion is an offer that blends product, price, and terms into a package of relevant and attractive benefits to the target user(s).

Customers respond to offers that provide appealing benefits. Such benefits are often physical attributes of a product, although they can just as easily be abstractions, such as the sense of security and reliability provided by a financial investment service. In either case, these benefits must be translated into tangible terms that meet real, felt needs. One of the oldest (and truest) sayings in marketing communications is that people don't buy drill bits, they buy holes; or, more precisely, the benefit from fulfilling the need to drill a quarter-inch hole. They don't buy power steering; they buy the ability to park an automobile more easily. And, as mentioned above, they buy security and dependability, not shares of a mutual fund.

This chapter will show how database marketers use information to identify the factors that influence their customers' and prospective customers' purchases and then examine how to construct promotions that address these.

Why People Buy

The *ability to buy* is usually attributed to income and wealth; the *propensity to spend* is most likely determined by benefits offered customers. The *willingness to buy* results from individual motives, attitudes, expectations, needs, and wants.

There are many different kinds of buyers motivated by many different kinds of influences. Studies by the Bureau of Labor Statistics have revealed that blue-collar workers spend differently than do professionals and managers, even at the same level of income. These studies show an above-average percentage of money income spent among lower-income families for food, tobacco, personal care, and medical care. Higher-income families, on the other hand, spend a smaller proportion of income on automobiles, housing, eating out, alcoholic beverages, clothing, recreation, education, and travel.

On the next level, these studies also found that particular product purchases—for Scotch whiskey, pianos and organs, and expenditures connected with recreational boating—are not, as one might expect, confined to those with high income or wealth. Such products are generally looked upon as symbolic of class status. Similarly, lower-income groups often purchase expensive, luxury brands.

Smart direct marketers using sophisticated databases have reported results like these BLS studies. Namely, lifestyle variances, peer values, and the influences of social class and culture exert a great deal of influence on the individual buyer's purchase decisions. Differences in economic and demographic factors alone do not adequately explain variations in buying behavior. Quantitative analysis of markets is not enough. Direct marketers need to know about the qualitative aspects of buyer behavior in order to create benefits that motivate customers to purchase.

Intra-Personal Influences:
Physiological and Psychological Needs and Motivations

Any study of customer behavior, consumer or business, must begin with the *individual* and his or her physiological (biogenic) and psychological (psychogenic) needs. It is inherent that a newborn baby cries when it is hungry. Later, though, it learns to cry to demonstrate that it is hungry. Direct marketing promotion techniques endeavor to affect the learned behavior of buyers. Learned needs evolve from the individual and the environment and are relatively slow to change.

A variety of **learning theories** have been presented in the literature of psychology. One of the best known is stimulus-response, demonstrated by Pavlov's experiments in which animal behavior patterns, influenced by rewards and punishments, ultimately became established habits. Seeing a perspiring athlete gulp down a soft drink in a television commercial, for example, might cause the observer to crave similar refreshment.

Another area of learning experiences that has relevance for directed marketers is that of Gestalt or field theory. Such theory is concerned with the whole observation: the total scene including the observer's participation in it. As an example of Gestalt psychology, most of those looking at the configuration below will see tracks, trees, poles or six pairs of parallel lines; rarely will they see simply 12 vertical lines:

In terms of Gestalt theory, individuals tend to blend into their environments, of which they themselves are a part. Peer groups influence their lifestyles; they associate ads with the credibility of the deliverer of such messages. Thus, a model in a hospital smock in a TV commercial implies medical authority.

Psychoanalytic theories, including those of Sigmund Freud, postulate that real buying motives may be hidden. Motivation researchers, using the technique of the in-depth interview, have thrived by providing their explanations of "hidden persuaders." Some psychoanalytic-based research has been controversial. In one motivation study done for the Forest Lawn Cemetery in California, it was determined that the bereaved prefer large plots so that the deceased will have room to move about. That research also found a strong preference for caskets with locks since many people fear that the dead will get out.

Abraham Maslow's Hierarchy of Needs developed a theory of motivation that ranked physical needs as basic; social needs next above, and actualization of self at the top of a pyramid. His ladder was labeled, bottom to top: physiological needs, safety needs, belongingness needs, esteem needs and self-actualization needs.

Interpersonal Influences:
The Impact of Environment on Behavior

Environmental influences—like class membership or that from family or other reference groups—also affect buyer behavior. In fact, some researchers see these factors as more significant determinants of customer behavior than current income or accumulated wealth.

Research suggests that these factors can even impact the behavior of B2B buyers.

Family and Household Reference Groups: Family and household groups of unrelated individuals living together influence each other's buying decisions. Most often spouses share the decision, but in great many cases, children are the ultimate determinants. Some researchers have contended that the family or households are more proper units for observation than are individuals, because the decision-making process among family or household members is a significant variable in buying behavior.

Other Face-to-Face Small Reference Groups: "What our friends own we own, too ... or shall soon own," said George Katona, economist at the University of Michigan's Institute for Social Research. That is because face-to-face small reference groups — work associates, social acquaintances, religious affiliations, and, of course, neighbors — influence customer decisions.

"Keeping up with the Joneses"" may explain why the prestigious *National Geographic* magazine mailed a subscription invitation to the next-door neighbors of its present subscribers. In substance, the direct-mail offer read: "Your next-door neighbor reads the *National Geographic*. Shouldn't you?"

Similarly, more than one automobile manufacturer has experienced success by inviting neighbors to local dealers with a letter calling attention to a new model of their brand " ... parked in your neighbor's driveway."

Referral selling, which uses a third party to recommend a product or service directly or indirectly, is a notable example of reference group influence that has special application for direct marketing. A customer is inclined to respect the judgments of friends or of an affinity group of which he or she is a member. That is why credit unions recommend products as diverse as insurance and automobiles to their members. That is also why oil companies sell socket wrench sets and luggage with inserts in their monthly bills going to their customers. And referral recommendations from present customers have been shown to account for 20 percent or more of new customers acquired by direct marketing organizations soliciting customer referrals.

Social Class Influences: A buyer can be strongly influenced by his or her social class or that to which he or she aspires. Noting that income level alone does not determine social class, researchers have pointed to type and location of housing, level of education, occupation, and source of income as being more important variables for defining social class membership. The beginning plumber and the just-out-of-school lawyer, for example, may have similar incomes but likely not the same social class.

From a three-year study of the social structure of metropolitan Chicago, a research team headed by W. Lloyd Warner developed this social classification scheme:

Social Class	Membership
Upper-Upper	Old families and the traditional leaders
Lower-Upper	Socially prominent new rich
Upper-Middle	Professional and managerial successes
Lower-Middle	White-collar workers
Upper-Lower	Blue-collar workers
Lower-Lower	Unskilled workers and transients

Using this classification scheme, Warner and his colleagues determined that where and what a customer buys will differ not only by economic values but also according to symbolic values. Studies such as this help explain the response power of an ego-building lead of a letter like this one: "The list on which I found your name tells me that you are above-average in ...."

Cultural Influences: Each of us is a product of our cultural heritage. We behave against the background of the culture from which we emerged, grew up, and lived. Unwittingly, we all respond—even as customers—to our cultural environment.

Many aspects of culture, such as courtship and status, are universal to all cultures. Some symbols, such as a young person's purchase of life insurance to signal independence, have telling influence on consumer behavior. The direct marketing copywriter needs to know which colors, phrases, or symbols are looked on favorably and which are taboo in a culture.

The Nature of Demand

Just as motivations influence response to an offer, so does marketplace demand. Price competition, so prevalent in the retail environment, matters less in direct marketing. More influential are the factors of *nonprice competition:* product life cycle, market segmentation, product differentiation and positioning as well as promotion that relates benefits to buyer characteristics.

Nonprice competition is particularly prevalent in database marketing. Price becomes subordinated to other benefits presented in a well-conceived and relevant promotion, including convenience, an

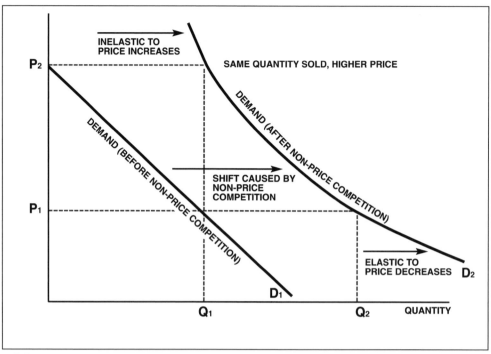

Exhibit 12-1: Nature of Demand

attractive product presentation, and the seller's prestige, service, and guarantees.

Price competition results in movements along a downward sloping demand curve, i.e., the lower the price, the greater the demand. The objective of nonprice competition, however, is to shift the entire demand curve so as to reflect an increase in total demand at all levels of price, as shown in Exhibit 12-1.

Exhibit 12-1 visualizes how nonprice competition can increase total demand, through shifting the total demand curve to the right, so that either a higher quantity of the product can be sold at the same price (P_1Q_2) or the same quantity can be sold at a higher price (P_2Q_1). Either is preferable to P_1Q_1!

A further objective of nonprice competition is to change the shape of the demand curve from a straight-line (D_1) to a parabola (D_2), demonstrating that it becomes *inelastic* to price increases and *elastic* to price decreases. Thus, increases in price result in relatively small decreases in demand; decreases in price result in relatively large increases in demand.

Sometimes a price increase stimulates demand for a product. This is true of products whose purchase is a way of impressing others—sometimes described as a "snob effect" or, as Thorstein Veblen called it, conspicuous consumption. Likewise, sometimes a decrease in the price of particular goods leads to a decrease in demand. Such goods are termed *inferior*. In contrast, *superior* goods are those with higher prices that result in higher demand. Potatoes have been presented as an example of this phenomenon: the quantity purchased was thought to decline as price declined. A 19th-century economist, after whom the so-called Giffen Paradox is named, observed a substitution effect of bread for potatoes whenever the price of potatoes decreased.

Customers, through such substitutions, demonstrate their superior or inferior reputability in associating with goods that themselves are perceived to be superior or inferior.

Offers and Benefits to Customers

The manner of presentation of a promotion, coupled with the request for a response, encompasses what is commonly called an *offer*. The offer is concerned not only with the product and its pricing—including its differentiation for market segments—but also payment methods and terms, guarantees, and a host of other devices including no-obligation trials, sweepstakes, contests, gifts, premiums, time limits and continuity clubs. Offers, incorporating customer benefits derived from a database, are structured to incite action and overcome human inertia.

Next to the product and its benefit for a particular market segment, the offer is a key determinant of success or failure of a promotion strategy.

The paragraphs in Exhibit 12-2 are from a 1932 direct-mail offer of oil leases. They demonstrate the use of *persuasion* copy.

Contrast this "Get rich quick" persuasion with the paragraphs in Exhibit 12-3, which also allude to riches, taken from a classic *benefit-oriented* offer written by Ed McLean and mailed extensively over a period of many years by *Newsweek* magazine.

These examples aptly illustrate the evolution of direct-response advertising. Direct marketing promotion experts now rely more on the selling value of benefits than on the hard sell of persuasion. Copy, design, and graphics are combined with arousing headlines and compelling offers in order to create an enticing impression, a favorable image.

The wise copywriter researches an audience before crafting words and graphics. Prior transactions and demographic/psychographic characteristics, as determined from a database, are important guides to effective writing.

The key sentence in the *Newsweek* letter shown in Exhibit 12-3 may very well be the question: "What, then, can *Newsweek* do for you?" In fact,

Dear Associate:

YOU MUST ACT THE VERY MINUTE YOU FINISH
READING THIS LETTER — or else! — IF YOU FAIL, — IF
YOU LET A SINGLE THING ON EARTH KEEP YOU OUT NOW —
——- YOU MAY BE TURNING DOWN THE GREATEST CHANCE OF
YOUR LIFE TO BECOME INDEPENDENTLY RICH — TO KNOW
THE BLOOD SURGING THRILL OF THE BIGGEST! — FATTEST!
— FORTUNE IN CASH PROFITS YOU HAVE EVER HAD A
CHANCE AT IN YOUR WHOLE LIFE!!

If you paid one bit of attention to my last
two letters to you — you have instantly recognized
that I am "ON THE TRAIL" of the very biggest thing
we have ever had a chance at!!

Now you HAVE GOT TO ACT!!

YOU HAVE GOT TO ACT QUICK! BY RETURN MAIL — IF
YOU ARE GOING TO GRASP THIS CHANCE TO PARTICIPATE
IN ABSOLUTELY THE BIGGEST AND MOST ASTOUNDING —
RECORD BREAKING, — PROFIT CLEAN UP WE HAVE EVER
KNOWN!!

In my last letter I gave you an "inkling" of
what I saw coming. I gave you a bare "thimble full"
of the utterly amazing — brain staggering — moun-
tainous mass of sensational advance information
that has come to me!!

You know what I am telling you IS RIGHT —
absolutely RIGHT! You KNOW the information I put in
your hands in my last letter is CORRECT because the
things I told you are IRREFUTABLE FACTS — FACTS....
I say! — that you can PUT YOUR FINGER ON —- THAT
YOU CAN EASILY...N-O-W...VERIFY!! — SITTING RIGHT
IN YOUR OWN HOME!!

Exhibit 12-2: Persuasion Copy Example

Dear Reader:

If the list upon which I found your name is any indication, this is not the first — nor will it be the last — subscription letter you receive. Quite frankly, your education and income set you apart from the general population and make you a highly rated prospect for everything from magazines to mutual funds.

You've undoubtedly "heard everything" by now in the way of promises and premiums. I won't try to top any of them.

Nor will I insult your intelligence.

If you subscribe to *Newsweek*, you won't get rich quick. You won't bowl over friends and business associates with clever remarks and sage comments after your first copy of *Newsweek* arrives. (Your conversation will benefit from a better understanding of the events and forces of our era, but that's all. Wit and wisdom are gifts no magazine can bestow.) And should you attain further professional or business success during the term of your subscription, you'll have your own native ability and good luck to thank for it — not *Newsweek*.

What, then, can *Newsweek* do for you?

Exhibit 12-3: Benefit Copy Example

asking this question about any product or service is a great way to pinpoint benefits.

One technique for identifying benefits is called FAB analysis (Features-Advantages-Benefits). An illustration of how FAB analysis works appears in Exhibit 12-4.

Translating Features of a Washing Machine into Advantages and then into Benefits

Features (what the product has):
compact size
high spin speed
wash temperature choice
range of colors
integrated tumble drier

Advantages (what the features do):
fits into a smaller space
clothes dry faster
accommodates a full range of fabrics
offers choice to consumer
moves from wash to dry automatically

Benefits (why customers buy):
space-saving
time-saving
does a good job
flexibility
convenience
economy
no more hand washing
choices

How to get from features to benefits:
imagination
technology
product design
common sense

Exhibit 12-4: Translating Features into Benefits

Nature of Promotion

Promotion is a part of the total marketing mix. However, it is not the process itself. Direct marketing is sometimes mistakenly equated with the promotion process, that is, as simply direct mail, or telemarketing or a website, or the use of some other print or broadcast medium. Direct marketing, of course, involves much more than just the promotion process.

It is in the nature of promotion to:

- fit products/services to needs/wants;
- achieve the unique selling proposition;
- integrate image/credibility with action/response;
- utilize databases effectively;
- maximize relevance through personalization;
- achieve ideal timing;
- measure response and be accountable for results.

Direct Response Advertising: Message and Media

Successful copywriters use the insights provided by databases to translate product features into advantages, the advantages into benefits and benefits into words, design, and graphics.

Vic Schwab, who has such a track record, described long ago the copywriting art as "learning to think like a horse":

A farmer lost his horse but found him again almost immediately. "How'd you find him so quickly?" asked a neighbor. To which the farmer replied: "Well, I just asked myself, if I were a horse, where would I go? I went there and there he was!"

Schwab's point was simple: Show people an advantage. This meant, to Schwab, that you had to know them. Today, database marketing provides that knowledge, enabling the trained copywriter to "think like a horse"—to relate the benefits of an offer to customers.

Geared to a database, a direct mail letter can substitute for a personal call. The formats are virtually unlimited:

Letter/Letterhead	Broadsides	Bulletins
Personalized	Brochures	Price Lists
Lift Letters	Booklets	Inserts
Memorandums	Catalogs	Reprints
Cards Circulars	Self-Mailers	Audio Records
Folders	Publications	Video Tapes

Invitations	Action Devices	Mailing Envelopes
Survey Research	Website Links	Package Inserts
Coupons	Order Forms	Billing Inserts
Tickets	Applications	Co-operative
Specialty Items	Reply Envelopes	Mailings
Calendars	Reply Cards	Syndicated
Novelties	Reply Labels	Mailings

The basic format, however, is this one:

- Mailing Envelope
- Letter (preferably, database-personalized)
- Circular (only if needed)
- Order Form
- Return Envelope

How long should a direct-mail letter be? Long enough to say what it has to say—no longer, no shorter. The old prejudice that no one reads long copy simply isn't true. People will keep reading if it is interesting to them, Some prefer to write letters by formula in order to keep the copy flowing in a logical manner. There are many formulas to choose from. One is labeled A-I-D-A:

- Attract Attention
- Arouse Interest
- Stimulate Desire
- Call for Action

Another formula is labeled P-P-P-P:

- Picture — get attention early in the copy
- Promise — describe the product's benefits to the reader
- Prove — show value of the product or service
- Push — ask for the order

Also, Bob Stone's Seven-Step Formula has stood the test of time:

1. Promise a benefit in your headline or first paragraph.
2. Immediately enlarge on your most important benefit.
3. Tell the reader specifically what he or she will get.
4. Back up your statements with proofs and endorsements.
5. Tell the reader what will be lost by not acting.
6. Rephrase your prominent benefits in the closing offer.
7. Incite action now.

The promotion formats of direct-response advertising other than direct mail can be basically categorized as:

- Print media—magazines and newspapers
- Broadcast media—television and radio
- Interactive electronic media—telephone, television, and personal computers

Direct response advertising in newspapers and magazines can be effective, but message space is limited compared to direct mail packages or catalogs. Like catalog copy, the headline must gain attention quickly and the body copy must tell the story completely yet concisely. The copy, as always, must be benefit-oriented and the graphic design should lead the reader through the ad's elements in the sequence intended. Illustrations augment copy. A response device must be provided, of course.

Television's limitations for direct-response advertisers have been its high cost and the short duration of an individual commercial message. Cable television, including emerging interactive features, has made possible more *directed* messages and desirable market segmentation. This has increased the effectiveness (results vs. costs) of the television medium.

Radio has had practical limitations, too. Most radio listeners are driving an automobile or are otherwise occupied, and telephones or pencil and pad are out of reach. Because radio does not provide the opportunity to visualize, it is most effective with known products or those that do not require demonstration. Both radio and television have been successfully used as a support medium, calling attention to forthcoming print or direct mail messages.

Interactive electronic media—notably, the telephone and, most recently, the Internet—are an integral part of direct marketing. These media, like direct mail but unlike print or broadcast, offer two-way communication: they can be utilized for response (inbound) as well as for advertising (outbound). Telephones, through a modem with personal computers, now provide visualization and demonstration along with a printed record. A similar alliance is occurring with FAX machines. Soon, black boxes will extend interactivity, wired and wireless, with TV.

An integral part of this interactivity has been and continues to be the salesperson. Personal selling—including selling by telephone—can provide person-to-person, two-way communication, because a salesperson can listen and use feedback to tailor promotional messages to individual buyers. While a personal sales call can be tremendously expensive, if a prospective customer is qualified, serious, and sincerely interested, a personal sales call can be worthwhile.

Direct marketing can incorporate elements of the personal sales call. The sales presentation may be contained in printed or broadcast direct-response advertising messages, or a mail-order package. A salesperson might speak to customers by telephone, or call on a qualified prospect that has been identified through a lead-generating program. Similarly, a catalog from a retail store might cause the recipient to visit the store, where a salesperson can complete the transaction.

Interactive Workshop 12-1:

Developing Targeted Promotions
Example A: Brown University

A targeted fundraising campaign developed for Brown University by Bachurski Associates is an example of a carefully segmented development campaign — and a model for how to appeal to specific segments within a customer/prospect database.

Brown University was doing just fine with its "hard-dollar" fundraising. But questions arose with its annual capital campaign. In fact, the exact same appeal was being sent to all 60,000 members of the university community's database!

Bachurski Associates created a base letter for the general mailing. And then, they fine-tuned it. Eighteen different versions of the letter and response form were sent as appeal mailings. These variations were derived from their database.

Copy sent to prospects that had never given before stressed the importance of their participation:

> Brown (with an endowment much smaller than those of many Ivy League universities) faces a serious challenge in recruiting and retaining faculty who are at the forefront of their disciplines. Competitive salaries are not enough; these pioneering intellectuals must also have outstanding library collections, research facilities and equipment, and in many cases the collaboration of outstanding graduate students.
>
> For the resources to attract top-notch faculty, Brown relies heavily on the support of the Brown Annual Fund. Today, Brown looks to you for support in the education of Brown students.

These words in the appeal to *previous donors,* sought upgrades:

> Thank you for your recent generous gift to the Brown Annual Fund. As we officially launch the 1995-96 campaigns, we hope you will consider increasing your support with a special gift, today. Remember, under the challenge grant described in the enclosed letter, your participation in the Brown Annual Fund this year will help bring Brown $1.5 million in matching funds.

Further customization was directed to *parents of present students* ("The education your son or daughter is getting is very special") and to *parents of students of prior years* ("Help sustain the institution that gave your child a great education").

Grandparents received special copy, too:

> The years your grandchild is spending at Brown will produce lifelong benefits. By making a tax-deductible gift to the Brown Annual Fund, you can ensure that these irreplaceable years are the best and most productive they can be. Remember that, under the challenge grant described in the enclosed letter, your participation in the Brown Annual Fund this year will help bring Brown $1.5 million in matching funds.

One part of the program included a lift letter from an alumnae fund chairman targeted to high-income alumnae stressing the tax value of capital gift giving. Another component included segmenting mailings along the size of past gifts.

This copy went to *recent Brown graduates:*

> While your years at Brown are still fresh in your mind, please remember that support from alumni is a cornerstone of the education you received. Your participation is especially important to Brown today; under the matching grant described in the enclosed letter, your gift to the Brown Annual Fund will help bring Brown $1.5 million in matching funds.

International graduates were singled out with this copy:

```
Wherever you travel in the world, wherever your
career may take you, you carry with you the fruits
of your years at Brown.
     You carry not only the information you
gathered here, but also the habits of mind, the
intellectual curiosity, and the skills that enable
you to extend your education throughout your life.
```

The end result of all this targeted (directed) writing was a dramatic rise in both the volume and the size of donations.

Exercises:

■ With reference to information contained in the Mountain & Valley Resort Ski Rental database of young skiers, detailed in Chapter 13, suggest a copy appeal to those who have neither affinity nor a prior connection with Brown University.

■ Suggest segments of the Mountain & Valley Resort Guest database, detailed in Chapter 14, which might derive benefit from a contribution the Brown University Annual Fund. What words would you use to convey this?

Example B: L. L. Bean

Bonner Slosberg, Inc., customized a direct-response advertising campaign for L.L. Bean that overlapped the company's customer base with the subscription lists of 20 national magazines, then varied the magazine ads according to what subscriber-customers had previously purchased from L. L. Bean.

Two people living next door, for example, receiving the same issue of the same magazine, might read two very different L. L. Bean ads. This experiment allowed the advertiser to gauge the effectiveness of their print advertisements by comparing a customer's past buying habits to purchases made or not made after the customer received the selective ad.

Exercises:

■ With reference to Chapters 13 and 14, how might Mountain & Valley Resort conduct a similar experiment (test)?

■ Suggest how copy going to each segment might be versioned for L.L.Bean. Do the same for Mountain & Valley Resort.

Example C: Hallmark Business Expressions

This versioned letter offered custom greeting cards targeted to a number of different market segments: marketing officers of banks, real estate firms, sports franchise marketing directors, insurance executives, etc. Each letter addressed the specific needs of the recipient. For bank executives, copy suggested that "Perhaps you'd like to welcome a new depositor ... celebrate a paid-off loan ... announce new rates or checking account benefits ... or communicate with branch managers and bank officers."

A typical letter sent to the CEO of a bank read:

```
I'd like to propose a unique business partnership
with you.
        Active as you are in the banking industry,
you recognize the value of forming productive,
lasting relationships with your banking customers
and employees ... and staying in touch with them
throughout the year.
        Hallmark, with our 85 years' successful
experience in relationship building, would like to
share our expertise with you - by designing
customer greeting cards to help you form, and
solidify, these vital bonds and consequently,
improve your bottom line.
```

Sent to the Marketing Director of the New England Patriots, that same paragraph read "Perhaps you'd like to welcome a new season ticket-holder ... thank a supplier ... celebrate a winning streak ...or salute outstanding employees and spur them on to win!"

Exercises:
- Study the industrial (business-to-business) segmentation alternatives in Chapter 9. Select three business clusters from the CD accompanying this book that might benefit from Hallmark Business Expressions.

- Write lead paragraphs translating features and advantages of Hallmark's product into benefits offered each segment.

IV
Cases

Chapter 13

The Mountain & Valley Resort (MVR) Ski Database

The CD-ROM accompanying this book summarizes the Ski customer database for Mountain & Valley Resort. Summary records permit more meaningful demonstration of data manipulation than individual records do. The database analysis tool links on the CD go through the process of database marketing analysis: merge/purge of individual customer records, transaction and demographic analysis, and report preparation based on cluster penetration.

Individual customer records, from which these summaries were derived, included transaction as well as enhancement data. Transactions were sequenced and timed. Appended Cluster codes, ZIP codes and GPS codes enabled identification of geographic, demographic and psychographic characteristics.

Statistical and analytical tools, (see Chapters 3, 5, 6, 7, and 10) are also included on the CD to enable correlation of such data with market penetration and response rates. Customers can be profiled, their lifetime value can be calculated, and targeted approaches to the most attractive market segments can be developed. Customer creation and cultivation can be planned. Experiments can be designed.

When you place the CD into your computer's CD drive, your default browser will automatically activate. You can then choose a specific Interactive Workshop from those listed on the Welcome page. These tools usually work best with a Netscape browser, and it is necessary to have an Adobe Acrobat Reader. If you do not have these installed on your machine, you can download them from the site links provided.

A database is a means for any organization to cultivate the customers it has already acquired and is also a means to create new customers whose profiles are like the most profitable ones it already has.

To achieve both of these objectives, a database must be much more than just a mailing list. It must categorize customer transactions, their demographic and psychographic characteristics as well as the environment of their locations. Objective research and testing, then, fuel inspired decision-making.

The following database model/simulation demonstrates how an organization can use its database to segment its markets.

The Mountain & Valley Resort Ski Database

Mountain & Valley Resort (MVR) is a family-oriented vacation destination and conference center as well as a weekend or permanent residence home for many. It encompasses 11,000 acres of land in the Blue Ridge Mountains of Virginia. Its market for vacationers as well as residents can be segmented by transactions and by customer characteristics. A more comprehensive description of MVR is contained in Workshop 8-1 in Chapter 8.

Each year about 200,000 people visit the resort, which now seeks to better understand the various segments of its customer database in order to become more efficient and precise in its marketing and to maximize response from its direct promotion offers. MVR seeks to profile market segments most like its current customers in order to target prospects in the future. And, MVR seeks to cultivate its present customers, through *continuity and cross-selling,* to find those most likely to visit again by developing predictable patterns of sequencing and timing, as well as purpose, of visits. It also is appropriate for MVR to calculate the Lifetime Value of a Customer so as to guide its ongoing marketing planning and budgeting.

MVR recognizes that customers are acquired and best served by those organizations that know the characteristics, as well as the sequencing and timing, of actions taken by their current buyers. And, since all customers are not alike, these need to be viewed as groups, as market segments. (The ultimate "group" contains just one member.) Such segments then become the focus of product differentiation and promotional positioning.

MVR Ski Database Availability

MVR knows that at direct marketing's core is a database. A recap of elements that could guide its database-directed customer creation and cultivation activities is presented in Exhibit 13-1.

DATA ELEMENTS	COMMENTS
Customer; Prospect:	**From MVR and/or Enhancement Databases:**
Identifier Number (PIN)	A unique ID number
Name	With title, i.e., Mr/Mrs/Miss/Ms/Dr
Address(es)	Physical and/or mailing address(es)
ZIP Code (+4) of Residence	An indicator of lifestyle and propensity to buy
Phone/Fax/E-mail Number(s)	From Experian or other (if not in MVR's)
Gender	From "given name" table
Ethnic Origin	From "surname" table
Age Indicator	As known or from enhancement databases
Other Demographic	As known or from enhancement databases
Psychographic Actions Interests Opinions	As known or from enhancement databases
Transactions; Sequence; Timing:	**First; Most Recent; 3-10 Years Limit:**
Source/Offer	Media, message, offer, publicity and/or other
Intermediary Booking	Plot origin/destination; DIR=direct; AGT=agent. GRP=group
Product (Line) … Activities	As applicable: ski, golf, tennis, family-oriented, nature, perf arts
Booking Date…Initial & Subsequent	Recency and frequency…sequencing and timing
Booking Revenue…Initial & Subsequent	Monetary
Number of Participants in Buyer Unit	Households, families, individuals, groups
Length of Stay	Number of nights
Credit Evaluation	Scored from Experian or Other + MVR's records

Exhibit 13-1: Mountain & Valley Resort Database Elements

MVR has provided these relational customer databases:

- 35,000+ ski equipment rental customers (virtually all day skiers rather than overnight guests at the resort) for the three most recent ski seasons. Individual records provide name/address; recency and frequency of rental; skier age, title, gender and type (cautious, moderate, aggressive); and when skied (date as well as midweek or weekend).
- 70,000+ resort guest customers database, some with records going as far back as ten years. Individual records (although not all of them) provide name/address; reservation detail; conference attendees; group bookings; participation in activities (ski, golf, tennis, family-oriented, performing arts, nature); demographics (title, age, gender); source (offer, media, agent); transactions data (revenues, recency, frequency/continuity, sequencing, timing).

Enhancements could be appended from external databases. Lifestyle Selector's proprietary database could provide household information such as foreign or domestic travel, family size, age, marital status, income, occupation, home ownership. Experian's credit records could provide financial evaluations and shopping indicators. Driver license records could provide age; automobile registrations could provide detail about cars owned; and, telephone directory records could provide mobility data.

An infinite number of variables can be derived for small geographic areas (Zip Codes or Block Groups) from Census and other sources such as Simmons and MRI. Coupled with multivariate statistical analysis, these can provide both explanation and prediction of market penetration. And, Geographic Information System (GIS) mapping can visualize the location of customers and the reach of travel agents.

Proposed MVR Ski Database Analysis

Market segmentation evaluates market penetration of customers versus defined market clusters or else response vs. directed promotion efforts, as the dependent variable. It then correlates the *dependent* variable with relevant *independent* (causation) variables. It is important that such market clusters, large enough to be statistically valid but still maintaining homogeneity, be *custom-developed,* so as to include only geographic areas relevant to MVR. Such custom clustering also enables identification of only those variables having potential impact on MVR market penetration.

While an infinite number of geographic, demographic and/or psychographic *independent* variables are obtainable from Census and other sources, only those relevant to MVR should be selected for analysis. Multivariate statistical techniques (correlation and regression, factor, cluster analyses) can then be used to relate those variables most reflective of lifestyle and the best predictors of buying behavior.

Analysis can be enhanced when coupled with demographic data about *individuals* and/or *households* and then further enhanced when cross-tabbed by customer transactions as well as by R/F/M (Recency/Frequency/Monetary) scoring. GIS (Geographic Information System) mapping, utilizing Census Bureau's TIGER (Topological Integrated Geographic Encoding and Referencing) System, can visualize reach and penetration of customers.

Analysis of the database can provide a definitive profile of the day skiers who are equipment rental customers, summarizing such variables as recency and frequency of rental; skier age, title, gender and type (cautious, moderate, aggressive); and when skied (date as well as midweek or weekend). An objective here would be to determine media and messages appropriate for finding new customers like those in the most profitable segment.

Much could be gained, in terms of the lifetime value of a customer, through study of how customer continuity can be improved. Many organizations are using frequency reward programs to tie customers to them. Some offer events and discounts to promote continuity. Best results seem to be achieved by those establishing affinity groups to cement ongoing relationships.

Market Segmentation and Customer Penetration of the MVR Ski Database

35,000+ transaction and demographic records of ski rental customers whose relationship with MVR was during a three-year period were provided. Duplicates were purged and individuals were merged to the household level, resulting in a net count of 31,906 households with transaction data. These 31,906 were matched to an external (Experian) database for enhancement with demographic data if/as available. Matches resulted on 21,436 individuals (67.18%) and 4,474 households (14.02%); the remaining 5,996 records (18.79%) could not be matched for enhancement. (This merge/purge process and some resultant customer records are demonstrated in Interactive Workshop 13-1 on the adjunct CD-ROM.)

Demographic enhancement provided from hits with the Experian database included these: inferred age grouping; dwelling type; households identified as direct mail responders; family type; gender; head-of-household status; ethnic markets code; homeowner/renter code; length-of-residence; and, estimated income range. Not all variables were available for all records when matched.

Characteristics of Ski Customer Households

Marketing thrives on information enabling practitioners to direct new business acquisition efforts to those prospects who have a high probability of becoming and remaining customers.

Such information comes from three main sources:

1. From within the organization's own customer database comes information about product preferences, purchase patterns (recency, frequency, monetary value), and certain demographics garnered in the course of doing business.

2. From data sources outside the organization comes enhancement information that can be appended to that already known about customers such as purchase actions taken with other firms, or public record data such as that about buying activity.

3. From environmental data sources, most notable being the Census of Population and Housing, comes information about small geographic areas, including ZIP Codes. Predictive and explanatory values of such information hinge upon the accepted principle that people with like interests tend to cluster and their behavior tends to be influenced by the environment of which they themselves are a part.

This analysis is concerned with the first and second sources listed: information derived from MVR's own ski rental customer database, as enhanced with data derived from the external (Experian) database. Frequency distributions of transaction and demographic variables identified within the ski rental customer database appear in Exhibits 13-2, 13-3 and 13-4. (These can be excerpted, too, from the CD, Interactive Workshop 13-1.) Since not all data variables could be identified for all records, the distribution totals vary. Note, too, that distributions are an allocation of records, not a measure of market penetration.

Ski Rental Transaction data summarized in Exhibit 13-2 are:

- Skier Type – aggressive, cautious, moderate
- When Skied – midweek, weekend
- Frequency Skied – number of times
- Average Ski Seasons – number of seasons
- Average Age – within age ranges
- Total Rental Amount – within monetary ranges

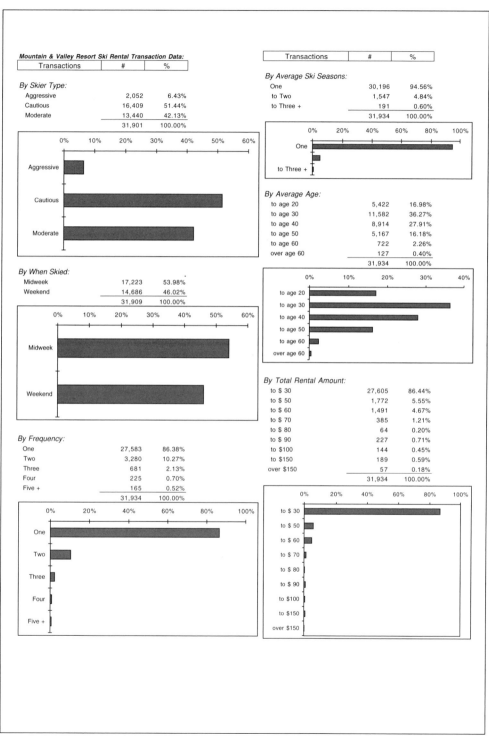

Exhibit 13-2: Ski Rental Customer Transaction Data

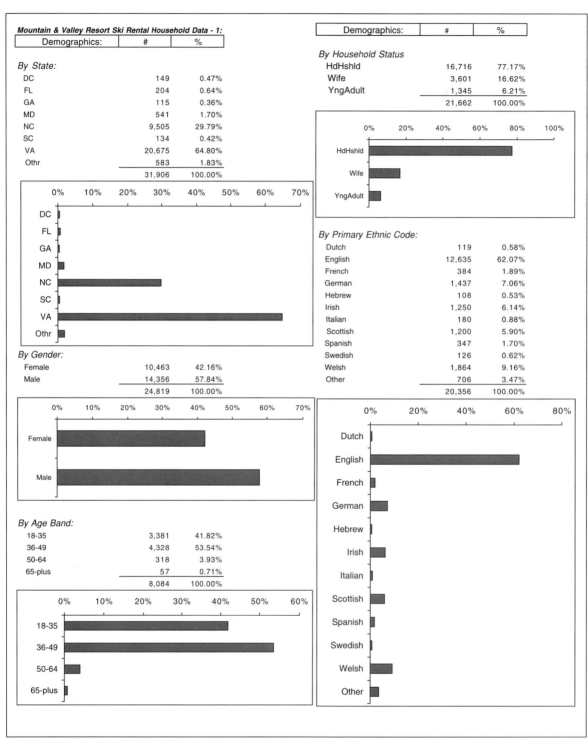

Exhibit 13-3: Ski Rental Customer Household Data (1)

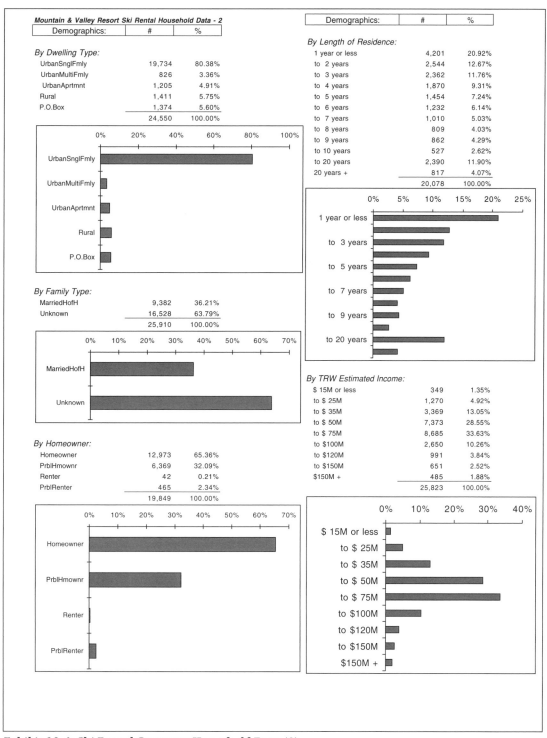

Mountain & Valley Resort Ski Rental Household Data - 2

Demographics:	#	%

By Dwelling Type:

	#	%
UrbanSnglFmly	19,734	80.38%
UrbanMultiFmly	826	3.36%
UrbanAprtmnt	1,205	4.91%
Rural	1,411	5.75%
P.O.Box	1,374	5.60%
	24,550	100.00%

By Family Type:

	#	%
MarriedHofH	9,382	36.21%
Unknown	16,528	63.79%
	25,910	100.00%

By Homeowner:

	#	%
Homeowner	12,973	65.36%
PrblHmownr	6,369	32.09%
Renter	42	0.21%
PrblRenter	465	2.34%
	19,849	100.00%

Demographics:	#	%

By Length of Residence:

	#	%
1 year or less	4,201	20.92%
to 2 years	2,544	12.67%
to 3 years	2,362	11.76%
to 4 years	1,870	9.31%
to 5 years	1,454	7.24%
to 6 years	1,232	6.14%
to 7 years	1,010	5.03%
to 8 years	809	4.03%
to 9 years	862	4.29%
to 10 years	527	2.62%
to 20 years	2,390	11.90%
20 years +	817	4.07%
	20,078	100.00%

By TRW Estimated Income:

	#	%
$ 15M or less	349	1.35%
to $ 25M	1,270	4.92%
to $ 35M	3,369	13.05%
to $ 50M	7,373	28.55%
to $ 75M	8,685	33.63%
to $100M	2,650	10.26%
to $120M	991	3.84%
to $150M	651	2.52%
$150M +	485	1.88%
	25,823	100.00%

Exhibit 13-4: Ski Rental Customer Household Data (2)

Ski Rental Demographics data in Exhibits 13-3 and 13-4 are:
- State of Residence – percent distribution
- Gender – female, male
- Age – range bands
- Household Status – head-of-household, wife, young adult
- Primary Ethnic Code – percent distribution
- Dwelling Type – urban/rural, single/multi/apartment
- Family Type – married, unknown
- Homeowner – known/probable homeowner, known/probable renter
- Length of Residence – years lived at given address
- TRW Estimated income – percent household distribution

Household Cluster Penetration Analysis of Ski Customers

The preceding presentation of the transaction and demographic characteristics of MVR's ski customer database is the basis of the customer profiling that follows.

An initial step in profiling of the MVR ski customers is the determination of market penetration within demographically and psychographically comparable clusters. A major reason for such clustering is to derive units containing sufficient observations to assure statistical validity of the determined predictions.

Once the statistical clusters are structured, the percentage of MVR ski customers in each cluster relative to its total customers is calculated. Similarly, the percentage of households in each cluster relative to total households is calculated. An index is then derived by dividing the ski customers percent into the universal household percent and multiplying that quotient by 100 for each respective cluster [(%Cust/%HH)*100]. An index value of 100 is average customer penetration of all households; a value above 100 is above average; a value below 100 is below average.

The Household Cluster Penetration Analysis ranks clusters in descending order of the index; it then records the degree of marketing effectiveness within each cluster and, cumulatively, within quintiles (20% groupings of clusters).

A bar chart relating penetration of ski rental customers and all households within the five quintiles of the Household Cluster Penetration Analysis Report is shown in Exhibit 13-5. Such visualization of the discrepancy of the customer and household percents in the high and low quintiles validates the benefits of clustering and the resultant selective prospect targeting. The chart in Exhibit 13-5 reveals that nearly 40% of MVR's ski rental customers are to be found among about 20% of the households.

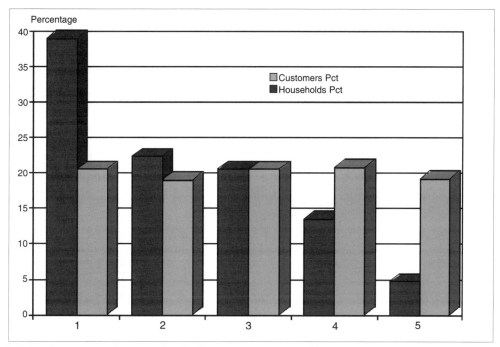

Exhibit 13-5: MVR Ski Household Cluster Penetration Chart

The key measurement in the Household Cluster Penetration Analysis shown in Exhibit 13-6 is the index derived by dividing the percent of all customers by the percent of all households. A clear pattern emerges from this evaluation. Penetration of ski customers within the top 20.51% of all households is 190.02% of the average penetration of all quintiles whereas that in the bottom 19.18% is 24.41%, a ratio of 1:7.78. The top cluster (#64) is 728.79% of the average of all clusters; the bottom cluster (#76) is 10.33% of average, a ratio of 1:70.55.

A definition of the demographic profile together with the lifestyle traits of each cluster can be found on the adjunct CD-ROM in Interactive Workshop 13-1. Simply click on the cluster code number in the Household Cluster Penetration Quintiles report to link to a description of that cluster. A summary of the characteristics of all clusters, rank ordered, appears in the Household Cluster Penetration Highlights report on the CD.

Quintile	Rank	Cluster Code	Customers	Customer Percent	Customer Total %	Households	Household Percent	Household Total %	Index	Cluster Universe
1	1	064	608	2.23	2.23	11,926	0.31	0.31	728.79	179,710
	2	015	643	2.36	4.59	26,274	0.67	0.98	349.85	489,705
	3	001	1,151	4.23	8.82	48,437	1.24	2.23	339.69	1,136,221
	4	036	316	1.16	9.98	17,789	0.46	2.68	253.93	639,608
	5	022	1,119	4.11	14.09	64,166	1.65	4.33	249.30	1,609,368
	6	043	105	0.39	14.47	6,396	0.16	4.49	234.69	278,880
	7	008	634	2.33	16.80	46,037	1.18	5.68	196.87	461,093
	8	029	54	0.20	17.00	4,203	0.11	5.78	183.71	224,378
	9	079	38	0.14	17.14	3,042	0.08	5.86	178.55	54,013
	10	016	790	2.90	20.04	63,897	1.64	7.50	176.74	1,151,684
	11	066	277	1.02	21.06	23,152	0.59	8.10	171.04	526,125
	12	009	765	2.81	23.86	64,212	1.65	9.75	170.31	891,479
	13	023	706	2.59	26.46	61,085	1.57	11.32	165.22	1,817,221
	14	002	966	3.55	30.00	95,748	2.46	13.78	144.22	1,877,576
	15	068	37	0.14	30.14	3,864	0.10	13.87	136.84	77,626
	16	004	95	0.35	30.49	10,157	0.26	14.14	133.72	123,941
	17	050	1,695	6.22	36.71	181,231	4.65	18.79	133.70	2,000,304
	18	037	250	0.92	37.63	27,052	0.69	19.48	132.11	835,823
	19	071	367	1.35	38.97	39,976	1.03	20.51	131.24	478,102
Quintile Totals:			**10,616**	**38.97**		**798,644**	**20.51**		**Quintile Index: 190.02**	**14,852,857**
2	20	044	46	0.17	39.14	5,072	0.13	20.64	129.66	269,307
	21	010	935	3.43	42.58	108,476	2.79	23.43	123.22	1,512,968
	22	012	793	2.91	45.49	93,664	2.41	25.83	121.03	1,552,143
	23	019	1,204	4.42	49.91	142,319	3.66	29.49	120.94	3,128,095

Exhibit 13-6: MVR Ski Household Cluster Penetration Quintiles

Quintile	Rank	Cluster Code	Customers	Customer Percent	Customer Total %	Households	Household Percent	Household Total %	Index	Cluster Universe
2	24	003	2,117	7.77	57.68	266,083	6.83	36.32	113.74	5,218,245
	25	017	988	3.63	61.31	126,676	3.25	39.57	111.50	2,237,083
Quintile Totals:			**6,083**	**22.33**		**742,290**	**19.06**	**Quintile Index:**	**117.15**	**13,917,841**
3	26	051	399	1.46	62.77	51,553	1.32	40.90	110.64	598,575
	27	024	1,430	5.25	68.02	185,126	4.75	45.65	110.42	5,461,613
	28	025	184	0.68	68.70	23,971	0.62	46.27	109.73	402,316
	29	011	267	0.98	69.68	36,464	0.94	47.21	104.67	308,851
	30	026	743	2.73	72.41	102,932	2.64	49.85	103.19	3,550,937
	31	018	1,083	3.98	76.38	155,954	4.01	53.85	99.27	1,630,752
	32	045	149	0.55	76.93	23,023	0.59	54.45	92.51	1,148,877
	33	005	1,041	3.82	80.75	169,530	4.35	58.80	87.78	3,710,270
	34	040	294	1.08	81.83	49,075	1.26	60.06	85.64	1,651,497
Quintile Totals:			**5,590**	**20.52**		**797,628**	**20.48**	**Quintile Index:**	**100.19**	**18,463,688**
4	35	038	535	1.96	83.79	91,080	2.34	62.40	83.97	2,689,430
	36	072	260	0.95	84.75	45,359	1.16	63.56	81.94	644,200
	37	052	1,265	4.64	89.39	228,997	5.88	69.44	78.97	3,583,469
	38	078	61	0.22	89.62	11,276	0.29	69.73	77.35	197,378
	39	082	52	0.19	89.81	9,920	0.25	69.99	74.93	192,265
	40	047	61	0.22	90.03	13,451	0.35	70.33	64.84	686,972
	41	054	306	1.12	91.16	69,559	1.79	72.12	62.89	919,020
	42	081	152	0.56	91.71	35,606	0.91	73.04	61.02	378,899
	43	080	67	0.25	91.96	16,215	0.42	73.45	59.07	299,773
	44	031	52	0.19	92.15	12,888	0.33	73.78	57.68	731,496
	45	053	85	0.31	92.46	25,732	0.66	74.44	47.23	194,781
	46	075	220	0.81	93.27	70,085	1.80	76.24	44.87	799,946
	47	073	558	2.05	95.32	178,217	4.58	80.82	44.76	2,356,630

Exhibit 13-6: MVR Ski Household Cluster Penetration Quintiles (continued)

Quintile	Rank	Cluster Code	Customers	Customer Percent	Customer Total %	Households	Household Percent	Household Total %	Index	Cluster Universe
Quintile Totals:			**3,674**	**13.49**		**808,385**	**20.76**	**Quintile Index:**	**64.97**	**13,674,259**
5	48	013	131	0.48	95.80	52,231	1.34	82.16	35.85	878,785
	49	020	231	0.85	96.65	101,394	2.60	84.77	32.57	2,230,269
	50	006	316	1.16	97.81	146,333	3.76	88.52	30.87	3,907,685
	51	027	249	0.91	98.72	150,097	3.85	92.38	23.72	5,266,438
	52	041	107	0.39	99.12	70,122	1.80	94.18	21.81	2,426,708
	53	055	158	0.58	99.70	111,769	2.87	97.05	20.21	1,814,467
	54	076	83	0.30	100.00	114,854	2.95	100.00	10.33	1,615,433
Quintile Totals:			**1,275**	**4.68**		**746,800**	**19.18**	**Quintile Index:**	**24.41**	**18,139,785**
Grand Totals:			**27,238**	**100.00**		**3,893,747**	**100.00**			**79,048,430**

Exhibit 13-6: MVR Ski Household Cluster Penetration Quintiles (continued)

Correlation of Cluster Penetration with Demographics and Lifestyles

After observing indexed differences, it remains to determine the reasons for such differences in terms of the demographic and psychographic make-up of clusters as well as the characteristics, described earlier, applicable to the MVR ski customer households.

The purpose of such determination is to be able to direct future customer acquisition and develop promotional efforts for those segments that have a high propensity for response or else to avoid expenditures on those segments that have a low probability for success. A related purpose is to be able to position products and create copy that will motivate those to whom such an offer is directed to respond.

Correlation analysis helps to *explain* the market penetration *rank orderings,* while step-wise multivariate regression analysis can predict the propensity of households within a cluster to respond to an offer made by MVR.

Exhibit 13-7, Correlation of Ski Rental Household Cluster Penetration with 128 Demographic Variables, rank-orders those variables having the highest correlation coefficients (Simple R Values) with cluster penetration—positive or negative—of MVR ski rental customers. Only the 49 most highly correlated demographic variables are shown in Exhibit 13-7. These variables can explain differences in penetration. They can also be used to direct market segmentation and guide advertising creation. The Regression Analysis of 128 Demographic Variables vs. Penetration, Exhibit 13-8, then becomes the statistical basis for defining clusters not now penetrated but which fit the demographic profiles of those which do.

Exhibit 13-9, Correlation of Ski Household Cluster Penetration with 1190 Lifestyle Variables, rank orders those variables having highest correlation coefficients (Simple R Values) with cluster penetration—positive or negative—of customers. Only the 49 most highly correlated demographic variables are shown in Exhibit 13-9. These variables can explain differences in penetration. They can also be used to direct market segmentation and guide advertising creation. The Regression Analysis of 1190 Lifestyle Variables vs. Penetration, Exhibit 13-10, becomes the statistical basis for defining clusters which fit the desired lifestyle profiles.

Reference to the Cluster Penetration and Characteristics Analysis section of Interactive Workshop 13-1 on the adjunct CD-ROM will disclose a link to a Demographic Analysis report. This report indexes and rank orders available demographic variables relating customer averages to U.S. averages. The top variable, indexed at 258.07% of average, is "military population;" the bottom variable, 21.59% of average, is "Hispanic population." That is, ski customers are more likely to come

Demography Simple R Correlation Report

Seq Num	Item Numr	REL_DETAIL_DESC	Simple R Value
1	62	Population age of 18 to 24 years	0.4833
2	36	Ratio of group quarters pop to total pop	0.4813
3	87	Never married population	0.2990
4	118	Population age of 18 years or older	0.2481
5	57	Non-white/non-black population	0.1890
6	113	Auto and auto repair expenditures	0.1789
7	128	Percentage of population with a male head of household	0.1779
8	55	White population	0.1740
9	43	1989 to 1996 Growth in Median Household Income	0.1655
10	111	Audio - video sales/rental/service expenditures	0.1610
11	124	Ratio of household income to total expenses	0.1567
12	82	Technical occupations	0.1520
13	75	Education - post-graduate degree	0.1446
14	120	Average years of education	0.1276
15	44	1996 to 2001 Growth in Median Household Income	0.1182
16	47	Household income of less than $20,000	0.1138
17	78	Percent of population not in labor force	0.1045
18	98	Housing of 10 to 49 units	0.0998
19	133	Percent of 1990 other families with no related children	0.0977
20	74	Education - Bachelor's degree	0.0974
21	95	Renter-occupied housing	0.0929
22	73	Education - Associate's degree	0.0854
23	92	Married population	0.0838
24	42	1996 to 2001 Change in Median Age	0.0686
25	97	Housing of 2 to 9 units	0.0684
26	41	1990 to 1996 Change in Median Age	0.0584
27	112	Pet shop and veterinary expenditures	0.0556
28	84	Agricultural occupations	0.0552
29	83	Service occupations	0.0535
30	126	Rural population	0.0506
31	45	1990 to 1996 Change in Median Value of Housing Unit	0.0496
32	121	Average Occupation	0.0448
33	76	Military population	0.0417
34	72	Education - some college	0.0401
35	38	1996 to 2001 population growth	0.0378
36	46	1996 to 2001 Change in Median Value of Housing Unit	0.0351
37	131	Percentage of married families without children	0.0312
38	100	Mobile home housing units	0.0263
39	37	1990 to 1996 population growth	0.0211
40	101	Restaurant expenditures	0.0197
41	105	Moving and storage expenditures	0.0162
42	39	Growth in Household Count from 1990 to 1996	0.0145
43	127	Seasonal population	0.0107
44	48	Household income of $20,000 to $34,999	0.0082
45	81	Professional occupations	-.0068
46	107	Florist expenditures	-.0116
47	51	Household income of $75,000 to $99,999	-.0318
48	52	Household income of $100,000 to $124,999	-.0369
49	26	Median Household Income, HHLDR age 55-64 (Computed)	-.0411

Exhibit 13-7: Correlation of Ski Household Cluster Penetration with 128 Demographic Variables (Only Top 49 shown here)

```
Statistical analysis <DBSTATS>          Time = 14:45:10

Job Description = Demography Simp        Y = Cust/HH
No. Obs. = 54       No. Var. = 129       F1 = 1.0          F2 = 2.0      Y var. # = 4
R =0.600664         R SQ. =0.360798      TOL = 0.001000    NUMBER STEPS = 2
F LEVEL = 8.7880    PROBABILITY = 0.99947
OVERALL SIGNIFICANCE F = 14.3935        PROBABILITY = 0.99999
STANDARD ERROR OF Y = 0.00633           Cust/HH           AVERAGE Y = 0.887279630E-02
CONSTANT TERM = 2.07575631142
```

VAR.NO.	COEFFIECENT	COEF S ERR.	r TO Y	T	PROB.
X- 88	0.158251101137E-01	0.539036E-02	-0.1387	2.936	0.9950
X-106	-2.08118455007	0.398672	-0.5028	-5.220	1.0000

VAR.DESC.	%CONTRIBUTION	AVG. X	%AVG.Y	STD.COEF
PP96A15PMAR	24.028	0.9656	0.2E+03	0.4777
PEX96_RENTAL	75.972	1.000	0.2E+05	-0.8494

PREDICTED VS ACTUAL RESULTS

OBS. NO.	ACTUAL	PREDICTED	DEVIATION	Code
1	0.23763E-01	0.10124E-01	0.13638663E-01	001
2	0.10089E-01	0.10148E-01	-0.59178787E-04	002
3	0.79560E-02	0.10118E-01	-0.21621380E-02	003
4	0.93530E-02	0.10105E-01	-0.75156963E-03	004
5	0.61410E-02	0.10180E-01	-0.40388885E-02	005
6	0.21590E-02	0.10142E-01	-0.79827411E-02	006
7	0.13772E-01	0.10052E-01	0.37203808E-02	008
8	0.11914E-01	0.10365E-01	0.15490988E-02	009
9	0.86190E-02	0.10267E-01	-0.16479113E-02	010
10	0.73220E-02	0.10109E-01	-0.27866012E-02	011
11	0.84660E-02	0.10351E-01	-0.18848346E-02	012
12	0.25080E-02	0.10270E-01	-0.77620107E-02	013
13	0.24473E-01	0.95484E-02	0.14924599E-01	015
14	0.12364E-01	0.97801E-02	0.25838763E-02	016
15	0.77990E-02	0.95229E-02	-0.17238907E-02	017
16	0.69440E-02	0.93837E-02	-0.24396961E-02	018
17	0.84600E-02	0.95625E-02	-0.11024681E-02	019
18	0.22780E-02	0.93584E-02	-0.70803817E-02	020
19	0.17439E-01	0.68518E-02	0.10587196E-01	022
20	0.11558E-01	0.73377E-02	0.42202990E-02	023
21	0.77240E-02	0.70638E-02	0.66024193E-03	024
22	0.76760E-02	0.71231E-02	0.55285473E-03	025
23	0.72180E-02	0.75070E-02	-0.28897822E-03	026
24	0.16590E-02	0.72934E-02	-0.56343554E-02	027
25	0.12848E-01	0.11451E-01	0.13972595E-02	029
26	0.40350E-02	0.11236E-01	-0.72011082E-02	031
27	0.17764E-01	0.72166E-02	0.10547395E-01	036
28	0.92410E-02	0.75804E-02	0.16605679E-02	037
29	0.58740E-02	0.71992E-02	-0.13252008E-02	038
30	0.59910E-02	0.77657E-02	-0.17746834E-02	040
31	0.15260E-02	0.74572E-02	-0.59311697E-02	041
32	0.16417E-01	0.89383E-02	0.74787322E-02	043
33	0.90690E-02	0.90641E-02	0.48685838E-05	044
34	0.64720E-02	0.89287E-02	-0.24567312E-02	045
35	0.45350E-02	0.91891E-02	-0.46540629E-02	047

Exhibit 13-8: Regression Analysis of 128 Demographic Variables vs. Penetration (Only 35 shown)

Smart Target - Simple R Correlation Report

Seq Num	STP_LS ID_NEW	STP_LS_DESCR	Simple R Value
1	0045	Listen to contemporary hit radio	0.6106
2	1143	Sold or changed home in the last year	0.5937
3	0751	Played/participated in bowling in the last year	0.5932
4	0754	Played/participated in billiards/pool in the last year	0.5896
5	1036	Drink ice beer	0.5864
6	0237	Have a personal loan for education	0.5845
7	0822	Went dancing in the last year	0.5821
8	0303	Moved into present residence in the last year	0.5787
9	1037	Drink full-calorie coolers (wine/malt/spirits)	0.5781
10	0870	Rented/bought a comedy movie	0.5696
11	0954	Bought jeans last year	0.5670
12	0041	Listen to album oriented rock (AOR) including modern rock radio	0.5619
13	0883	Bought alternative rock records/discs/tapes in the last year	0.5592
14	0772	Participated in overnight camping trips in the last year	0.5576
15	0782	Played/participated in basketball in the last year	0.5566
16	0882	Bought heavy rock records/discs/tapes in the last year	0.5560
17	0120	Ordered records/CD's/tapes/videos through mail/phone in the last year	0.5556
18	0894	Bought 1970's rock records/discs/tapes in the last year	0.5499
19	0774	Participated in mountain bicycling in the last year	0.5492
20	0783	Played/participated in baseball in the last year	0.5490
21	0828	Painting, drawing, sculpting in the last year	0.5476
22	1117	Tried to stop smoking through gradual reduction	0.5444
23	0753	Played/participated in racquetball in the last year	0.5409
24	0786	Played/participated in hockey in the last year	0.5399
25	1157	Expect to sell or change home in the near future	0.5376
26	1062	Drink Coca-Cola	0.5367
27	0869	Rented/bought an action/drama adventure movie	0.5354
28	0827	Played a musical instrument in the last year	0.5323
29	0773	Participated in mountain/rock climbing in the last year	0.5303
30	0046	Listen to classic rock radio	0.5300
31	0897	Belong to records/discs/tapes club	0.5293
32	0878	Rented/bought a romantic comedy movie	0.5249
33	0768	Participated in target shooting in the last year	0.5241
34	0809	Went to a comedy club in the last year	0.5215
35	0899	Joined a records/discs/tapes club through a direct mail solicitation	0.5192
36	0787	Played/participated in soccer in the last year	0.5188
37	0933	Bought men's work boots (leather/leather type) in the last year	0.5187
38	0928	Spent under $50 on games and toys in the last year	0.5137
39	0930	Played board games in the last year	0.5137
40	0932	Bought men's western or cowboy boots (not rubber) in the last year	0.5133
41	0687	Purchased microwave oven last year	0.5123
42	1021	Fast Food Restaurants Most Often Used - Pizza	0.5073
43	0029	Highly Loyal Reader of the *Cosmopolitan*	0.5069
44	0776	Went street/dirt/trail motorcycling in the last year	0.5054
45	1139	Changed job for lower level of pay in the last year	0.5044
46	0081	Watch ice hockey on TV frequently	0.5023
47	0200	Acquired a credit card in the last year	0.5008
48	0813	Attended country concert in the last year	0.5001
49	0755	Participated in in-line roller skating in the last year	0.4990

Exhibit 13-9: Correlation of Ski Household Cluster Penetration with 1190 Lifestyle Variables (Only top 49 shown here)

```
Statistical analysis <DBSTATS>                                    Time = 15:23:40

Job Description = Lifestyles                    Y = Cust/HH
No. Obs. = 54          No. Var. = 399          F1 = 1.0            F2 = 2.0      Y var. # = 4
R =0.765148            R SQ. =0.55451          TOL = 0.001000      NUMBER STEPS = 2
F LEVEL = 1.5395                               PROBABILITY = 0.78421
OVERALL SIGNIFICANCE F = 23.5377               PROBABILITY = 1.00000
STANDARD ERROR OF Y = 0.00515                  Cust/HH
CONSTANT TERM = -0.15742616727279E-01                              AVERAGE Y = 0.887279630E-02
```

VAR.NO.	COEFFIECENT	COEF S ERR.	r TO Y	T	PROB.	VAR.DESC.	%CONTRIBUTION	AVG. X	%AVG.Y	STD.COEF
X- 50	0.179580531083E-01	0.237686E-02	0.6106	7.555	1.0000	RDO_CONTEMPORARY	61.691	1.052	0.2E+03	0.7050
X-165	0.119731062316E-01	0.336527E-02	0.1644	3.558	0.999	MD_11+_PR_LGDST	13.680	1.088	0.1E+03	0.3580
X-300	-0.675032819318E-02	0.141403E-02	-0.1959	-4.774	1.0000	OW_CONDOMINUM	24.629	1.081	-0.8E+02	-0.4906

Exhibit 13-10: Regression Analysis of Lifestyle Variables

from geographic areas with heavy military, as opposed to Hispanic, populations.

Lifestyle traits are evaluated in links to Strong Lifestyle Analysis and Weak Lifestyle Analysis reports on the CD. These reports reveal strongest correlation with the variable "visited a gambling casino in Europe in the last year," indexed at 198.03% of average. Weakest correlation is with the variable "belong to American Association of Retired Persons (AARP)," indexed at 71.71%

Media Analysis

Exhibit 13-11, Media Analysis, lists lifestyle variables that can help define media reading, viewing and listening habits of MVR ski customers. The Media Categories section of this report ranks general media types based on their use by ski customers. The Media Details section expands the data. Only the most-highly-correlated reading and viewing variables are shown in Exhibit 13-11. The complete listing is contained on the CD.

Reference to this report, on the adjunct CD in its entirety, reveals that the most likely media for reaching the MVR Ski market segment would be alternative/adult alternative or adult contemporary/new age radio. Following these would be motorcycle publications, jazz radio, and computer publications. Least likely to generate response would be listeners to nostalgia/big band radio or television viewers of bowling or "Dr. Quinn Medicine Woman." These revelations, of course, warrant experimentation!

Frequency Distribution of Ski Customers by State

MVR ski customers travel primarily from Virginia, North Carolina, Maryland, and the District of Columbia. Origin of ski customers by state is shown in Exhibit 13-12, Frequency Distribution by State. Customer origin and penetration by 5-digit ZIP Code area is graphically presented on the adjunct CD-ROM.

MEDIA CATEGORIES

Rank	STP ID	Description	Customer Percent	U.S. Percent	Lifestyle Index
12	1196	Magazine & Newspaper Reader	35.37	33.80	104.64
18	1197	Radio Listener	20.89	20.22	103.30
51	1198	Television Watcher	27.88	29.28	95.22

MEDIA DETAILS

Rank	STP ID	Description	Customer Percent	U.S. Percent	Lifestyle Index
24	0043	Listen to alternative/adult alternative radio	8.35	6.74	123.83
40	0052	Listen to new adult contemporary/new age radio	3.26	2.70	120.82
51	0014	Read motorcycle publications	5.09	4.25	119.75
55	0061	Listen to jazz radio	3.26	2.73	119.37
62	0006	Read computer publications	16.62	13.98	118.88
71	0041	Listen to album oriented rock (AOR) including modern rock radio	13.35	11.28	118.33
75	0004	Read business & finance publications	32.44	27.46	118.15
92	0046	Listen to classic rock radio	9.87	8.44	116.92
102	0012	Read men's publications	27.75	23.85	116.33
105	0047	Listen to classical radio	5.13	4.42	116.18
119	0018	Read sports publications	26.84	23.25	115.44
127	0001	Read airline/in flight publications	7.85	6.82	115.08
128	0013	Read metropolitan/regional/state publications	5.06	4.40	114.97
148	0003	Read boating & yachting publications	4.35	3.81	114.19
159	0045	Listen to contemporary hit radio	11.83	10.41	113.63
160	0005	Read child rearing/parenthood publications	31.20	27.46	113.61
166	0056	Listen to soft contemporary (lite/soft rock) radio	1.99	1.75	113.42

Exhibit 13-11: Media Analysis (part only)

State	Count	Percent
AK	0	0.00%
AL	0	0.00%
AR	0	0.00%
AZ	0	0.00%
CA	0	0.00%
CO	0	0.00%
CT	0	0.00%
DC	149	0.48%
DE	0	0.00%
FL	0	0.00%
GA	0	0.00%
HI	0	0.00%
IA	0	0.00%
ID	0	0.00%

State	Count	Percent
IL	0	0.00%
IN	0	0.00%
KS	0	0.00%
KY	0	0.00%
LA	0	0.00%
MA	0	0.00%
MD	541	1.75%
ME	0	0.00%
MI	0	0.00%
MN	0	0.00%
MO	0	0.00%
MS	0	0.00%
MT	0	0.00%
NC	9,505	30.79%

State	Count	Percent
ND	0	0.00%
NE	0	0.00%
NH	0	0.00%
NJ	0	0.00%
NM	0	0.00%
NV	0	0.00%
NY	0	0.00%
OH	0	0.00%
OK	0	0.00%
OR	0	0.00%
PA	0	0.00%
PR	0	0.00%
RI	0	0.00%
SC	0	0.00%

State	Count	Percent
SD	0	0.00%
TN	0	0.00%
TX	0	0.00%
UT	0	0.00%
VA	20,675	66.97%
VI	0	0.00%
VT	0	0.00%
WA	0	0.00%
WI	0	0.00%
WV	0	0.00%
WY	0	0.00%
Invalid		%

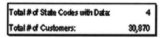

Total # of State Codes with Data:	4
Total # of Customers:	30,870

Exhibit 13-12: Frequency Distribution by State

Interactive Workshop 13-1:
Demonstration of Utilization of the MVR Ski Database

> To get the greatest benefit from this workshop, please be sure to read the instructions at the beginning of this chapter for accessing and analyzing the Mountain & Valley Resort database as well as working with the statistical tools and techniques that are contained on the CD-ROM accompanying this book.

- Excerpt from the MVR Ski database only those ski customers who are identified as "cautious." How many are there? Do the same thing for those who ski midweek as opposed to weekends. Distinguish customers by frequency of visit and dollars spent.

- Identify those skiers age 30 and under. Do this for those who have lived at their present residence less than a year. Distinguish ski customers by gender and household status and ethnic origin. Where do they come from? Do they own their own homes or do they rent ... and in what type of dwelling to they reside? What can you say about their estimated income?

- Determine household cluster penetration statistics for ski customers. What are the characteristics of those clusters with high penetration compared with those with low penetration? What can you say about lifestyles of these respective clusters?

- In what media should MVR advertise to attract ski customers?

- Design an experiment to determine, in a statistically valid manner, the response to a special promotional offer to be sent to the "cautious" skiers. Anticipating a 2% response to the offer, assuming a 95% confidence level and a maximum acceptable variance of 15%, calculate the required sample size.

- How would you design an experiment to determine a difference in response to the offer between midweek and weekend skiers? How would you measure the difference in response statistically?

Chapter 14

The Mountain & Valley Resort (MVR) Guest Database

The CD-ROM that accompanies this book summarizes the Guest Customer database for Mountain & Valley Resort. Summary records permit more meaningful demonstration, manipulation, and use of data than individual records. The database analysis tool links on the CD track the process of database marketing analysis: merge/purge of individual customer records, transaction and demographic analysis, and report preparation based on cluster penetration.

Individual customer records, from which these summaries were derived, include transaction as well as enhancement data. Transactions are sequenced and timed. Appended Cluster codes, ZIP codes, and GPS codes enable identification of geographic, demographic and psychographic characteristics.

Statistical and analytical tools (see Chapters 3,5,6, and 7) are also included on the CD to enable correlation of such data with market penetration and response rates. Customers can be profiled, their lifetime value can be calculated, and targeted approaches to the most attractive market segments can be developed. Customer creation and cultivation can be planned. Experiments can be designed.

When you place the CD into your computer's CD drive, your default browser will automatically activate. You can then choose a specific Interactive Workshop from those listed on the Welcome page. These tools usually work best with a Netscape browser, and it is necessary to have Adobe Acrobat Reader. If you do not have these installed on your machine, you can download them from the site links provided.

Mountain & Valley Resort (MVR) seeks to better understand segments of its Guest database by profiling market segments most like its current customers in order to target its future promotion more precisely and thus maximize response and profitability. In addition, the company wants to identify those guests most likely to make repeat visits and upsell or cross-sell them. It seeks to develop predictable patterns of sequencing and timing of visits, so that the Lifetime Value of a Customer can be defined and exploited. It also wants to identify the most profitable promotion offers and media for acquiring new customers.

The company's objective is identification of market segments in which response to new customer acquisition as well as continuity and cross-selling of current customers, with an emphasis on response advertising utilizing appropriate media, can be maximized.

The Mountain & Valley Resort Guest Database

The MVR database (described in Chapter 13) includes 70,000 guest reservation records. Duplicates were purged, individuals were merged to the household level and commercial accounts were deleted. This netted out to 12,043 households with complete transactions data during the period 1996-1998. (This merge/purge process and some resultant customer records are demonstrated in Interactive Workshop 14-1 on the CD-ROM.)

The 12,043 households with transaction data were then matched to the Experian database for enhancement with individual demographic and lifestyle data if/as available. Matches resulted on 8,979 individuals (74.56%) and 1,293 households (10.74%); the remaining 1,771 records (14.71%) could not be matched for enhancement. Individual transactions, demographic and lifestyles variables are those for head-of-household.

Market Segmentation and Customer Penetration
of MVR Guest Database

The origin of MVR Guests is shown in Exhibit 14-1, which shows a frequency distribution by three-digit ZIP Code area. Frequency distributions of transaction and demographic variables identified within the guest customer database appear in Exhibits 14-2, 14-3, and 14-4 (CD-ROM, Interactive Workshop 14-1.)

Transaction variables for each guest included these, as shown in the frequency distributions in Exhibit 14-2:

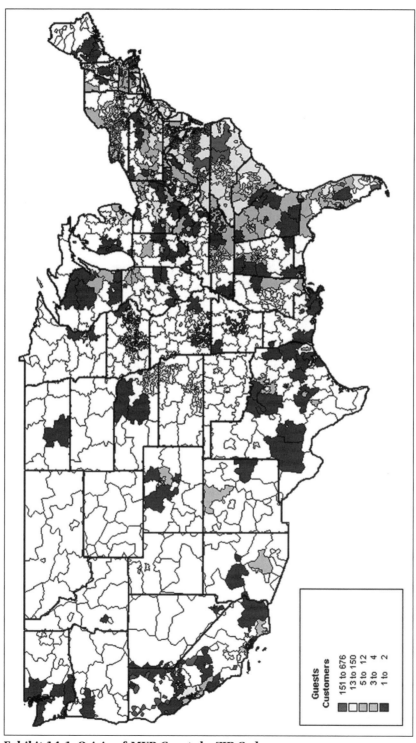

Exhibit 14-1: Origin of MVR Guests by ZIP Code

- Booking Type – Direct, Agent, Group
- Package Type – Family, Golf, Ski, Arts, Other
- Participants per Stay – Average Number
- Nights per Stay – Average Number
- Reservation Value – Average Dollars
- Repeat Visits – Number of Visits

Demographic/lifestyle enhancements were provided from matches (or hits) with the Experian database. These included: age group, gender, household status, family type, ethnic market code, dwelling type, homeowner/renter indicator, length-of-residence, and estimated income. Not all variables were available for all records.

Frequency distributions of demographic/housing variables identified within the customer database appear in Exhibits 14-3 and 14.4. Since not all data variables could be identified for all records, the distribution totals vary. These distributions are not a measure of market penetration, but rather an allocation of records. These variables are presented:

- State of Residence—percent distribution
- Gender—female, male
- Age—range bands
- Household Status—head-of-household, wife, young adult
- Primary Ethnic Code—percent distribution
- Dwelling Type—urban/rural, single/multi/apartment
- Family Type—married, unknown
- Homeowner— known/probable homeowner, known/probable renter
- Length of Residence—years lived at given address
- TRW Estimated income—percent household distribution

Household Cluster Penetration Analysis of Guest Households

Analysis of the demographic and lifestyle characteristics of MVR's Guest database is introductory to customer profiling.

An initial step in profiling the MVR Guest database is to determine market penetration within demographically and psychographically comparable clusters. A major reason for such clustering is to create units large enough to assure the statistical validity of predictions. The first step in doing so is establishing clusters of all households within an area. Since putting a customer household into a cluster involves geo-coding (i.e., global positioning), those records whose address locations are not published or available (post office boxes, military bases, etc.) must be deleted from market penetration analysis.

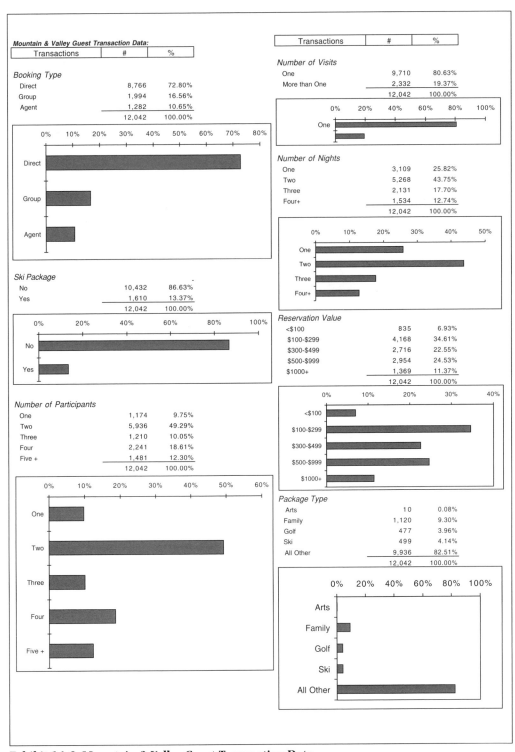

Exhibit 14-2: Mountain & Valley Guest Transaction Data

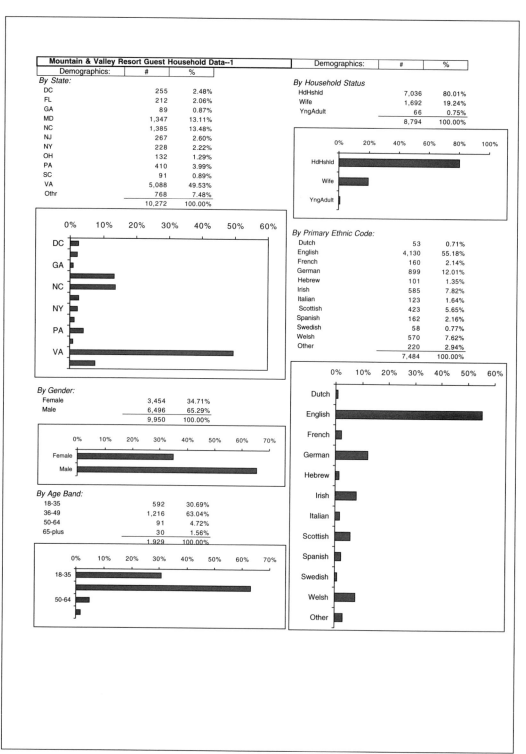

Exhibit 14-3: Mountain & Valley Guest Household Data (1)

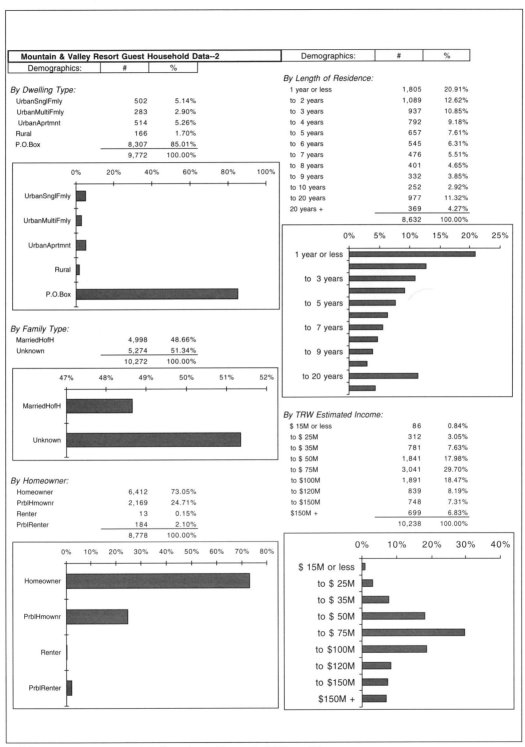

Mountain & Valley Resort Guest Household Data--2			Demographics:	#	%
Demographics:	#	%			

By Dwelling Type:

	#	%
UrbanSnglFmly	502	5.14%
UrbanMultiFmly	283	2.90%
UrbanAprtmnt	514	5.26%
Rural	166	1.70%
P.O.Box	8,307	85.01%
	9,772	100.00%

By Length of Residence:

	#	%
1 year or less	1,805	20.91%
to 2 years	1,089	12.62%
to 3 years	937	10.85%
to 4 years	792	9.18%
to 5 years	657	7.61%
to 6 years	545	6.31%
to 7 years	476	5.51%
to 8 years	401	4.65%
to 9 years	332	3.85%
to 10 years	252	2.92%
to 20 years	977	11.32%
20 years +	369	4.27%
	8,632	100.00%

By Family Type:

	#	%
MarriedHofH	4,998	48.66%
Unknown	5,274	51.34%
	10,272	100.00%

By TRW Estimated Income:

	#	%
$ 15M or less	86	0.84%
to $ 25M	312	3.05%
to $ 35M	781	7.63%
to $ 50M	1,841	17.98%
to $ 75M	3,041	29.70%
to $100M	1,891	18.47%
to $120M	839	8.19%
to $150M	748	7.31%
$150M +	699	6.83%
	10,238	100.00%

By Homeowner:

	#	%
Homeowner	6,412	73.05%
PrblHmownr	2,169	24.71%
Renter	13	0.15%
PrblRenter	184	2.10%
	8,778	100.00%

Exhibit 14-4: Mountain & Valley Guest Household Data (2)

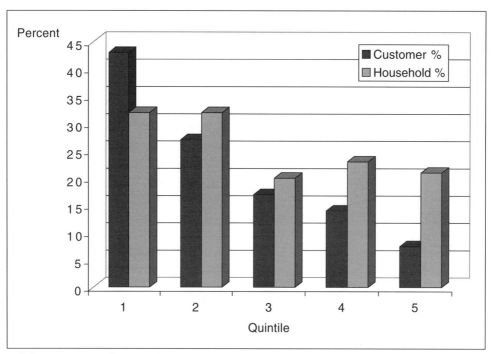

Exhibit 14-5: Distribution of Mountain & Valley Resort Guests within All Households

Once the statistical clusters have been developed, guest customer households are indexed to all households within these clusters by quintiles (20 percent groupings)using Household Cluster Penetration Analysis. These groupings indicate the degree of cumulative marketing effectiveness. Quintiles with a high percentage of matches or hits indicate a high degree of penetration; a low percentage indicates a low penetration. The degree of difference is then rank-ordered. The next step is to identify the reasons for the differences, which involves matching and comparing the demographic and psychographic make-up of the entire clusters with the characteristics of MVR customer households. That is determined through regression and correlation analysis.

The purpose of such determination, of course, is to direct future customer acquisition and to develop promotions whose offers and appeals will be more likely to generate high response rates and avoid promotional expenditures into those segments with a low probability for success. Such profiles help to position specific products (i.e., Ski vs. Golf) and create advertising messages.

Quintile	Rank	Cluster Code	Customers	Customer Percent	Customer Total %	Households	Household Percent	Household Total %	Index	Cluster Universe
1	1	081	395	5.10	5.10	65,733	1.38	1.38	368.58	360,262
	2	018	943	12.17	17.26	206,619	4.35	5.73	279.94	1,473,039
	3	015	213	2.75	20.01	48,671	1.02	6.75	268.43	605,846
	4	079	41	0.53	20.54	10,287	0.22	6.97	244.48	64,832
	5	011	157	2.03	22.56	44,145	0.93	7.90	218.14	306,313
	6	001	104	1.34	23.91	30,358	0.64	8.54	210.13	1,157,357
	7	025	124	1.60	25.51	37,206	0.78	9.32	204.42	415,196
	8	082	100	1.29	26.80	33,733	0.71	10.03	181.84	217,766
	9	016	284	3.66	30.46	97,238	2.05	12.07	179.14	1,232,851
	10	019	690	8.90	39.36	250,027	5.26	17.33	169.27	3,189,019
	11	064	55	0.71	40.07	23,798	0.50	17.83	141.76	230,216
	12	036	50	0.65	40.72	22,282	0.47	18.30	137.64	743,340
	13	009	165	2.13	42.85	74,387	1.56	19.87	136.06	953,794
Quintile Totals:			3,321	42.85		944,484	19.87		**Quintile Index:** 215.67	10,949,831
2	14	022	245	3.16	46.01	113,156	2.38	22.25	132.80	2,048,486
	15	008	143	1.84	47.85	66,311	1.39	23.64	132.27	588,074
	16	012	262	3.38	51.23	130,516	2.75	26.39	123.13	1,626,987
	17	053	74	0.95	52.19	37,691	0.79	27.18	120.42	230,360
	18	017	361	4.66	56.84	200,538	4.22	31.40	110.42	2,460,954
	19	021	68	0.88	57.72	38,468	0.81	32.21	108.43	287,183
	20	023	124	1.60	59.32	70,947	1.49	33.70	107.20	1,963,499
	21	040	85	1.10	60.42	49,873	1.05	34.75	104.54	1,704,430
	22	026	240	3.10	63.51	146,449	3.08	37.83	100.52	3,640,500
	23	037	38	0.49	64.00	23,617	0.50	38.32	98.70	888,446

Exhibit 14-6.1: Mountain & Valley Resort Guests Household Cluster Penetration Analysis

Quintile	Rank	Cluster Code	Customers	Customer Percent	Customer Total %	Households	Household Percent	Household Total %	Index	Cluster Universe
2	24	002	93	1.20	65.20	59,845	1.26	39.58	95.32	2,078,332
Quintile Totals:			**1,733**	**22.36**		**937,411**	**19.72**	**Quintile Index:**	**113.39**	**17,517,251**
3	25	010	219	2.83	68.03	143,350	3.02	42.60	93.70	1,771,006
	26	051	88	1.14	69.17	59,561	1.25	43.85	90.62	686,392
	27	078	86	1.11	70.27	61,782	1.30	45.15	85.38	241,808
	28	050	406	5.24	75.51	311,368	6.55	51.70	79.98	2,748,384
	29	005	163	2.10	77.62	126,023	2.65	54.35	79.34	4,035,227
	30	071	49	0.63	78.25	40,999	0.86	55.21	73.31	603,451
	31	080	72	0.93	79.18	61,146	1.29	56.50	72.22	355,111
	32	054	106	1.37	80.54	93,866	1.97	58.47	69.27	1,041,952
Quintile Totals:			**1,189**	**15.34**		**898,095**	**18.89**	**Quintile Index:**	**81.20**	**11,483,331**
4	33	003	177	2.28	82.83	165,104	3.47	61.95	65.76	6,230,411
	34	020	232	2.99	85.82	217,086	4.57	66.51	65.55	2,724,194
	35	024	225	2.90	88.72	246,572	5.19	71.70	55.97	6,666,692
	36	052	297	3.83	92.56	328,903	6.92	78.62	55.39	5,103,532
	37	083	70	0.90	93.46	84,906	1.79	80.40	50.57	443,507
Quintile Totals:			**1,001**	**12.91**		**1,042,571**	**21.93**	**Quintile Index:**	**58.89**	**21,168,336**
5	38	038	77	0.99	94.45	93,997	1.98	82.38	50.24	3,309,632
	39	013	65	0.84	95.29	89,835	1.89	84.27	44.38	1,147,520
	40	055	114	1.47	96.76	203,507	4.28	88.55	34.36	2,598,721
	41	027	138	1.78	98.54	262,314	5.52	94.07	32.27	6,480,539
	42	006	66	0.85	99.39	129,082	2.72	96.78	31.36	5,322,697
	43	073	47	0.61	100.00	152,941	3.22	100.00	18.85	3,056,243

Exhibit 14-6.2: Mountain & Valley Resort Guests Household ClusterPenetration Analysis

Quintile	Rank	Cluster Code	Customers	Customer Percent	Customer Total %	Households	Household Percent	Household Total %	Index	Cluster Universe
Quintile Totals:			**507**	**6.54**		**931,676**	**19.60**	**Quintile Index:**	**33.38**	**21,915,352**
Grand Totals:			7,751	100.00		4,754,237	100.00			83,034,101

Exhibit 14-6.3: Mountain & Valley Resort Guests Household Cluster Penetration Analysis

Once the clusters have been developed, the degree of market penetration can follow. Market penetration itself is measured by dividing customers within a cluster by the total number of households in each such cluster or, similarly, dividing direct mail responses by the number of solicitation pieces mailed. Certain key statistics are thus derived, such as a Customer/Household or Response/Mailing index (whose base is an overall mean of penetration) on which the clusters are then rank ordered, with subtotals at quintiles representing 20% of households or mailings.

A graphic portrayal of household segmentation indexing distribution by quintiles of MVR Guest households within all households is shown in Exhibit 14-5.

The MVR Guest Household Cluster Penetration Analysis, grouped by quintiles of all households, is shown in Exhibit 14-6. The key measurement in this analysis is the index derived by dividing the percent of all customers by the percent of all households. A clear pattern emerges from this evaluation. Penetration of guests within the top 19.87% of all households is 215.67% of the average penetration of all quintiles, whereas that in the bottom 19.60% is 33.38%, a ratio of 1:6.46. The top cluster (#81) is 368.58% of the average of all clusters; the bottom cluster (#73) is 18.85% of average, a ratio of 1:19.55.

A definition of the demographic profile and the lifestyle traits of each cluster can be found on the CD-ROM in Interactive Workshop 14-1. Simply click on the cluster code number in the Household Cluster Penetration Quintiles report to link to a description of that cluster. A summary of the characteristics of all clusters, rank ordered, appears in the Household Cluster Penetration Highlights report on the CD.

Next, we need to determine, through correlation of cluster penetration with both the demographic and the lifestyle variables associated with these clusters, why penetration of top quintiles of clusters is better than average. We also need to determine, too, which advertising media are most suitable for reaching prospective guests.

Correlations of Cluster Penetration with Demographics and Lifestyles

Correlation analysis helps to explain the market penetration rank orderings. Multivariate regression analysis can predict the propensity of guest prospect households within a cluster to respond to an offer made by Mountain & Valley Resort.

Simple correlation coefficients (R-value) of 128 demographic variables (derived from U. S. Census data) and 100 lifestyle variables (derived from Simmons Study of Media and Markets data)—relative to

C112 Demography Simple R Correlation Report

Seq Num	Item Num	REL_DETAIL_DESC	Simple R Value
1	20	Median Household Wealth	0.5603
2	18	Median Household Income, HHLDR age 80-84	0.5357
3	19	Median Household Income, HHLDR age 85 and older	0.5338
4	23	Median Household Income, HHLDR age 15-34 (Computed)	0.5266
5	9	Median Household Income, HHLDR age 15-24	0.5256
6	17	Median Household Income, HHLDR age 75-79	0.5245
7	25	Median Household Income, HHLDR age 45-54 (Computed)	0.5234
8	24	Median Household Income, HHLDR age 35-44 (Computed)	0.5202
9	10	Median Household Income, HHLDR age 25-34	0.5194
10	27	Median Household Income, HHLDR age 65 and older	0.5190
11	52	Household income of $100,000 to $124,999	0.5184
12	26	Median Household Income, HHLDR age 55-64 (Computed)	0.5151
13	53	Household income of $125,000 to $149,999	0.5142
14	11	Median Household Income, HHLDR age 35-44	0.5099
15	12	Median Household Income, HHLDR age 45-54	0.5097
16	14	Median Household Income, HHLDR age 60-64	0.5079
17	13	Median Household Income, HHLDR age 55-59	0.5067
18	15	Median Household Income, HHLDR age 65-69	0.5007
19	16	Median Household Income, HHLDR age 70-74	0.4906
20	116	Catering expenditures	0.4659
21	113	Auto and auto repair expenditures	0.4599
22	22	Standard Deviation of 1996 Age	0.4535
23	51	Household income of $75,000 to $99,999	0.4505
24	120	Average years of education	0.4361
25	81	Professional occupations	0.4324
26	65	Population age of 45 to 54 years	0.4297
27	54	Household income of $150,000 or more	0.4278
28	74	Education - Bachelor's degree	0.4275
29	108	Home expenditures	0.4234
30	92	Married population	0.4206
31	104	Lawn care service/lawn mower expenditures	0.4182
32	117	Travel expenditures	0.4175
33	121	Average Occupation	0.4172
34	75	Education - post-graduate degree	0.4039
35	94	Owner-occupied housing	0.3933
36	34	Median home value	0.3767
37	8	Per capita income	0.3755
38	30	Median age of Households with income of $35,000 to $50,000	0.3738
39	6	Median age of males	0.3713
40	32	Median age of Households with income of $75,000 or more	0.3709
41	31	Median age of Households with income of $50,000 to $75,000	0.3690
42	96	Single-unit housing	0.3674
43	21	Total household expenditures	0.3482
44	107	Florist expenditures	0.3416
45	133	Percent of 1990 other families with no related children	0.3288
46	88	Married population	0.3281
47	66	Population age of 55 to 64 years	0.3201
48	115	Accounting and legal services expenditures	0.3189
49	29	Median age of Households with income of $25,000 to $35,000	0.3188
50	110	Jewelry expenditures	0.3151
51	35	Median age	0.3124
52	55	White population	0.2914
53	102	Liquor expenditures	0.2774
54	7	Median age of females	0.2722
55	57	Non-white/non-black population	0.2692
56	112	Pet shop and veterinary expenditures	0.2374
57	33	Median age of head of household	0.2189
58	122	Household size	0.2133
59	28	Median age of Households with income of less than $25,000	0.1715
60	42	1996 to 2001 Change in Median Age	0.1628
61	79	Percent of labor force that is employed	0.1436
62	38	1996 to 2001 population growth	0.1429
63	50	Household income of $50,000 to $74,999	0.1354
64	37	1990 to 1996 population growth	0.1331

Exhibit 14-7.1: Regression/Correlation Analysis of Market Penetration vs. 128 Demographic Variables

C112 Demography Simple R Correlation Report

Seq Num	Item Num	REL_DETAIL_DESC	Simple R Value
65	59	Percent Growth in Median Household Wealth from 1996 to 2001	0.1295
66	39	Growth in Household Count from 1990 to 1996	0.1288
67	82	Technical occupations	0.1211
68	67	Population age of 65 to 74 years	0.1201
69	118	Population age of 18 years or older	0.1093
70	73	Education - Associate's degree	0.0824
71	64	Population age of 35 to 44 years	0.0819
72	41	1990 to 1996 Change in Median Age	0.0684
73	131	Percentage of married families without children	0.0613
74	77	Percent of population in labor force	0.0611
75	106	Rental service expenditures	0.0555
76	111	Audio - video sales/rental/service expenditures	0.0533
77	125	Urban population	0.0477
78	72	Education - some college	0.0369
79	119	Population age of 65 years or older	0.0322
80	61	Population age of 12 to 17 years	0.0278
81	127	Seasonal population	0.0256
82	36	Ratio of group quarters pop to total pop	0.0169
83	62	Population age of 18 to 24 years	-.0169
84	78	Percent of population not in labor force	-.0443
85	126	Rural population	-.0485
86	68	Population age of 75 years or older	-.0560
87	130	Percentage of married families with related children	-.0611
88	105	Moving and storage expenditures	-.0790
89	40	Population density per square mile	-.0972
90	99	Housing of 50+ units	-.0998
91	123	Population age of 17 years or younger	-.1077
92	114	Healthcare and health insurance expenditures	-.1121
93	84	Agricultural occupations	-.1574
94	87	Never married population	-.1608
95	60	Population age of 11 years or younger	-.1733
96	76	Military population	-.1849
97	45	1990 to 1996 Change in Median Value of Housing Unit	-.1866
98	46	1996 to 2001 Change in Median Value of Housing Unit	-.1883
99	109	Laundry and cleaning expenditures	-.2038
100	98	Housing of 10 to 49 units	-.2319
101	100	Mobile home housing units	-.2433
102	90	Widowed population	-.2618
103	58	Hispanic population	-.2727
104	56	Black population	-.2849
105	101	Restaurant expenditures	-.2968
106	128	Percentage of population with a male head of household	-.3217
107	85	Crafts/trade occupations	-.3235
108	103	Beauty salon and barber shop expenditures	-.3443
109	71	Education - high school graduate	-.3479
110	44	1996 to 2001 Growth in Median Household Income	-.3494
111	132	Percent of 1990 other families with related children	-.3537
112	43	1989 to 1996 Growth in Median Household Income	-.3610
113	63	Population age of 25 to 34 years	-.3689
114	97	Housing of 2 to 9 units	-.3693
115	95	Renter-occupied housing	-.3775
116	89	Separated population	-.4025
117	69	Education - less than 8th grade	-.4055
118	129	Percentage of population with a female head of household	.4087
119	124	Ratio of household income to total expenses	-.4095
120	86	Machine operators/labor occupations	-.4140
121	47	Household income of less than $20,000	-.4199
122	49	Household income of $35,000 to $49,999	-.4223
123	93	Other population	-.4247
124	83	Service occupations	-.4421
125	70	Education - 9-12 grades	-.4471
126	80	Percent of labor force that is unemployed	-.4525
127	91	Divorced population	-.4779
128	48	Household income of $20,000 to $34,999	-.5088

Exhibit 14-7.2: Regression/Correlation Analysis of Market Penetration vs. 128 Demographic Variables

Job Description = C112 Demography Simp			Y = Cust/HH	

No. Obs. = 43   No. Var. = 129   F1 = 1.0   F2 = 2.0   Y var. # = 4
R =0.610332   R SQ. =0.372505   TOL = 0.001000   NUMBER STEPS = 10
F LEVEL = 1.5386   PROBABILITY = 0.77287
OVERALL SIGNIFICANCE F = 11.8728   PROBABILITY = 0.99991
STANDARD ERROR OF Y = 0.00100   Cust/HH   AVERAGE Y = 0.194200000E-02
CONSTANT TERM = 0.320748635568E-02

VAR. NO.	COEFFICIENT	COEF. S ERR.	r TO Y	T	PROB.
X- 20	0.234468271445E-02	0.677616E-03	0.5603	3.460	0.9987
X- 65	-0.374842102646E-02	0.194016E-02	0.4297	-1.932	0.9395

VARIABLE DESC.	% CONTRIBUTION	AVG. X	% AVG. Y	STD.COEF	
MHW96	76.234	1.183	0.1E+03	1.1628	
PAGE96_4554	23.766	1.078	-0.2E+03	-0.6492	

PREDICTED VS ACTUAL RESULTS

OBS. NO.	ACTUAL	PREDICTED	DEVIATION	C112 Code
1	0.34260E-02	0.15531E-02	0.18728966E-02	001
2	0.15540E-02	0.15931E-02	-0.39083261E-04	002
3	0.10720E-02	0.15607E-02	-0.48865716E-03	003
4	0.12930E-02	0.16068E-02	-0.31379651E-03	005
5	0.51100E-03	0.15713E-02	-0.10602698E-02	006
6	0.21570E-02	0.18707E-02	0.28634409E-03	008
7	0.22180E-02	0.19534E-02	0.26462588E-03	009
8	0.15280E-02	0.19279E-02	-0.39992505E-03	010
9	0.35560E-02	0.18880E-02	0.16680120E-02	011
10	0.20070E-02	0.19481E-02	0.58870730E-04	012
11	0.72400E-03	0.19260E-02	-0.12020121E-02	013
12	0.43760E-02	0.27816E-02	0.15944489E-02	015
13	0.29210E-02	0.27643E-02	0.15672680E-03	016
14	0.18000E-02	0.27963E-02	-0.99628861E-03	017
15	0.45640E-02	0.30078E-02	0.15562064E-02	018
16	0.27600E-02	0.27952E-02	-0.35199864E-04	019
17	0.10690E-02	0.28446E-02	-0.17756014E-02	020
18	0.17680E-02	0.30562E-02	-0.12881884E-02	021
19	0.21650E-02	0.16306E-02	0.53440518E-03	022
20	0.17480E-02	0.18400E-02	-0.91996895E-04	023
21	0.91300E-03	0.17399E-02	-0.82686840E-03	024
22	0.33330E-02	0.18620E-02	0.14709919E-02	025
23	0.16390E-02	0.19174E-02	-0.27842695E-03	026
24	0.52600E-03	0.18757E-02	-0.13496651E-02	027
25	0.22440E-02	0.15360E-02	0.70804125E-03	036
26	0.16090E-02	0.16046E-02	0.44196795E-05	037
27	0.81900E-03	0.15487E-02	-0.72971272E-03	038
28	0.17040E-02	0.16578E-02	0.46153848E-04	040
29	0.13040E-02	0.85214E-03	0.45185999E-03	050
30	0.14770E-02	0.94799E-03	0.52900723E-03	051
31	0.90300E-03	0.87952E-03	0.23479392E-04	052
32	0.19630E-02	0.71269E-03	0.12503106E-02	053
33	0.11290E-02	0.91571E-03	0.21328680E-03	054
34	0.56000E-03	0.84434E-03	-0.28433642E-03	055
35	0.23110E-02	0.24362E-02	-0.12516732E-03	064
36	0.11950E-02	0.13178E-02	-0.12280211E-03	071
37	0.30700E-03	0.13414E-02	-0.10343877E-02	073

Exhibit 14-7.3: Regression/Correlation Analysis of Market Penetration vs. 128 Demographic Variables

market penetration—reveal comfortably high relationships, both positive and negative. While penetrations shown in this study are arithmetically derived within clusters, correlation and regression analysis are used to both explain the differences in penetration among clusters and also to predict future marketing effectiveness through definition of areas providing high probability of response to future MVR promotions.

Exhibit 14-7 presents a Regression/Correlation Analysis of Market Penetration vs. 128 Demographic Variables. This reveals, in rank order, the correlation coefficients of 128 demographic variables relative to market penetration, positive or negative, for MVR Guest households. These variables explain observed penetration differences. They can be used to direct future market segmentation and guide creation of future advertising.

Exhibit 14-8 presents a Regression/Correlation Analysis of Market Penetration vs. Lifestyle Variables. This reveals, in rank order, correlation coefficients of 98 lifestyle variables relative to market penetration, positive or negative, for MVR Guest households. These variables, which also explain observed penetration differences, can be used to direct future market segmentation and guide creation of future advertising.

The Cluster Penetration and Characteristics Analysis section of Interactive Workshop 14-1 on the CD-ROM has a link to a Demographic Analysis report. This report indexes and rank orders available demographic variables relating customer averages to U.S. averages. The top variable, indexed at 402.3% of average, is "ratio of population in group quarters/population in individual housing units"; the bottom variable, 17.2% of average, is "percent of industry in mining." That is, guest customers are more likely to come from geographic areas with mainly individual housing units and are least likely to come from areas where the mining industry is concentrated.

Lifestyle traits are evaluated in links to Strong Lifestyle Analysis and Weak Lifestyle Analysis reports. These reports reveal strongest correlation with the variable "visited a gambling casino in Europe in the last year," indexed at 227.91% of average. Weakest correlation is with the variable "carry insurance from Medicare/Medigap/Medicaid," indexed 71.27%

Media Analysis: Categories and Lifestyle Preferences of Customers

Exhibit 14-9, Media Analysis, lists lifestyle variables that can help define media reading, viewing and listening habits of MVR Guest customers. The Media Categories section of this report ranks general media types based on their use by Guest customers. The Media Details section expands the data. Only the most-highly correlated reading and

Smart Target - Simple R Correlation Report

Seq Num	STP_LS_ ID_NEW	STP_LS_DESCR	Simple R Value
1	0465	Traveled domestically for business in the last year	0.6119
2	0376	Took domestic business trip in the last year	0.6119
3	0184	Spent $50 or more on cellular phone bill last month	0.5942
4	0179	Use a cellular phone for business purposes	0.5938
5	0554	Stayed in domestic hotel/motel 10 or more nights for business	0.5908
6	0792	Spend $25 or more on golf balls in the last year	0.5813
7	1069	Belong to a business club	0.5811
8	0463	Traveled by plane for 4 or more domestic business trips last year	0.5759
9	0791	Spent $100 or more on golf clubs in the last year	0.5732
10	0195	Used an American Express card in the last 30 days	0.5710
11	0516	Currently enrolled in a frequent guest program for domestic hotel	0.5707
12	0952	Spent $1150 or more on men's apparel last year	0.5666
13	0369	Rented car for business use three or more times in the last year	0.5644
14	0722	Own a fax machine at home	0.5634
15	0342	Own a European car	0.5625
16	0607	Carry loss of income through medical/disability insurance	0.5621
17	0122	Ordered computer software through mail/phone in the last year	0.5569
18	0358	Belong to priority/private car rental club	0.5558
19	0359	Last car rented away from home	0.5553
20	0943	Spent $30 or more on a men's regular dress shirt	0.5531
21	0004	Read business & finance publications	0.5489
22	0662	Purchased custom made drapes/curtains for $250 or more last year	0.5470
23	0716	Use a personal computer at home for personal financial management	0.5470
24	0706	Used an on-line/interactive computer service in the last 30 days	0.5465
25	0757	Participated in downhill snow skiing in the last year	0.5445
26	0794	Bought golf shoes in the last year	0.5439
27	0189	Have an American Express card	0.5404
28	0723	Own a copying machine at home	0.5392
29	0488	Stayed at a ski resort in the last year	0.5375
30	0448	Traveled by rented car for foreign travel in the last 3 years	0.5371
31	0937	Spent $200 or more on a men's winter suit	0.5350
32	0486	Currently enrolled in a frequent flyer program	0.5320
33	0718	Use a personal computer at home for taxes	0.5302
34	0287	Have $5,000 or more stock in employers' company	0.5275
35	0210	Used travel & entertainment card in the last 30 days	0.5266
36	0357	Rent cars for business/personal use	0.5262
37	1034	Drink light/low calorie imported beer (cans/bottles)	0.5257
38	0939	Spent $100 or more on men's dress shoes (leather/leather type)	0.5241
39	0615	Used interior decorating service in the last year	0.5225
40	0444	Traveled by first class or business class on plane for foreign trv	0.5209
41	0684	Own an electric espresso/cappuccino maker	0.5196
42	0941	Spent $40 or more on a men's sweater	0.5158
43	0950	Spend $50 or more on slacks (males)	0.5137
44	0264	Use a discount brokerage firm for brokerage account	0.5125
45	0460	Used travel agent for hotel reservations for foreign travel	0.5093
46	0609	Carry $200,000 or more in home/tenant insurance	0.5091
47	0370	Rented car for personal use two or more times in the last year	0.5073
48	0341	Own a Volvo	0.5035
49	0440	Spent $3,000 or more on last foreign trip	0.4976
50	1094	Made a charitable gift or contribution in the last year educ. org	0.4940
51	0793	Spent $25 or more on golf gloves in the last year	0.4937
52	0294	Have investment property	0.4932
53	0253	Have a Keogh account	0.4867
54	1033	Drink regular imported draft beer	0.4861
55	0267	Use a mutual fund company for mutual fund accounts	0.4847
56	0372	Bought $1,000 or more worth of travelers cheques in the last year	0.4833
57	0959	Bought sport coat/blazer last year (males)	0.4805
58	0272	Own money market funds at a brokerage firm	0.4777
59	0956	Bought lightweight summer suit last year (males)	0.4732
60	0384	Visited Mexico in the last 3 years	0.4716

**Exhibit 14-8.1: Regression/Correlation Analysis of Market Penetration
vs. 98 Lifestyle Variables**

Smart Target - Simple R Correlation Report

Seq Num	STP_LS_ID_NEW	STP_LS_DESCR	Simple R Value
61	0274	Own common stock in company (other than employers')	0.4705
62	0344	Own a foreign luxury car	0.4667
63	0459	Used travel agent for flight reservations for foreign travel yr.	0.4639
64	0945	Spent $100 or more on sport coat/blazer (males)	0.4637
65	0378	Took three or more foreign round trips in last 3 years	0.4629
66	0285	Have $5,000 or more in mutual funds	0.4628
67	0711	Own an apple computer	0.4603
68	0708	Used a World-Wide-Web service in the last 30 days	0.4560
69	0632	Hired professional painter for exterior painting in the last year	0.4542
70	1075	Belong to a country club	0.4528
71	0717	Use a personal computer at home for personal networking/e- mail	0.4466
72	0286	Have $5,000 or more stock in company other than employers'	0.4550
73	0560	Visited a gambling casino in the Caribbean Islands last year	0.4436
74	0960	Bought winter/all year suit (separates) last year (males)	0.4116
75	1102	Made a charitable gift or contribution of $200 or more in the yr	0.4315
76	0330	Own an Acura	0.4272
77	1043	Drink imported dinner/table wines	0.4205
78	0013	Read metropolitan/regional/state publications	0.4185
79	0283	Made 6 or more stock transactions (not including empl co)last yr	0.4184
80	0262	Have a brokerage account	0.4164
81	1077	Belong to an environmentalist organization	0.4164
82	0277	Own $100,000 or more in securities	0.4149
83	0397	Visited Eastern Europe in the last 3 years	0.4141
84	0801	Played tennis 10 or more times in the last year	0.4138
85	0047	Listen to classical radio	0.4119
86	0412	Visited Russia in the last 3 years	0.4111
87	0270	Own bonds (other than U.S. Savings Bonds)	0.4030
88	0346	Own a convertible bought new	0.4026
89	0383	Visited Hawaii in the last 3 years	0.4109
90	1093	Made a charitable gift or contribution last yr to arts/culture	0.3932
91	0263	Use a full service brokerage firm for brokerage account	0.3883
92	0042	Listen to news radio	0.3823
93	0426	Visited African countries in the last 3 years	0.3690
94	0631	Hired professional painter for	0.3528
95	0417	Visited Asia in the last 3 years	0.3430
96	0425	Visited South Pacific (Oceania) in the last 3 years	0.2760
97	0414	Visited the Middle East in the last 3 years	0.2522
98	0561	Visited a gambling casino in Europe in the last year	0.0182

Exhibit 14-8.2: Regression/Correlation Analysis of Market Penetration vs. Lifestyle Variables (98 shown)

viewing variables are shown in Exhibit 14-9. The complete listing is contained on the CD.

Reference to the entire report (on the CD) reveals that the most likely media for reaching the MVR Guest market segment would be business and finance publications. Following these would be news and classical radio, metropolitan/ regional/state publications, and airline/in-flight publications. Least likely to generate response would be viewers of daytime quiz/audience participation television or readers of women's publications. These revelations would warrant experimentation.

Statistical analysis <DBSTATS> Time = 13:07:10

Job Description = C112 Lifestyles Plus   Y = Cust/HH
No. Obs. = 43   No. Var. = 101   F1 = 1.0   F2 = 2.0 Y var. # = 4
R =0.638127   R SQ. =0.407206 TOL = 0.001000   NUMBER STEPS = 10
F LEVEL = 0.9807   PROBABILITY = 0.61611
OVERALL SIGNIFICANCE F = 13.7385   PROBABILITY = 0.99997
STANDARD ERROR OF Y = 0.00097   Cust/HH   AVERAGE Y = 0.194200000E-02
CONSTANT TERM = 0.891970645171E-03

VAR. NO.	COEFFICIENT	COEF. S ERR	r TO Y	T	PROB.
X- 41	0.170862172667E-02	0.553654E-03	0.6119	3.086	0.9963
X- 89	-0.110161752154E-02	0.740624E-03	0.5158	-1.487	0.8553

VARIABLE DESC.	% CONTRIBUTION	AVG. X	% AVG. Y	STD.COEF.
TK_DMSTC_BUS_TRP	81.149	1.465	0.1E+03	1.1209
SP_$40+_MN_SWTR	18.851	1.319	-0.7E+02	0.5402

PREDICTED VS ACTUAL RESULTS

OBS. NO.	ACTUAL	PREDICTED	DEVIATION	C112 Code
1	0.34260E-02	0.13808E-02	0.20451923E-02	001
2	0.15540E-02	0.17195E-02	-0.16549365E-03	002
3	0.10720E-02	0.13041E-02	-0.23214812E-03	003
4	0.12930E-02	0.17886E-02	-0.49560465E-03	005
5	0.51100E-03	0.10834E-02	-0.57239557E-03	006
6	0.21570E-02	0.18838E-02	0.27323293E-03	008
7	0.22180E-02	0.20943E-02	0.12365110E-03	009
8	0.15280E-02	0.20060E-02	-0.47795358E-03	010
9	0.35560E-02	0.35129E-02	0.43121097E-04	011
10	0.20070E-02	0.22087E-02	-0.20171251E-03	012
11	0.72400E-03	0.18534E-02	-0.11293861E-02	013
12	0.43760E-02	0.18914E-02	0.24845796E-02	015
13	0.29210E-02	0.21947E-02	0.72627107E-03	016
14	0.18000E-02	0.21000E-02	-0.30004882E-03	017
15	0.45640E-02	0.38995E-02	0.66453352E-03	018
16	0.27600E-02	0.24084E-02	0.35156793E-03	019
17	0.10690E-02	0.18454E-02	-0.77637727E-03	020
18	0.17680E-02	0.20465E-02	-0.27850384E-03	021
19	0.21650E-02	0.13850E-02	0.78001799E-03	022
20	0.17480E-02	0.17549E-02	-0.68861214E-05	023
21	0.91300E-03	0.12992E-02	-0.38615460E-03	024
22	0.33330E-02	0.38716E-02	-0.53855428E-03	025
23	0.16390E-02	0.18483E-02	-0.20929312E-03	026
24	0.52600E-03	0.10477E-02	-0.52165269E-03	027
25	0.22440E-02	0.12693E-02	0.97467040E-03	036
26	0.16090E-02	0.15287E-02	0.80299302E-04	037
27	0.81900E-03	0.11706E-02	-0.35160111E-03	038
28	0.17040E-02	0.15264E-02	0.17757475E-03	040
29	0.13040E-02	0.14527E-02	-0.14874645E-03	050
30	0.14770E-02	0.17341E-02	-0.25705568E-03	051
31	0.90300E-03	0.14298E-02	-0.52676722E-03	052
32	0.19630E-02	0.35802E-02	-0.16172216E-02	053
33	0.11290E-02	0.17923E-02	-0.66326081E-03	054
34	0.56000E-03	0.12505E-02	-0.69052732E-03	055
35	0.23110E-02	0.23111E-02	-0.57643966E-07	064

Exhibit 14-8.3: Regression/Correlation Analysis of Market Penetration vs. 98 Lifestyle Variables

MEDIA CATEGORIES

Rank	STP ID	Description	Percent	U.S. Percent	Lifestyle Index
7	1196	Magazine & Newspaper Reader	40.03	33.80	118.42
50	1197	Radio Listener	19.33	20.22	95.62
53	1198	Television Watcher	25.84	29.28	88.26

MEDIA DETAILS

Rank	STP ID	Description	Percent	U.S. Percent	Lifestyle Index
42	0004	Read business & finance publications	45.01	27.46	163.92
46	0042	Listen to news radio	6.84	4.26	160.60
49	0047	Listen to classical radio	7.03	4.42	159.15
74	0013	Read metropolitan/regional/state publications	6.69	4.40	152.10
112	0001	Read airline/in flight publications	9.85	6.82	144.46
118	0051	Listen to jazz radio	3.92	2.73	143.56
134	0006	Read computer publications	19.58	13.98	140.02
139	0007	Read Epicurean publications	13.34	9.60	138.94
158	0043	Listen to alternative/adult alternative radio	9.22	6.74	136.73
160	0019	Read travel publications	10.44	7.65	136.49
164	0052	Listen to new adult contemporary/new age radio	3.65	2.70	135.23
172	0066	Own a TV 30 inches or larger	10.19	7.57	134.61
189	0003	Read boating & yachting publications	5.07	3.81	133.08
242	0053	Listen to news/business news/talk radio	20.96	16.36	128.10
276	0018	Read sports publications	29.00	23.25	124.74
284	0017	Read science/technology publications	8.38	6.77	123.73
299	0073	Watch college basketball on TV frequently	11.51	9.40	122.46
323	0083	Watch tennis on TV frequently	3.78	3.12	121.06

Exhibit 14-9: Mountain & Valley Resort Guest Media Analysis

Interactive Workshop 14-1:

Calculating Customer Penetration and Building a Profile of MVR Guests

Read the instructions at the beginning of this chapter for accessing and analyzing the Mountain & Valley Resort database as well as working with the statistical tools and techniques contained on the CD-ROM accompanying this book.

The principles of taxonomy—the grouping of individuals or objects—are straightforward. If a researcher tests a model, all people in the sample are assumed to behave according to the model and its parameters. When there is strong a priori reason to believe nonconforming individuals are present, these individuals should be removed and grouped separately. An example of taxonomy is the definition of animals into classifications such as mammals. birds, amphibians, and rodents. Certain species fit easily. But, how does one classify a bat? Is it a rodent or a bird?

Factor analysis and cluster analysis are statistical techniques for grouping characteristics, actions, persons, or objects into natural aggregations. Factor analysis is a means of data reduction combining variables into groups called factors. Cluster analysis groups persons or entities having the same underlying traits into common elements called clusters. These techniques are used in tandem by the researcher to examine the properties of the data as well as of the population studied.

The objective is to classify entities into homogeneous groups based on the information available. Such grouping implies that subgroups behave differently in response to stimuli such as market segmentation, product differentiation and promotion. Regression and correlation analysis within derived clusters is used for prediction as well as explanation.

This workshop provides an opportunity to work with a "live" customer database and apply the tools and techniques discussed in this chapter.

- Develop a customer profile of those who have been guests at the Mountain & Valley Resort two or more times

- Develop a customer profile of those guests whose market codes identify them as members of a group booking.

■ Study the booking codes distribution. Isolate those guests whose visit resulted from direct booking as a result of seeing an advertisement in appropriate media such as golf, ski or business publications. Do profiles of these customers differ from that of customers derived from group bookings?

■ Compare demographically and psychographically the Ski Rental database with the Guest database.

■ See if you can fit your own numbers into the examples of spreadsheets provided in this chapter and on the CD-ROM.

---

(1) Customer Retention Rates:

Visit 1 =	100.00%		Visit 6 =	47.11% of Visit
Visit 2 =	14.36% of Visit 1		Visit 7 =	52.63% of Visit
Visit 3 =	28.50% of Visit 2		Visit 8 =	56.67% of Visit
Visit 4 =	34.42% of Visit 3		Visit 9 =	70.59% of Visit
Visit 5 =	41.02% of Visit 4		Visit 10 =	83.33% of Visit

(2) Revenues per Guest Visit:

	# Active Customers		Visit Rev. /Customer		GrossVisit Revenues
Visit 1 =	100.00	X	$574	=	$57,400
Visit 2 =	14.36	X	$740	=	$10,626
Visit 3 =	4.09	X	$876	=	$3,585
Visit 4 =	1.41	X	$999	=	$1,407
Visit 5 =	0.58	X	$901	=	$521
Visit 6 =	0.27	X	$688	=	$187
Visit 7 =	0.14	X	$992	=	$142
Visit 8 =	0.08	X	$811	=	$66
Visit 9 +	0.06	X	$599	=	$34
Visit 10 =	0.05	X	$706	=	$34

(3) Fulfillment Costs:

Costs of Goods Sold=	0.50
Gen./Admin. Costs =	0.20
Total Costs =	0.70

(4) Future Gross Profits = Contributions to Acquisition Cost

(5) Present Value of Future Sales = Discounted Value of Future Profits

PROJECTION OF THE LIFETIME VALUE OF A NEW MOUNTAIN & VALLEY RESORT CUSTOMER:

# Active Customers (1)	GrossVisit Revenues @ (2)	Total Costs X (3)=Net Revenues		Gross Profits (4)(=1-3)	X	10%Disc Factor %	PresValue Customers = (5)
100.00	$57,400	70.00%	40,180	$17,220		0.9524	$16,400.33
14.36	$10,626	70.00%	7,438	$3,188		0.9070	$2,891.44
4.09	$3,585	70.00%	2,510	$1,076		0.8433	$907.00
1.41	$1,407	70.00%	985	$422		0.8433	$356.02
0.58	$521	70.00%	364	$156		0.7655	$119.56
0.27	$187	70.00%	131	$56		0.7655	$43.01
0.14	$142	70.00%	99	$43		0.6938	$29.58
0.08	$66	70.00%	46	$20		0.6938	$13.71
0.06	$34	70.00%	24	$10		0.6293	$6.48
0.05	$34	70.00%	24	$10		0.6293	$6.37

Present Value of 100 New Customers:	$20,773.50

(6) Present Value of One Newly-Acquired Customer (divide by100):   **$207.74**
(= Lifetime Value of One Newly-Acquired Mountain & Valley Resort Customer)
(= Amount to be Spent to Acquire a New Mountain & Valley Resort Customer)

Exhibit 14-10: Calculation of the Lifetime Value of a Newly-Acquired Mountain & Valley Resort Customer

Interactive Workshop 14-2:

Calculating the Lifetime Value of an MVR Guest

> Read the instructions at the beginning of this chapter
> for accessing and analyzing the Mountain & Valley
> Resort database as well as working with the statistical
> tools and techniques contained on the CD-ROM
> accompanying this book.

Derived from the MVR database, the calculation of the Lifetime Value of a Newly Acquired Mountain & Valley Resort customer is shown in Exhibit 14-10; customer continuity is displayed in Exhibit 14-11.

It has been said that the most important sale an organization makes to a customer is the second one, rather than the first. The observation that just 14.36% of those visiting Mountain & Valley Resort for the first time come back for a second visit points up the need for regular directed promotional efforts to the MVR customer database. It is not enough to simply acquire new customers. These assets must be cultivated through both continuity selling and cross-selling of new products.

Operations:

- In Exhibit 14-10, on the adjunct CD, increase the number of guests who return to MVR for a second visit by 20 percentage points (to 34.46%); then, increase the retention rates by ten percentage points for each visit following the second. What impact does such cultivation of customers have on the amount of money that can be spent to acquire a new customer?

- What impact does increasing the average revenue per visit have on the lifetime value of a customer?

- Conduct other "what if?" experiments in Exhibit 14-10. For example, decrease the costs of goods sold — and note the impact on the bottom-line.

- Referring to Exhibit 14-11, what can you say about customer continuity and the time between visits as customers develop relationships and affinity with an organization?

Guest Continuity	1st Visit	2nd Visit	3rd Visit	4th Visit	5th Visit	6th Visit	7th Visit	8th Visit	9th Visit	10th Visit	Total 2++
# Guest Visits	41,872	6,013	1,714	590	242	114	60	34	24	20	8,811
% of First Visit	100.00%	14.36%	4.09%	1.41%	0.58%	0.27%	0.14%	0.08%	0.06%	0.05%	21.04%
% of Prior Visit	100.00%	14.36%	28.50%	34.42%	41.02%	47.11%	52.63%	56.67%	70.59%	83.33%	na
Time Between Visits (Days)	0	261	231	195	174	153	126	115	102	59	1416.00
Avg Revenue per Visit	$574	$740	$876	$999	$901	$688	$992	$811	$599	$706	$7,312

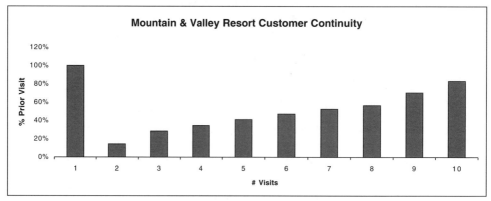

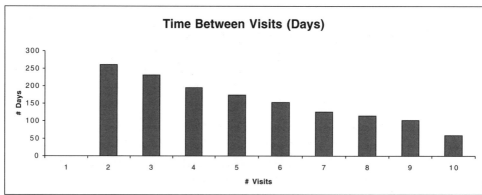

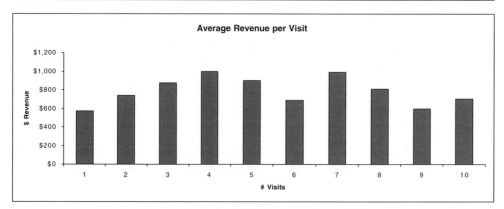

Exhibit 14-11: Mountain & Valley Resort Guest Customer Continuity

Suggested Readings

Martin Baier. *How to Find and Cultivate Customers Through Direct Marketing.* Lincolnwood, IL: NTC Business Books, 1996

Donna Baier-Stein. *Write on Target.* Lincolnwood, IL: NTC Business Books, 1997

Mike Berry. *The New Integrated Direct Marketing.* London: Gower, 1998

Bill Bishop. *Strategic Marketing in the Digital Age.* Lincolnwood, IL: NTC Business Books/American Marketing Association, 1997

Robert Bly. *Business-to-Business Direct Marketing.* Lincolnwood, IL: NTC Business Books, 1998

George Duncan. *Streetwise Direct Marketing.* Boston: Adams Media, 2001

John Fraser-Robinson. *Customer-Driven Marketing.* London: Kogan-Page, 1994

Seth Godin. *Permission Marketing.* New York: Simon & Schuster, 1999.

Arthur M. Hughes. *The Complete Database Marketer.* New York: McGraw-Hill, 1995

Victor Hunter. *Business-to-Business: Creating a Community of Customers.* Lincolnwood, IL: NTC Business Books, 1997.

Robert Jackson and Paul Wang. *Strategic Database Marketing.* Lincolnwood, IL: NTC Business Books, 1995.

Russell Kern. *S.U.R.E.-Fire Direct Response Marketing.* Lincolnwood, IL: NTC/Contemporary Books, 2000.

Herschell Gordon Lewis and Robert E. Lewis. *Selling on the Net.* Lincolnwood, IL: NTC Business Books, 1996.

Bernard Liautaud. *E-Business Intelligence.* New York: McGraw-Hill, 2000.

Graeme McCorkell. *Direct and Database Marketing.* London: Kogan-Page, 1997.

Chuck Martin. *Net Future: The 7 Cybertrends That Will Drive Your Business, Create New Wealth, and Define Your Future.* New York: McGraw-Hill, 1999.

R.A. Moeller. *Distributed Data Warehousing Using Web Technology.* New York: Amacom, 2000.

Edward Nash. *Database Marketing: The Ultimate Marketing Tool.* New York: McGraw-Hill, 1993.

―――――. *Direct Marketing: Strategy, Planning, Execution.* Fourth edition. New York: McGraw-Hill, 2000.

Stewart Pearson. *Building Brands Directly.* New York: New York University Press, 1996.

Mark Peck. Integrated *Account Management: How Business-to-Business Marketers Can Maximize Customer Loyalty and Profitability.* New York: Amacom, 1997.

Don Peppers and Martha Rogers. *The One-to-One Manager: Real-World Lessons in Customer Relationship Management.* New York: Doubleday, 1999.

Stan Rapp and Chuck Martin. *Max e-Marketing in the Net Future.* New York: McGraw-Hill, 2000.

Olivia Par Rud. *Data Mining Cookbook: Modeling Data for Marketing, Risk, and Customer Relationship Management.* New York: Wiley & Sons, 2000.

Christopher Ryan. *High-Performance Interactive Marketing: New Technique s and Technologies for Winning and Keeping Customers.* Evanston, IL: Racom Communications, 2001.

Jack Schmid and Alan Weber. *Desktop Database Marketing.* Chicago: NTC, 1997.

Don E. Schultz and Philip Kitchen. *Communicating Globally: An Integrated Marketing Approach.* Lincolnwood, IL: NTC Business Books, 2000.

Dick Shaver. *The Next Step in Database Marketing—Customer-Guided Marketing.* New York: Wiley & Sons, 1996.

David Shepard Associates. *The New Direct Marketing: How to Implement a Profit-Driven Database Marketing Strategy.* Third edition. New York: McGraw-Hill, 1999.

Barry Silverstein. *Business-to-Business Internet Marketing.* Third edition. New York: Maximum Press, 2000.

Jim Sterne. *World Wide Web Marketing.* Third edition. New York: Wiley & Sons, 2001.

Bob Stone. Successful *Direct Marketing Methods.* Seventh edition. Lincolnwood, IL: NT Business Books, 2001.

Index